RUN AT DESTRUCTION

"Run at Destruction *is a tragic — yet fascinating — true story of an unfathomable death in the Heartland of America. It happened in a wholesome community of runners and educators, perhaps the last group you would expect to be involved, however tangentially, in secret affairs, deception, and infidelity. Except for the bond between mothers and their children, there may be nothing stronger than women friends who are there to pick up the pieces when the world explodes, and to listen with true concern. Author Lynda Drews writes of her lost friend, and of her own efforts to find justice for Pam Bulik. Readers will find themselves walking along with Drews as she describes an enviable friendship, her grief when it ended suddenly, and the layers she peeled away to find the truth. Wonderfully written. A must for true-crime readers."*

> — **Ann Rule,** author of The Stranger Beside Me,
> Small Sacrifices, *and* Mortal Danger

"Reader groups everywhere will find Run at Destruction *intriguing and thought-provoking. The characters struck a familiar chord inspiring endless discussion.*"

> — **Lora Stemke,** Titletown Teachers Reader's Group

"Run at Destruction *is written with the beat of a runner's heart: steady intensity racing toward an inevitable finish. Drews is the John Grisham of the running world, pulling readers into a unique subculture where the drama unfolds.*"

> — **Sean Ryan,** Race Director, Cellcom Green Bay Marathon

RUN AT
DESTRUCTION

A True Fatal Love Triangle

Lynda Drews

Run at Destruction
A True Fatal Love Triangle
Copyright ©2009 by Lynda Drews

TitleTown Publishing LLC
P.O. Box 12093
Green Bay WI 54307
920-737-8051
www.titletownpublishing.com
www.lyndadrews.com

Book design and production by Mick Magenta/ Cypress House
Cover design by Elizabeth Petersen

The names of some individuals and street addresses in this book have been changed. Those names are indicated by an asterisk (*) the first time each appears in the book.

Grateful acknowledgement is given to the following for permission to reprint certain photos: Bill and Bonnie Metzger, Sue (Christensen) Weimer, and Wesley Norman, Ph. D.

Publisher's Cataloging-in-Publication Data

Drews, Lynda.
   Run at destruction : a true fatal love triangle / Lynda Drews. -- 1st. -- Green Bay, WI : TitleTown Publishing, 2009.
      p. ; cm.
   ISBN: 978-0-9820009-2-2
   1. Murder--Wisconsin--Green Bay--Case studies. 2. Triangles (Interpersonal relations)--Case studies. 3. Runners (Sports)--Wisconsin--Green Bay--Biography. I. Title.
   HV6534.G74 D74 2009   2009927471
   364.15230973--dc22 0908

Printed in the United States of America by Thomson-Shore

9 8 7 6 5 4 3 2 1

Dedicated to
Jim and my boys
For their patience, encouragement, and love

And to
Pam and Beezie
My forever-cherished friends

Acknowledgments

This is a work of nonfiction. Any material not derived from my own memories is either taken from official records or is the result of interviews with the persons directly involved. Even though these individuals are identified within the text, I would be remiss if I didn't express my heartfelt gratitude. Without their support and co-operation, this book could not have been written. In addition, I want to thank my publisher, Tracy Ertl, for believing in me.

Lynda Drews

Contents

1

Unexplained Absence

For me, April 7, 1984 would forever belong to Pam. Repeatedly I squinted at my watch and rolled high on my toes, searching the crowd for my best friend Pamela Bulik. Familiar faces from the Green Bay community and surrounding area milled in and out of the Joggers Joynt, a running-gear store that sponsored local races. Notoriously indifferent about running fashion, the group resembled Goodwill shoppers.

Pam (Metzger) Bulik

Approaching the registration table I sipped my addiction, a cooling mug of coffee. Its scent mingled with the odor of runners' sweat from early warm-ups, and menthol gels being liberally applied to leg muscles. Dick Lytie sprawled behind a rickety table, wearing a psychedelic jacket and matching tights taken right off his store's closeout rack, yet modeling the best shoes money could buy. Affectionately known as our local running guru, he looked like a mountain man with his salt-and-pepper shaggy beard and frizzy hair.

As Dick checked in runners for his Spring Classic half marathon, he handed out numbers, safety pins, and a long-sleeved T-shirt. My drawers were stuffed with dozens, but this was my first black one. Even though many participants donned their funeral-appearing attire, the atmosphere swung to the other extreme. While stretching inside and out they burped, farted, and gulped down fluids. Conversely, runners lined up by the Joynt's one-stall bathroom for last-minute pit stops to void their fluids. Nervous excitement flowed on this sunny 45-degree day.

Where was Pam? I kept expecting to hear, "Hey, girl" followed by her nudge and memorable smile. Perhaps she was sick or overslept. Maybe one of her two children had a problem that she'd needed to deal with. There had to be a logical explanation. Once again her husband, Bob, was at his Marine Corps Reserve weekend in Denver, leaving family issues to fall on her shoulders.

Close to starting time, hyped-up runners crossed the street and gathered next to St. Bernard's Church. I scurried back to the car to lock my mug inside, placing it next to Pam's gift. It wasn't her birthday. It was simply a token of friendship—to remind her how special she was to me.

I then corralled Dick to see if I'd missed Pam in the process.

"No," he frowned. She'd never checked in. Because she'd pre-registered, he too agreed her absence was strange. He purposely held up the start, still anticipating her arrival. As runners got antsy, Dick could wait no longer. At 11:10 he raised the gun.

The crowd quieted. Only the wind whispered through leafless trees.

Then the shot exploded.

Caffeine-wired, I took off—without Pam. I knew her disappointment at missing this experience would gnaw at her. Near the end of the race the course wove near her home. Since she wasn't at the start I figured she might be there to cheer us on.

Over the last eight months there'd been many painful reasons why Pam hadn't completed a decent-length race. To generate a renewed sense of fulfillment and pride I'd convinced her to tackle the Green Bay Marathon in May. For months we'd methodically increased our training to nearly fifty miles a week. Today's race was to be a hard training run toward that goal. Now, due to Pam's absence, I decided to race competitively and assumed my seven-and-a-half-minute pace. Because I'd figured our conversation would have filled the miles and passed the time, I'd left my running radio at home and had to settle for my own thoughts.

As I scaled the first steep incline, the breeze felt odd against my bare legs after months of cold-weather running. Through the towering oaks of Preble Park the bright cloudless sky cast a filigree of light, thawing lingering snow. The sound of racers pounding the pavement mingled with the melt gushing down along the curb. What a wonderful day for a run – spring eavesdropping on the tail end of winter, bringing back nostalgic memories of a similar day...

While attending the University of Wisconsin La Crosse I'd dated my husband, Jim Drews, an all-American cross country runner. To show interest in his passion and to impress him a little I'd reluctantly taken up the sport. In the past I'd double tied my shoes, pulled on a comfortable sweatshirt, and completed an uncomfortable jog. But that particular day something was different. With Jim in my mind and heart I was determined to run to French Island and back. I still could recall the cool, crisp air on my face, the pungent smell of the Mississippi River, and the sound of my breathing. It was the first day I'd felt uniquely empowered. Boredom, pain, and fatigue had been non-existent. A clear sense of my future had emerged. On that day I'd found my natural pace and become a runner for life.

Remarkably, on our runs together, Pam experienced this same euphoric high—making me miss her all the more today.

I wound past Tudors, Cape Cods, and ranches, until I reached the three-mile mark at Preble High School where Pam's husband first taught and my friend, Sylvia Madden, still did. I gained a temporary partner as my image jogged along beside me, mirrored in the two blocks of classroom windows.

Back in 1974, Jim had accepted a teaching and coaching job

at Green Bay East High School, and I'd been hired as a systems engineer at IBM. Before moving to Green Bay, this city held such mystique for me. During televised Packer games broadcasters would laud it, showing fans gladly shoveling out the seats of the stadium for free, wearing green and gold with pride, and even choosing to be buried in Packer caskets below their cherished frozen tundra. Everyone said the people of Green Bay were honest, sincere, and friendly. I knew this was true, but our first year here as a newly married couple was lonely for me. My job was male dominated, so it was difficult for me to establish any close female friends—and find a running buddy. At Jim's school parties the women were nice, but I hadn't connected. Within this community I had yet to discover the right woman to shift a casual relationship into a significant friendship.

However, that changed. At an East High track meet in the spring of '75 the former coach's wife told me she knew a woman about my age who was also a runner. Two days later, I tentatively pulled into the driveway of her two-story white clapboard home, parking behind another vehicle. Nervously, I dashed up four stairs, two steps at a time, and then adjusted the paisley headband in my naturally curly brown hair. With timid determination, I was now ready to meet the enthusiastic woman I'd called. I took a deep breath, poised my index finger, and pushed the bell.

As the door swung open, I realized I shouldn't have worried. A perky gal greeted me, grabbing my extended hand in both of hers. "Hi, you! I'm Barb Delong. You must be Lynda." She then turned and introduced me to her friend, Pamela Bulik.

An arresting smile lit up Pam's beautiful heart-shaped face. Surrounded by short hair the color of variegated sand, her warm intelligent eyes gazed directly at me.

I caught my breath, feeling an immediate connection.

As we three jogged that day, the miles flew by. I immediately started to care about these women. We were excited to discover that our husbands were also runners. Our conversation became intimate as we swapped college stories—how we'd each

**Three Running Friends
Lynda Drews, Pam Bulik,
and Barb Delong**

experienced a sense of ardor and tenderness for our spouses-to-be that had developed into an irresistible attraction. It was their unique brew of intellectual, spiritual, emotional, and of course physical aspects. We admired their lean, firm bodies that didn't contain a pinch of fat. We wickedly admitted to groin sensations when we'd watch them run, especially on steamy Wisconsin days when they wore only skimpy shorts, socks, and shoes. Even in May, we three women heated up discussing the sweat that glistened on their bare chests as their graceful limbs moved to their own internal rhythm.

This was whom the three of us were drawn to, and it's what we hoped would continue to draw our husbands to us. Jokingly, though, since none of us was quite as svelte, we trusted they'd focus primarily on our more engaging attributes. Pam was the most outspoken. Unlike Barb and me she was large-boned and muscular. At five foot seven she was also two inches taller than me. She complained about the weight she'd gained since the birth of her two children, though I thought she carried the extra thirty pounds well. Constantly dieting, Pam said she'd tried every weight-loss program, paying a fortune to lose and gain the same pound. Finally, she'd realized that running produced the best results—and what's more, it was free.

That day I realized a void in my life might be filled. Barb was demonstrative while Pam's exterior was a little rough as she hid her tender side. I'd met Pam by chance, because I'd taken the initiative to call Barb, but our friendship grew close by choice.

By the six-mile mark in today's race my mouth felt like paste. The moldy dampness of last fall's leaves still hung in the air as the meandering course now paralleled Baird's Creek, splashing among the rocks, teasing me. I checked my watch. I was right on pace. Directly ahead I could see the most challenging hill. At least the reward of a water stop would be at its crest. I tried to concentrate on my breathing. My leg muscles burned as I charged the endless incline. I missed Pam's presence at my side, to help urge me on. Exhausted, I reached the top, grabbed a cup of water, took several swallows, and splashed the rest on my face, grateful that the worst was behind me. Three miles ahead, I anticipated hearing Pam's encouraging voice.

Those first five years in Green Bay I'd lived within a mile of Pam. Even though my race times were faster than hers, we could train together. Often we left our houses at the same time and met in the middle. Then, jogging at a comfortable pace, we delved into every imaginable topic. There was nothing like a run, with miles of roads stretching out in front, to give us uninterrupted time to really talk.

Until I met Pam, I was reluctant to share some secrets from my family's past, but our discussions became therapeutic, providing a launching pad for eventual disclosure to others.

Compared to many families I had little to complain about. I grew up fairly pampered, and though my life wasn't perfect, there was lots of love and outward affection from both of my parents.

I knew my dad was an alcoholic. He and a friend would consume beer while reloading shotgun shells in the basement. My dad left for hunting weekends in search of ducks, pheasants, or deer and could drink to his heart's content. When the situation became unbearable, he left for treatment centers in Milwaukee to dry out.

On a scorcher of a day, Pam had empathized with me, nudging my arm, as we'd run side-by-side. "Hey, Lynda, you're not alone. My father's an alcoholic, too."

"Really?" I glanced sideways at my friend's caring face. She was wiping sweat out of her eyes using the red bandana she always kept tucked in the waistband of her running shorts.

"Afraid so. At least, though, it wasn't that bad until I was in high school."

"How did your mom deal with it?"

"She's deeply religious. I think that helped. But she often kept her feelings to herself. She was a teacher—very bright, creative and disciplined. I definitely knew she loved me, and of course, still does, but growing up, I probably got more hugs from Mrs. Christensen, my best friend, Sue Weimer's mom."

I squeezed Pam's arm. It was the best I could do as we plodded along.

Metzger Family - 1952
Bill (10), William Sr., Pam (3)
and Myrtle (Myrt)

"You've said you have an older brother? Were you two close?"

"It would've been nice, but Bill and I are seven years apart. I know I was a damn nuisance to a guy who wanted to be cool. He picked on me an awful lot," she caught my eyes, "and dubbed me Baby Huey. I just hated that."

"You mean that cute cartoon duck that wears a baby bonnet and a diaper?" I tried to deflate the image.

"Lynda, you're being kind! That duck is fat!" Pam tried to laugh. "I've always felt that Bill was my parents' favorite. It wasn't that I was denied things, but I knew the sun rose and set on my big brother."

"So, when he started high school, you must've been in about third grade," I said, before quickly pointing out a bad pavement crack.

"Thanks," Pam said, avoiding it. "Yeah. My parents were part of a very social group that partied a lot. Most often, they included me, but I've got to confess, sometimes I felt like an afterthought. When I was about eight, I'll never forget having to holler and chase their car down the block until they stopped and let me in."

I cringed at that mental picture.

During my sophomore year in high school, I told Pam, my dad had finally been admitted into a month-long alcohol treatment program in rural Minnesota. After his release I was utterly amazed when he'd fully abstained. "From that point on," I said, "my parents' marriage really improved."

"Lynda, you're so lucky." Her voice caught. "Mine divorced after I married Bob."

Now reaching the eight-mile mark in today's race, I filed those memories of Pam in the back of my mind so I could focus on the target ahead. I was gaining on Dr. John Kiser, a good friend, my general practitioner, and someone I frequently tried to beat. Sirens filled the air as a rescue squad pulled up alongside him. John perplexingly climbed in.

About ten minutes later I neared the corner by Pam's home. An uneasiness crept through me. What was going on? She'd missed the start and now was absent from this spot. I strained my neck looking up the hill, which then turned left into the Buliks' hidden cul-de-sac. There appeared to be a cluster of neighbors near the top, but I didn't see Pam. I had a weird premonition that something was terribly wrong.

The effect of my pre-race caffeine had vanished, and a trudging heaviness enveloped my legs. A cluster of blackbirds, perched high on the crossbar of a light pole, cawed at me, their beaks jerking left and right, temporarily drowning out my raspy breathing. I tried to focus, but thoughts of Pam kept getting in the way.

Finally, the end was in sight. Place did not matter – first or last, runners and spectators would cheer. But today there was little applause. An uncanny quiet surrounded much of the black T-shirted group. Furtive glances from friends felt targeted my way.

Relieved to be crossing the finish line, I heard Dick announce 1:39:10. I was pleased.

But instead of congratulatory words, my friend gave me a despairing look, sliding his arm around my sweaty back, supporting me. "Lynda, there's no easy way to tell you this."

A stab of anxiety cut through me. "Tell me what?"

"They found Pam."

I stumbled at his words, my worried eyes finding Dick's. "What do you mean?"

"They found her at home." He tightened his grip on me and heaved a body-racking sigh. "Lynda, Pam's dead."

~

Runners clustered around at the finish line, weeping and whispering. Through my own tears I mentioned my earlier premonition, how, when Pam had not been at the corner, I'd somehow thought, *I hope she didn't commit suicide.*

Friends attempted to console me. Dr. John Kiser was now among them. Another friend had driven him back to the finish. John worked in the local hospitals' emergency rooms, and knew the paramedics who'd coincidentally picked him up. They'd been responding to a 911 call and asked for his assistance. John had been troubled when they'd turned down the Buliks' driveway. Even though another rescue squad had beat them to the scene they'd entered the home and been directed to the master bathroom off the foyer.

John paused so I could prepare myself. My heart beat spastically, dreading what I'd hear next.

Near the Buliks' 4×6 foot whirlpool bathtub, he said that a white hospital blanket had covered a body. Kneeling beside it, the coroner had uncovered Pam's face.

A soft moan escaped my lips. I visualized my friend just last weekend, so alive. I'd told Pam how proud I was of her and then had given her a hug, feeling her warm breath against my neck. Of course we weren't sisters, but the way I'd felt about her was as dear as that bond.

My pained eyes caught John's. "Do you know how she died?"

"Apparently, Lynda, she drowned."

"Drowned?" I could not comprehend.

~

Chilled from the race and shivering from shock, I drove home, the traffic blurred by my tears. Pam was dead because she had drowned? It didn't make sense. And why did thoughts of suicide enter my mind? Did I really think Pam could have killed herself? And now, knowing she'd drowned, I found it hard to believe she would choose that way. Pam was so modest about her body. She'd never want to be found naked. But maybe she wasn't. John saw only her face. Overwhelmed, I felt incapable of trying to understand.

With the backdoor propped open, my husband leaned against its frame, his forehead creased under his mop of blond curls, waiting and watching. Pam's death had already made the news. I could tell he'd been crying.

"Oh Jim..." My words dissolved into tears as I buried my face in his comforting shoulder. Until my crying subsided, he ran his fingers through my tangled hair, his soft mustache resting on my wet cheek.

Eventually, legs stiffening from the race, I hobbled upstairs to where our two-year old, Collin, was napping. Gently, I gathered our sleepy boy into my arms, breathing in his sweet smell, once again bringing on tears.

He cuddled close, seeming to sense something was wrong.

It was hard to imagine this was something Pam would never experience again. How were her children going to deal? Abby* was only nine and Alex*, eleven. And what about Bob? I couldn't point to a specific person that he would say was his "best friend"—someone to provide him that critical on-going support. My husband liked Bob, but he wasn't in Jim's tight circle of free-spirited running buddies. Pam's husband was an enigma and didn't fit the norm. To most, he seemed aloof and withdrawn.

At my high school reunions, former classmates claimed that was how they'd perceived me. I'd never felt I was, it was just shyness that had made me seem that way. I believed that about Bob, too.

As a woman, I couldn't help but notice his good looks. With

high Slavic cheekbones, thick coffee-colored hair, penetrating almond shaped eyes, and muscular physique, Bob stood out like a yellow finch among sparrows. At parties we'd dance together, and he might innocently flirt. So would I—among good friends it was allowed.

When we would discuss favorite films, Bob seemed to prefer love stories to action flicks. He liked to work with plants and cook. He was patient with his children, gently coaching them along. Often Bob seemed more at ease with women than men, and frequently ran with Kathy Kapalin, by far the best woman runner among our friends. But during their many miles together, Kathy said he'd never discussed any private thoughts, just races they'd run or planned to.

Eagle River weekend with the Buliks (Bob, Pam, Abby, Alex, and Scottie Misty) and Drewses (Lynda, Jim, Collin, and Springer Spaniel Fletcher)

Until the Bulik family spent a weekend at my family's cottage near Eagle River, Wisconsin, my relationship with Bob had been pretty impersonal, too, but in the summer of '82, amidst the towering pines, it changed. While we adults dangled our feet from our dock into Stormy Lake, and the Bulik children floated on tubes, the atmosphere prompted childhood memories from the group. With Collin dozing in my lap, I reminisced about some of mine and then asked Bob about his.

He actually opened up, recalling how he and his younger brother used to camp, fish, and swim with their parents. He grew up in a happy home in Kenosha, Wisconsin, and attended St. Casimir Elementary School where he confessed to being shy and having some difficulty making friends. He'd been an altar boy, played the trumpet, and participated in swimming and tennis while attending St. Joseph's High School. Since the rest of us had been raised Protestant, I teased him saying, he was the only one who could claim Catholic guilt.

Bob was also the only one who'd lost a parent. His mother had passed away from a stroke a few years earlier. When he went home, he said, he missed her presence. In their household she'd been the dominant personality.

Pam's adoring eyes had remained glued to Bob's face as he talked. For as long as I'd known Pam, she'd idolized Bob. She now patted his bare thigh and left her hand there, saying, that since his mom's death he'd been such a good son to his dad. When Bob placed his hand over Pam's, I noticed how she dissolved at his touch. She'd told me he'd dated a few women in high school and college, but she'd been his "first."

That weekend was the most I'd heard Bob discuss his personal life. Finally, I'd reached the point where my feelings for him ran more than skin deep. Today, I worried about Bob. How were he and the kids ever going to cope with Pam's death? Admittedly, over the past year, due to the Buliks' marital issues, my relationship with Bob had suffered some. Since Valentine's Day, however, other than a small fluke, he and Pam had seemed to be doing so well.

Rapid footsteps approached. Jim entered Collin's room followed by Beezie MacNeil. Her shiny fudge hair, always worn in a bob, was disheveled, her face blotchy, and eyes red.

Jim took Collin from my arms and discretely left the room.

Beezie reached for me, and our bodies convulsed in grief. Throughout this difficult year, she had been there for Pam more than me.

We eventually crossed the hallway and entered the master bedroom, decorated in soothing shades of green. Sinking down on the bedspread, I hugged a pillow to my chest and gazed up at Beezie. "Do you think they've reached Bob in Denver?"

"Lynda, he's home. Sylvia saw him this morning when he passed her in their van."

We didn't understand why Bob was home, but we were glad he was for their children's sake. They'd been dropped off at Sylvia and Tom Madden's house. It wasn't until the Buliks' pastor arrived with some officers that Abby and Alex were told Pam was dead.

"Why officers?" I gave Beezie a worried glance.

"I'm sure it's routine."

I fingered the edge of the pillow, not looking at her and said, "It's been nearly a week since I last talked to Pam. Maybe things would've been different if I'd called." Already the familiar guilt was crawling up inside of me, the shameful kind that rumbled below the surface.

Beezie sat down beside me and slipped her arm around my sticky body. "I know, Lynda, I feel the same."

My eyes connected with hers. "Do you think Pam took pills and somehow ended up in the tub?" Beezie had always been an opinionated dynamite. I knew I'd get the truth from her.

"I don't believe for a minute she tried to kill herself!" Beezie was positive Pam had accidentally drowned.

I wanted to believe it too.

∞∞∞∞∞∞∞∞∞∞∞∞∞∞∞∞∞∞

In search of a waterway to the Orient, Jean Nicolet discovered La Baye Verte in 1634. His historic meeting with the Winnebago Indians opened the gates to Jesuit missionaries and French fur traders, helping to launch the oldest community in Wisconsin, now known as Green Bay.

By 1862 the Chicago Northwestern Railroad had laid tracks into the area and the harbor was improved. The timber needs of Chicago and Milwaukee deforested the surrounding area and gave rise to the first paper mills. Employment agencies met boats in New York and offered transportation and two weeks free room and board to entice workers to the local mills and factories, thus attracting the city's major ethnic makeup of hardy Germans, Belgiums, and Scandinavians.

When Curly Lambeau gathered some husky young athletes inside the *Green Bay Press-Gazette*'s editorial room in 1919, the Packers were organized. Ten years later they won their first national championship and placed the city on the country's map.

By the mid-eighties, for most of the 100,000 Green Bay residents, living here was not something transient—it was lifetime. That engendered a community spirit and a deep-rooted respect for your neighbor. This solidly middle-class city had a down-to-earth culture, strong family values, and no pretenses of urban-chic. It also prided itself on its extraordinary low crime rate—50 percent below the national average.

≈

In 1984, a Green Bay detective's job was to manage about seven to ten cases. Some years a serious incident never occurred, but when one did come along, all others were put on the shelf. That's what happened to Detective Sergeant James Taylor on April 7.

For Taylor, becoming a cop happened by chance. After graduating from Green Bay East, he'd married his high school sweetheart and taken a job at Northern Paper Mill. Within a month of packing 120 cases of toilet paper each day, he knew this life wasn't for him. In 1965 the town of Preble was annexed into the city of Green Bay, and with this came the need for additional police officers. Taylor applied, got the job, and took a cut in pay. Now, at age forty-two, he was one of the twenty detectives on the Green Bay Police force. Even though he'd been one since 1976, he'd worked the night shift, so it was rare to land a major case. Previously he'd caught only one, the abduction and rape of a young girl, but this year Taylor moved to the day shift.

Today, when he'd answered the call for detective's assistance at 251 Traders Court* it had sounded familiar. As Taylor headed down the 200 feet of steep driveway, into the wooded ravine lot, filled with birch and white ash, he made a sharp right, paralleling the plank fence that lined the drive. Finally, he reached the

L-shaped multilevel home with beige siding and brown trim that matched the stained cedar of the entrance wing. Now he remembered this unique secluded home, seemingly miles away from the city's lights and limits. He'd been here eight months ago. *Uh-oh,* Taylor thought, *what happened now? Did the intruder return?*

Bulik home looking down from cul-de-sac

The rescue squad and coroner's vehicle had already arrived, so Taylor knew it didn't look good. He drove up behind a silver and maroon van parked inside the left stall of the garage. A late-model blue Monza was pulled up within inches of the closed right-hand garage door. He checked his watch. It was now 11:35 a.m.

Dressed neatly in a navy sport coat, plaid shirt, tie, and khakis, Taylor climbed out of his unmarked brown Chevy. With flared nostrils, slight jowls, and bags below his eyes—evidence of frequent late hours living the detective's life—he looked a bit like the Cowardly Lion from the 1939 film *The Wizard of Oz*. Before entering

Sergeant James Taylor's unmarked brown Chevy parked behind the
Buliks' van and next to the Buliks' blue Monza

the home's attached garage, he ran his fingers through dark thin-
ning hair, which crowned ample sideburns. Then, squeezing by
the van, he crossed the empty garage stall, and climbed the six
wooden steps leading into the house proper. Immediately to his
left was a half bath and laundry room. Ahead was an open-con-
cept kitchen and family room. Its French patio doors opening out
to a bench-lined deck with a hot tub.

By the kitchen desk he met Officer Chuck Peterson, who had
requested a detective to the scene. "So officer," Taylor said, "can
you explain the situation?"

Peterson nodded. "At about 11:15, I was dispatched to this
home in reference to the drowning of a woman. When I arrived,
I rang the front doorbell and a male subject greeted me. I now
know his name is Robert Bulik."

Taylor remembered the guy. "Where is Mr. Bulik now?"

"In the living room with Sergeant Baenen."

"And the drowning victim?"

"I'll show you."

Taylor followed him down the hall from the kitchen toward the front entrance. To their right was a formal dining room. On their left was an open staircase that led up to the children's second-floor bedrooms and bath.

"Were the Bulik children here when you arrived?" Taylor asked with paternal concern.

"No, sir."

His shoulders relaxed a bit.

Next to the stairs, Peterson pointed out a cozy living room where Sergeant Donald Baenen was stationed beside an emotional Bob Bulik. He was on his knees and leaning over a tropical-print couch. Even though this trim muscular man was in his mid-thirties, his dark thick hair held no hint of gray. On the floor beside him a Scottish terrier lay, seemingly puzzled by her master's emotions.

Taylor didn't pause. He wanted to gather more information before talking to Bulik.

Off the foyer, an entrance provided access to the master bedroom on the left and a bathroom to the right. Across from the toilet and shower was a vanity with a sink. Adjacent to the vanity was a narrow door-free entrance into an adjoining transom-windowed room where an in-ground whirlpool tub was located. From that room, a second similar entrance circled back into the master bedroom.

The body of a woman lay on the carpeted floor next to the large bathtub. It appeared as if she were simply asleep. That's where, Peterson said, he'd found her when Mr. Bulik let him into the home.

The rescue squad team was in the room with Deputy Coroner Genie Williams. In her standard pantsuit attire and blond hair sheared short, she was known for her warm and compassionate heart, certainly a great asset in the kind of work she performed. But the detectives also appreciated how she kept mum about details surrounding a death. Instead of the politics, Genie liked the bodies. In an investigation of a suspicious death, she knew how important it was to hide certain facts from the public.

Genie told Taylor, "I'm about to begin a cursory exam." When the case involved a death, Wisconsin state law dictated that the coroner was in charge of determining the what, when, where, and how behind it. Genie would share anything she discovered with the police.

"Is the victim Mrs. Bulik?" Taylor asked.

Peterson nodded. "Yes sir, it is."

Back on August 18, 1983, Taylor had received a 10:30 p.m. call about an intruder at the Bulik home. That night, he'd taken only Bob's statement. Because the case had been turned over to day-shift detectives, Taylor had never met Bob's wife. Today, looking at her in death, the detective closed his eyes. This was never easy. Luckily, this kind of situation was rare in Green Bay. He wondered what had caused this beautiful young woman's death—an accident, a suicide, or something more?

Taylor was pulled back from his thoughts as Lieutenant Richard Katers from the Green Bay Fire Department rescue squad said, "When we arrived at 11:20, I checked the victim for vital signs but found none. Based on her color and the mottling to her throat, she looked like she'd been in the water for some time. Her hair was still wet, and her fingers, toes, and feet were wrinkled."

"What about electrical appliances?" Taylor asked.

"We checked for electrical cords along the tub and found none."

Taylor returned to the vanity area with Officer Peterson. They noticed two hair dryers resting on the counter. Both were dry and unplugged.

Peterson then related what he'd learned from the husband. "Once the rescue squad arrived, I went into the bedroom and asked Mr. Bulik when he'd last talked to his wife. He said he didn't know, but about 8:30 this morning he'd put water in the tub."

"What was his demeanor like?"

"He was kneeling at the bedside crying and sobbing. He said that his wife was a runner and was having trouble with her legs and wanted to soak before she ran today."

"Was she on any medication?"

"I asked him if his wife took any … or had been sick. He said yes, but could not tell me where the medication might be." Peterson pointed out the bottom drawer of the vanity where he'd found two prescription bottles.

Taylor located them, noting that one was a bottle of Tylenol with codeine and the second was a container of Dalmane—a sleeping medication. "Did you ask Mr. Bulik if his wife took the sleeping pills on a regular basis?"

Peterson nodded. "He said only when he was out of town. Mr. Bulik is in the Marine Corps Reserve and got back at about 10:30 last night."

To make Bob more comfortable, Peterson had then helped Bob from his bedroom to the living room. "I was trying to console him when Sergeant Baenen arrived, also in response to the 911 call." Peterson checked his notes. "Sergeant, right before you arrived, a Jean Weidner phoned the home. Apparently, she's the Buliks' marriage counselor."

Taylor frowned. First there was Peterson's information. Second was the absence of electrical items around the tub. Third, the victim apparently hadn't been on any regular medication and due to her running, had been in good physical condition. Lastly, there was the past incident. Given all this, Taylor considered Pam's death suspicious and decided to call it in. He was told that Deputy Chief Richard Rice would be summoned from the funeral of Brown County lawman John Baye.

Due to the deputy chief's delay, Sergeant Baenen was instructed to remain with Bob while Taylor and Peterson inspected the grounds. It was now noon. They circled the exterior of the home and then returned to the blue Monza they'd been told was the Buliks' car. The vehicle's engine was very cold. Entering the garage, Peterson then opened the front passenger door of the Buliks' van.

Taylor did the same to the driver's door. This vehicle's firewall was warm. While backing out, the two detectives were confused at discovering a wet van seat. They reentered the house and checked the laundry room. On top of the washing machine was a green sweat suit. Its top was dry, however, both the pants portion and the panties wrapped inside them were wet. In addition, the panties were streaked with either body waste or outside dirt. In the washer, a print nightgown and two pair of blue jeans were still wet following the spin cycle.

Taylor notified the deputy coroner about their discoveries.

Genie said she'd use filter paper to blot the wet van seat and then submit it to St. Vincent Hospital's lab for analysis. To determine Pam's time of death, she'd checked for rigor in the victim's dependant parts and now had been recording the temperatures for the body, room, and bathwater. "I've also informed Dr. Darrel Skarphol that a detailed autopsy needs to be performed today. He'll be arriving to view the body before it's transported to St. Vincent's morgue."

Taylor was finally ready to question Bob. Now seated on the living room sofa, he seemed more composed. The detective first confirmed Peterson's earlier conversation and then asked, "Mr. Bulik, when you drew your wife's bath water this morning, how did she appear?"

"Groggy."

"What do you mean by groggy?"

Bob mumbled the same word and then convulsed into sobs.

Unable to question him further, the detective once again placed Sergeant Baenen on Bob's watch. Taylor then returned to the garage to search for additional evidence, hoping to decipher the reason for the wet van seat. Inside the right-hand stall, where the blue Monza normally parked, he found a patch of grease and oil. There appeared to be two marks that traveled through it as if someone had dragged their feet. At one point, Taylor looked up and thought he caught a glimpse of Bob through the window of the door leading into the house. The detective frowned. Baenen was supposed to be on Bob's constant watch.

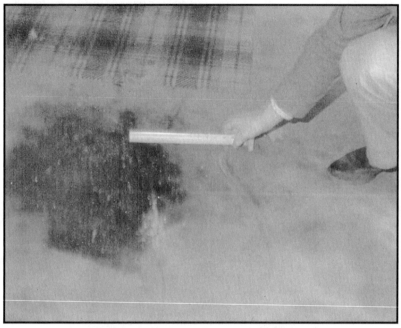

Sergeant Taylor measuring garage marks

Deputy Chief Richard Rice eventually arrived accompanied by Sergeant Stanley Keckhaver from Photo-Identification. A roll of yellow tape stating "Do Not Cross Police Line" was immediately placed across the front of the Buliks' driveway at the top of the hill.

Bob was told he was not under arrest, however, the deputy chief explained that Officer Peterson would now be transporting Bob to police headquarters for further questioning. Because the case was being handled as a suspicious death, District Attorney Peter Naze had been alerted and had sent Assistant DA Royce Finne to the scene. Detective Lieutenants Robert Langan and Tom Hinz then arrived and had Taylor familiarize them with the case details before the two headed downtown to conduct Bob's interview.

Taylor and Keckhaver were now ready to videotape and photograph the entire scene. They started outside, moved into the garage and finished up inside the house. Taylor pointed out the evidence to be photographed, then logged it, and marked it. With no way of knowing what evidence might be important to the investigation, the rule of thumb was to take too much rather than too little.

Sergeant Jim Taylor pointing at the location in the living room where he interviewed Bob Bulik

Samples of leaves, dirt, and grease were gathered from inside the garage. From the washing machine the sweat suit, panties and a leaf were bagged. On the floor of the dining room a man's tan jacket was secured along with a pair of men's red Saucony jogging shoes, their soles covered in mud. From two different locations within the home, a matched pair of women's Etonic running shoes was collected.

In the master bath, a wastebasket containing an empty prescription bottle was secured. All other medication in the home was also gathered. A brown towel lying on the bathroom floor was collected, as were a leaf and dirt located on the floor of the master bedroom and bathroom. The contents of the wastebaskets from the master bedroom and the bathtub area were garnered along with some hairs from the northeast side of the tub's edge. The depth of the bath water was measured and water samples were taken from the filled tub. After it was drained, any debris from the bottom was secured.

Evidence was also collected from Pam's body. This included nail scrapings and a black hair caught between her left and middle finger.

Taylor finally shut all the windows in the house, locked the doors, and climbed into his car. He'd also had the Buliks' Scottie taken to the dog pound for safekeeping. For more than four hours Taylor had combed the spacious home. If he'd missed something he knew the only way he could return would be with a search warrant.

≈

The duty officer in charge at the Green Bay Police Station was Sergeant Anderson. Coincidentally, he'd been the day-shift detective who'd conducted the follow-up investigation on the Buliks' August incident. Before Lieutenants Langan and Hinz talked with Bob Bulik, Anderson filled them in on those details. Then, at 3:00 p.m., the two detectives escorted Bob into a small room that held a table and three chairs. Around 5:40, Bob's interview was completed and he was driven home. At that point, he voluntarily provided his maroon bathrobe to be added to the case evidence.

By this time, Lieutenant Langan had joined Sergeant Taylor to discuss the outcome of Bob's interview. Langan said, "When Tom Hinz and I walked into the room, we weren't quite sure what we had. It was a difficult position to be in. We didn't know if we were interrogating someone who was a possible suspect in the death of his wife or also a victim who'd just lost a loved one." Advised of his rights, Bob had waived them. After first answering questions, he'd provided a written statement. This detailed his activity beginning on Friday, April 6, with his departure to Glenview, Illinois, to catch a military flight for his Marine Corps Reserve weekend in Denver, and ended with his 911 call on Saturday, April 7.

"Bob was cooperative," Langan said, "but Hinz and I were concerned with particular areas that he couldn't recall or give good answers to. Overall, Bob didn't appear incapacitated or impaired in any way. He did break down a few times, but primarily acted like—*let's get this over with. I've got nothing for you.* He seemed awfully cold, but people react differently in crisis situations."

Langan frowned. "Tom's a really good interrogator. We're supposed to be after nothing but the facts, but we still have feelings and hunches and opinions. If we didn't we probably wouldn't be good at what we do." Even though Langan didn't have all the facts, he said, "It didn't smell right to me."

Earlier in the day, when Taylor had familiarized him with the Bulik scene, Langan already knew this case was different. Here was the home of professionals—both Buliks were teachers. None of the Green Bay detectives had worked this kind of suspicious death before. They'd had fatal bar fights, a shooting at the YMCA, and other gruesome family situations, but there'd been nothing like this—"somebody up on the hill with a fancy bathroom."

2

Close-Knit Running Community

Portion of Fun Run Group at 1980 Marquette Marathon.
Front: Mary Tieman, Wayne Hubbard, Barb Delong, Chuck Pankratz,
Beezie and Bruce MacNeil, Daryl Kapalin, Leroy Vogt
Second: Sue Vogt, unknown, Pam Bulik, Dan Graham, unknown,
Bernice and Dick Lytie, Jim Drews, Bob Delong, Lynda Drews, Leo
Tieman, Larry Boehm, Sue Hyde, Bob Bulik
Back: Arlyss Hubbard, Kathleen & Rod Leadley, Sandy Johnsen,
Kathy Kapalin, Per Johnsen

B
ack in 1976, Jim and I had attended the Montreal Olympics
with Beezie MacNeil and her husband, Bruce, a fellow teacher
of Jim's from East High School. That was where the idea to establish a Green Bay community Fun Run had been hatched. Fashioned
from a *Runner's World* magazine program, Bruce's goal had been

to bring local people together with this common interest. Because the MacNeils had children, the runs became a family event. Of course, the Buliks and Delongs were included in the mix. Every Wednesday night, from April to September, Bruce organized the runs in a park located about a mile from Lambeau Field. Over the years, the group had also begun gathering at rotating homes throughout the winter months.

These weekly runs united our group of around fifty friends. There were no officers or structured meetings. To participate you just showed up. No one was judged by financial status, education, sexual orientation, political views, race, or religion. If some calamity befell a member, only one call was needed and the group would respond. Each asked how the other was doing, and honestly cared.

The Sunday morning after Pam's death, I slipped out of bed, listening to the gentle conversation of mourning doves perched high on our eaves. The outside thermometer read 40 degrees. The day was moving toward beautiful. I remembered the tide of anticipation that had washed over me before yesterday's race. Today it was just a sucking whirlpool of loss.

Last evening the Fun Run group had exchanged concerned phone calls, but nobody had yet heard from Bob. Beezie and I had discussed how Pam would've wanted somebody looking out for him like she'd asked my husband to do in the past. We'd insisted that both of our husbands go and check on Bob later today.

I grabbed the *Green Bay Press-Gazette* from the porch steps. Pam's death was front-page news. I read the article and then read it again. Something wasn't right.

Jim entered the family room with Collin and mussed my hair. "I hope you feel better than you look."

"I do a little, but listen to this. It says Pam's death is puzzling the local authorities. Before they rule her death accidental or criminal they need to wait for the Wisconsin Crime Lab's analysis of Pam's autopsy results."

Jim's brow wrinkled. "They used the word 'criminal?'"

I nodded. "But get this—their van was impounded." I told him that the Buliks' August incident had also been mentioned, but the police said there was no evidence linking it to Pam's death.

At this point, we'd nearly forgotten about it...

∞∞∞∞∞∞∞∞∞∞∞∞∞∞∞

On Friday, August 19, 1983, I headed for our detached garage where the carriage house once stood. After climbing into my blue Cutlass, I started its noisy engine. Because of the promise of better mileage I drove a diesel.

I thrived on stress. This morning, before heading to IBM, I'd spent time with Collin and his seventy-year old nanny. I'd checked my watch several times, not wanting to waste a minute by leaving too early. Now I'd cut it too close and ended up speeding.

I drove down Monroe Street taking sips of coffee between bites of bagel as *Billie Jean* played on the radio. The breeze through the open windows was hot and the sulfur emission from Fort Howard Paper mingled with the scent of the Fox River.

Stopped at a light the news began. "A Green Bay couple was assaulted last evening in their home at 251 Traders Court. The suspect remains at large."

My heart leapt. That was the Buliks' address.

Within five minutes I was at my desk and called their home.

The machine picked up.

Since St. Vincent Hospital handled emergencies, I tried it first.

Three rings and the receptionist answered.

"Can you please tell me, if you have a Pam or Bob Bulik assigned to a room?" My stomach knotted.

"Let me check... I see only a Pamela Bulik, but she's in the ICU and isn't accepting visitors."

≈

Distraught about my friend, over the next four days I'd managed to speak with the anxious Bulik children a few times, but not

Bob. Understandably, Alex and Abby were upset and, of course, they said, so was their dad, who'd been on a nearly constant vigil at the hospital with Pam. I was sick to hear that she'd sustained a life-threatening skull fracture and concussion. But last night, Pam had finally been moved out of the ICU.

Over the noon hour the hospital's fourth floor hallway was congested. I dodged nurses, other visitors, and carts from central supply, pharmacy, and maintenance while being greeted by the smell of disinfectant blended with the aroma of patients' food trays.

There was a lot of commotion in the room next to Pam's. A boisterous family overflowed into the hallway with flowers, balloons and gifts—quite a contrast to Pam's dimly lit room. I tapped on the partially closed door and peeked in. Her back was to me. White gauze covered a shaved spot near the crown of her matted hair.

I set down a small gift near a stack of greeting cards, a few plants, and a vase of roses. Note cards were propped up against them. As expected the roses were from Bob and one plant was from the Fun Run Group. I was surprised that the remaining ones were not from Pam's family. Maybe everything hadn't been moved from intensive care yet.

"Pam," I whispered, gently tugging at her foot through the blanket. "It's Lynda."

She cautiously turned and winced in the process of propping herself up. Her eyes were wet and dark.

"I've been so worried." I gave Pam a careful hug. Then perching on the edge of her bed, I squeezed her hand, reassured when she returned the squeeze.

"I know you have…" she slurred, apparently from her head injury or medication. Pam said her neurosurgeon, Dr. Bruce Breseler, had told her that he didn't believe there'd be any permanent brain damage. "In addition to a pounding headache, I can't smell anything, Lynda, so nothing even tastes good."

"One way to lose some weight!" I forced some humor.

She tried to smile.

"The news said you were attacked … how did it happen?"

Pam moistened her mouth from a nearby glass of water and then said, "Bob and I had been celebrating our thirteenth wedding anniversary downtown, with a couple of drinks, before we got home around dark."

"The kids were at Y-camp, right?"

"Yeah, luckily. We opened a bottle of wine and grilled chicken outside. After eating, we started to exercise on the family room floor."

I looked dubious. "Like sit-ups?"

Pam shook her head, and then cringed at the painful mistake. "Bob was teaching me some passive stretching exercises he'd learned at reserves." She spoke slowly and precisely, finding it difficult to form some words. "I don't remember Bob getting up or leaving, but he told me later that he heard a noise and started from the family room. That's where this guy in his late teens confronted him."

"Could he be one of the troubled students Bob has worked with?" At Edison Junior High, he taught special education to emotionally disturbed children, like he'd previously done at Preble High School.

"Bob doesn't think so, though he just caught a glimpse of the guy before he was struck in the stomach and blacked out. When Bob came to, he found me lying on the floor." She briefly rested and then continued. "I don't recall getting hit, but I do remember throwing up." Gingerly, she touched the dressing on her head. "I needed ten stitches."

Her troubled eyes found mine. "Lynda, a detective stopped in to see me today. He insinuated Bob could've done this to me."

My neck jerked back. "You're kidding! How could the police ever suggest that?"

≈

Jim and I discussed my conversation with Pam. He agreed that Bob could definitely not be involved. Since arriving in Green Bay, Jim had worked at East High, Howe Elementary, and Fort

Howard Elementary, all inner-city schools. He was trained to recognize abused children, who often lived in homes where domestic violence among their caregivers was also the norm. A large percentage of the violent crimes against these students' mothers were committed by an intimate partner, usually the husband or boyfriend. Of course the police worked from those same statistics, but we knew the Buliks didn't fit this standard mold. There was absolutely no indication that Pam had ever been abused. We saw the family weekly at Fun Runs. She wore revealing running clothes. If this were an ongoing issue Pam could never have hidden her bruises. In this situation, the police were way off base.

Before I'd left the hospital, Pam had asked me if Jim would give Bob a call. Now that she was out of danger, she felt certain that Jim would be able to reach him. Pam was worried about Bob's reaction to the assault. He felt he should've protected her, yet she didn't see how, since he'd gotten hit himself.

My husband has always been a sensitive and thoughtful guy. He'd often notice a news article, cut it out, write a note, and mail both to a friend congratulating them on their achievement, providing a condolence, or just saying "Hi, I see you're doing well." In this way he was similar to Pam. But this was different—Pam wanted Bob to share his feelings with Jim. I knew Jim would never confide in Bob. I had my doubts that this would be successful, but because Pam asked, I knew Jim would try.

Awkwardly, he did talk to Bob. Because he was a marine, Jim could tell that Bob was embarrassed about not stopping the guy. Bob also related that earlier this summer, some minor items had been stolen out of their backyard including a bug zapper and one of Pam's potted plants. In their neighborhood, a peeping Tom had been reported, and two doors down from the Buliks' a car and a bike were recently stolen right out of the driveway. After Jim hung up we discussed it. On the night of the assault the Buliks' front lights had been off. Any of the individuals, who had committed the earlier crimes, could have been surprised at finding Bob and Pam home and simply overreacted.

~

Pam was discharged the Thursday before Bob's teacher in-service began for the 1983-84 school year. To put Bob's mind at ease, Beezie offered to spend Friday with Pam at the Buliks' home. Close to noon, I also drove over from IBM and pulled up in front of their garage.

Since the police hadn't caught the intruder, I looked around a bit warily. From here, I couldn't see the Buliks' neighbors on either side. It certainly would have been easy for someone to break-in undetected.

I carried chicken salad and croissants for lunch. Normally I entered through the garage, but the doors were down. To my right was the elevated front entrance. I tried the front door, but it was locked. Because a knock or the doorbell might waken Pam, I decided to walk around the house, figuring I could catch Beezie's attention in the kitchen or family room. As I did, I nervously checked the wooded terrain, but thankfully spotted only chipmunks scuttling under brush and gray squirrels scurrying up trees. Stepping up on the deck, I tried the double French patio doors. They, too, were locked.

I put my face up to the glass and could see the twenty feet of hearth. It ran below the floor to ceiling natural stone fireplace to the left and the dark plank paneling to the right where the TV was nestled. Beezie was seated in a plaid chair, her back to me, working on some stitchery. As I gently rapped, I saw it fly into the air.

She turned toward me, her eyes like saucers, covering her mouth to hold back a scream.

I bent over laughing.

She unbolted the door and slapped my arm. "Lynda, stop that! It's not funny. You scared me half to death!"

"I noticed!" I entered still amused. "I didn't want to wake Pam."

"I can't believe I didn't hear you drive down. It's creepy being here, knowing what happened."

I agreed and relocked the door before setting the lunch down on the counter that separated the kitchen from the family room.

"So how's Pam doing?"

"Some of her color's back, but she still has horrendous headaches."

As if on cue, Pam emerged from her bedroom shampooed and showered. She was wearing sunglasses to reduce the impact of the bright room.

I gave her a hug and stood back. "You look just like a movie star in your robe and clean fluffy hair."

Pam cracked her beautiful smile, giving me goose bumps. It looked like she was on her way to recovery.

She noticed the food. "I'm so embarrassed." More color appeared on her cheeks. "I can't pitch in for lunch. Until my disability insurance starts, we're a little short on money."

"Don't even think about it," I said. "It's our treat."

For the fall semester, Pam said she'd be on medical leave. Like her parents, who both had been educators in Wisconsin Rapids, Pam had earned a teaching degree, but it wasn't until the Buliks built their beautiful home that financial need had compelled Pam to find a job in her field. Similar to Bob, she'd accepted a special education position focused on emotionally disturbed children and taught at a high school in Freedom, a small town twenty miles south of Green Bay. Pam was a great advocate for her students, but made them toe the line and she believed they respected her for it. Even though Pam enjoyed teaching, ironically, because of the assault, she was temporarily resuming her preferred lifestyle as a stay-at-home mom, gourmet cook, and connoisseur of crafts.

Today, as I dished up our plates and laid them on the family room's coffee table, Beezie helped Pam to the couch. She needed a cane for balance. While picking at her food she basked in the sunlight. Fortunately our conversations were starting again, but it was obvious she wouldn't be running anytime soon.

"Pam," I said, scratching Misty behind her little black ears, "what was your parents' reaction to your attack?" Beezie and I both knew our mothers would've been there in an instant to help, and we wondered where Pam's was.

Her evident discomfort with my question made me feel terrible that I'd asked. Pam said her dad planned to drive over from Wisconsin Rapids sometime this week, and her mother was still checking into airfares from her home in Florida. Pam also seemed frustrated. She still couldn't remember the details of the assault and was mortified that the police continued to believe Bob might be responsible. "A detective's talked to me twice and asked both Bob and me to take lie-detector tests. I told him I couldn't see any use to that!" But then she asked for our opinions.

June 1970 College Graduation for Pam with her parents, Myrtle and William, and Grandmother Blanche Metzger.

We discussed the pros and cons. Beezie and I thought, since they had nothing to hide, both Buliks should take the polygraph.

Pam had asked her brother the same question.

Now a captain in the navy, Bill lived in Bellevue, Washington, with his wife, Bonnie, and their three daughters. The Metzger siblings' relationship had improved since Bill's return from his tortuous years in Vietnam.

Near the end of Pam's freshman year in college, Bill had taken off in a F-8 Crusader on a combat mission to Hanoi. His plane had crash-landed after being hit by anti-aircraft artillery. Suffering a broken right leg and torn left arm and leg, Bill was captured. During his six years in prison, Bonnie, Pam, and often Bob, spoke at organizational meetings and fairs to promote a national letter-writing campaign urging the Vietnamese to take care of their POWs. The Metzger family also started the Wisconsin chapter of the POW MIA Organization. Bill felt his family's efforts had definitely helped secure his, and others' safe release in March 1973.

Last night on the phone, similar to Beezie's and my recommendation, Bill had told Pam that a lie-detector test would refocus
the authorities on finding the real perpetrator.

≈

In mid-September, Pam told friends the polygraph questions
she'd been asked. Did she know what had caused her August head
injury? Was she purposely withholding any information about
how she'd received it? And did she know who had caused it? Of
course she'd answered no to each.

The next day the Buliks got the news: the polygraph results
confirmed the truth had been told, and with nothing else to go
on, the police department was filing the case as unsolved.

∞∞∞∞∞∞∞∞∞∞∞∞∞∞

The first forty-eight to seventy-two hours of any investigation
were the most important. Because Sergeant Taylor had been
the initial detective to respond to the apparent drowning at the
Bulik home, it was now his case. Yesterday, after securing the evidence in a station locker, he'd begun divvying out assignments to
other Green Bay detectives. As many interviews as feasible were
now being conducted with anyone that knew anything about the
Buliks. The goal was to gather information before an individual's memory was clouded by other people's opinions and recollections. When anything pertinent was discovered, Taylor would
re-interview that individual. His job was to get into the hearts
and heads of the Buliks.

Taylor had to admit that when he'd driven up to the Buliks'
home yesterday, he'd initially been worried that the department
had possibly screwed up handling the earlier August case. Maybe
the purported intruder had returned. But when he'd confirmed
that this was not so, his gut had told him that Bob was somehow
involved in Pam's death. Taylor knew, however, that keeping an
open mind was a necessity. Tunnel vision could lead a case entirely
in the wrong direction. He credited his wife, Judy, for frequently

straightening him out. Since his perspective was often jaded, Judy became his conscience, instructing him to look for the good in people, not just the bad.

At 10:25 a.m. on Sunday, April 8, the second phase of Pam's autopsy was underway. Dr. Skarphol was performing an additional gross examination to check for bruises that might have become more apparent since last evening's autopsy.

Taylor knew that there were three possible ways Pam could have died: accident, suicide, or homicide. If it was the latter he was looking for what he called the MOM factor—the motive, opportunity, and means. Was there a reason that Bob had wanted to harm Pam? He'd already admitted to being in the house. That gave him the opportunity, and the bathtub certainly provided the means.

Since marriage discord often drove motive, the detective had immediately followed up with the Buliks' counselor, Jean Weidner. She, along with Dr. O'Neill and Dr. Reinhard, made up Psychiatric Services of Green Bay and had each worked with the Buliks over the past eight months. Dr. Michael O'Neill had prescribed sleeping pills for Pam, but at present, did not have her on any medication. In response to Taylor's concern about the Bulik children's welfare, Weidner said that she believed they'd be safe with their dad. That was all she'd divulge, however, until Bob's written permission was secured. Taylor was working on that obstacle. This wasn't the case for Dr. O'Neill, Pam's individual therapist. He'd agreed to meet this afternoon.

Back in August, Green Bay detectives had felt that Pam's head injury had most likely been the result of spousal issues. Taylor now wondered if Pam had started to remember those details, and fearing her accusations and the possible repercussions, Bob had been forced to quiet his wife.

In the midst of Pam's initial autopsy, Dr. Breseler had arrived at the hospital and provided some insight about the August incident. When Pam had been in the ICU, he said that Bob had hung around her room a great deal. It surely could've been the act of a very concerned husband, but Breseler's impression was that Bob had seemed more anxious about Pam's recollection concerning the assault than about her vital signs or whether she'd be all right.

As Taylor gathered other viewpoints on this August premise, he was addressing the suicide question, too. In the days immediately preceding Pam's death, had anyone believed she'd been in a mindset to take her own life?

Pam's only sibling had called this morning, shocked about his sister's death. Bill Metzger had last spoken to Pam the previous Friday, after Bob had left for a weekend in Yuma, Arizona, with his Denver reserve unit. At that time, she'd seemed somewhat depressed, though Bill didn't believe his sister had been suicidal. He said he had mixed emotions about Bob's possible involvement in Pam's death.

William Metzger Sr. had also contacted the station, deeply distressed over the loss of his daughter. Pam and his grandchildren were to have visited him today in Wisconsin Rapids.

Around noon, Nancy Gloudeman, a fellow teacher from Freedom High School, called. Yesterday she'd been making food for their Saturday night faculty party when the TV announced that Pamela Bulik, age thirty-five, was dead from a possible suicide. Nancy didn't feel that could be true. When they'd left school on Friday, Pam had been in good spirits and was looking forward to the party. At Freedom High School, Pam had been well liked, a sweetheart, with great staff rapport. As a teacher, she'd had a definite effect on her special education students and dealt well with difficult situations, such as, when one student had thrown a chair at her while another pulled a knife. But her own children had been the center of Pam's world. For this reason, Nancy couldn't believe her friend would take her own life.

Nancy used the word "strange" in conjunction with the media's account that the Buliks' large bathtub was involved in Pam's death. Previously, Pam had complained how costly it was to fill, so the family most often used the one upstairs.

The two women had talked in great length about Pam's August assault. Although Pam didn't remember being hit by Bob, she'd told Nancy that she'd had thoughts about him doing it. During Pam's four years at Freedom, though, Nancy said she'd never noticed any bruises on her friend.

Nancy's call started a domino effect providing names of other teachers to contact. On Monday and Tuesday, April 2 and 3, Linda Maves said she'd met Pam at an educators' conference in Milwaukee. Earlier, Pam had related to Linda that she believed that someone had been hired to get her in August, but she'd never named Bob as the party responsible for arranging the hit. Because Pam couldn't remember the incident, she'd told Linda she'd been living in fear. Following the August assault, Linda had asked Bob if their dog had barked at the intruder. Every time she'd visited the Buliks' home, the Scottie would bark at her. Bob had told her that Misty never barked at anyone. His comment still bothered Linda.

In January of '84, when Pam returned from her disability leave, another teacher, Debbie Ehlers, said Pam had been pretty stressed out. She'd confided that she thought Bob might've been involved in the assault, but hadn't been sure. Debbie thought Bob was arrogant, standoffish, and rather controlling. She felt Pam had been afraid she might do something wrong when he was around.

Debra Fantini, also a Freedom colleague, had last seen Pam on Thursday, April 5. Since Debra was a runner, the two women had periodically worked out together. Like Nancy, she'd never noticed any bruises on Pam. At yesterday's Jogger's Joynt race, Pam and Debra had made plans to meet, but Debra had stayed home due to a cold.

Pam had told another teaching associate, Diane Richardson, that when the assailant had entered the Buliks' home, she and Bob had been exercising. Pam said she'd been struck, while on all fours and facing the carpet. Again, Pam had never accused Bob.

At first glance, Taylor's hypothesis that Pam's August memory had possibly resurfaced wasn't holding water, but so far there hadn't been any evidence that Pam had been mired in depression and planning to take her own life either. On the contrary, it appeared as if Pam had instead scheduled a full and enjoyable weekend of activities. And her planning had moved beyond this weekend. Pam's 1984 golf-league sign-up form, dated this week, had been dropped off at the station. Pam marked that she wouldn't be participating this summer and explained why:

> I will be out of state and therefore believe it to be unfair to take up a place when someone else could golf more. Please extend my deepest gratitude to all the wonderful people who sent me cards, and kept me in their prayers as I recovered from my accident last summer. Their thoughts and concerns touched me and were a great source of comfort and strength. I am as close to being 100% recovered, as I probably will ever get. (I'm running in the UWGB's 26-mile marathon in May). Will miss seeing everyone this summer, but am looking forward to travel with my family.
> *Pam Bulik*

While calls relating to Pam's death kept coming into, and going out of the station, Sergeant Keckhaver began a custodial inspection of the Buliks' van. At Bob's interview with detectives, he'd signed a consent form allowing the police to search it after it had been towed into the police garage. As in the home, there was no way to know what evidence might be important to the case, so some inconsequential items, most likely, would be photographed, marked, and bagged from the Buliks' silver and maroon vehicle.

First, Keckhaver collected any additional foreign material from the van's seats. Then, on the console between the two front captain's chairs, a box of Puff tissues and a table fork were noted. In the glove compartment were two medicine bottles: one of extra strength Tylenol and one, with no label, that smelled like cough medicine. The floor area of the driver's side was very clean, but the passenger side floor was dirty with leaves, mud, and a used tissue. Also, the running board leading into the passenger seat area contained a substantial amount of dirt-type material. The floor between the captain's chairs included parts of leaves, dirt material, and a white plastic bucket. Behind the chairs were a multicolored umbrella and an ice scraper with a brush. On the floor behind the second row of seats were a blue blanket and a white towel.

With activities now in motion at the station, Sergeant Taylor began canvassing the Buliks' neighborhood, taking notes in his ever-present pocket notebook. Later, he'd transfer pertinent information to the official GBPD Detail Sheets, keeping his private comments to himself. If a case went to trial, he didn't want the defense to have the benefit of his personal thoughts during their discovery phase.

Taylor first contacted the Ghents*, who occupied the home just to the left of the Buliks'. They'd recently moved in and hadn't conversed with Pam and Bob other than to say hello. On the morning of Pam's death they hadn't seen or heard anything unusual, but Sandy Ghent did hear something at around nine o'clock the evening before. She'd been putting out their dog when she'd noticed some talking coming from the woods located behind both their home and the Buliks'. She hadn't been able to understand the words, so she didn't know if it had been an argument, but the voices had continued for at least fifteen minutes.

Another neighbor, Mrs. Sara Weston*, had seen Pam and Bob running on Wednesday or Thursday, but not together. Pam would sometimes take naps and leave her home unlocked. Because Mrs. Weston knew about the Buliks' previous home assault, she said, this made no sense to her.

Taylor next stopped at the Maddens'. Tom said his wife, Sylvia, wasn't home, but had been a very close friend of Pam's. Sylvia worked as a special education teacher, too. A tentative interview for her was scheduled after school ended on Monday.

The remaining homes within one block of the Buliks' residence were checked. Most claimed that Pam and Bob's only close friends were a group they jogged with—some kind of running club—maybe it was associated with the Jogger's Joynt. It was interesting, Taylor noted, that the Buliks' running friends had yet to contact the station, while Pam's teaching colleagues had.

Could it be that the Freedom teachers swore allegiance only to Pam, while their running friends might protect both Buliks?

Our Astor Park home

On the Sunday afternoon following Pam's death, Collin and I were stacking blocks while Fletcher, our Springer spaniel, dozed in the sunlight coming through the beveled windows of our Astor Park home. In the 1890s Green Bay had been in the midst of its boom years, and Astor was its most prestigious residential neighborhood. Victor I. Minahan, a co-founder of the *Green Bay Press-Gazette*, was one of our home's early owners, though, by the 1970s, it had been turned into a home for delinquent boys. For a pittance we were able to purchase our 1899 Queen Anne Victorian, with its beautiful open gables, original slate roof, tiled fireplaces, and back and front staircases. Jim and I were now gradually returning our home to its original grandeur.

From the window, I could see Bruce MacNeil arrive in his rusting green rambler, nicknamed Scout. I yelled up the front stairway to Jim. All day I'd known the impending visit to Bob's was making him uncomfortable. The two men had roped Dick Lytie in, too.

While Jim was gone I had a neighborhood girl watch Collin so I could complete a slow jog. I hoped it would reduce the pain in my legs from yesterday's race, and do the same for my soul. I let my tears come as I thought about Pam. This was the first weekend in months I hadn't run with her and realized my tears were also for me. At that memorable Saturday back in 1975, there had been three. Now Pam was unbelievably dead and because Barb's husband, Bob, had recently accepted a promotion, this week would be her last in Green Bay. I couldn't curb the penetrating ache realizing that by next Saturday I'd have lost both of my original soul mates.

Back from my jog, I followed behind Collin, pedaling his Big Bird tricycle down the sidewalk. Between the pickets in our fence, protecting Fletcher from vehicles, I could see his sad eyes. He wanted to play. The loud rumblings of an approaching car filled the air as Bruce, looking like a rabid dog, pulled into our driveway. Behind his normally gruff manner was a caring man with firm character and boisterous laugh. He also became easily agitated over any injustice, causing spittle to accumulate at the corners of his mouth. Today, on top of their frustrating meeting with Bob, he said that Scout's tailpipe had fallen off.

Jim climbed out, ready to explain, as Bruce hot-rodded away.

Because the guys had believed that relatives would be at the Buliks', Jim said they'd parked on their cul-de-sac and walked down the long driveway. At the bottom there'd been no vehicles and the garage doors had been closed. "Honestly, Lynda, I hoped Bob wasn't home. Dick and I nominated Bruce to ring the bell and then he dashed back to join us."

I could just picture the scene: the three of them must have looked like a firing squad, ready to shoot poor Bob.

"He finally opened the front door," Jim said, bending down to straighten Collin's tricycle out.

"How did he look?"

"Just awful. He didn't say a thing. Dick finally broke the ice and said how sorry we were about Pam. I felt foolish standing there, shuffling my feet with no idea what to say."

I leaned against the fence, feeling Fletcher's nose nudge my legs. "Did you go in?"

"No. It was like Bob wanted us to leave, but wouldn't say so. We agreed that it was one of the strangest situations we've ever encountered."

"I'm still glad you made the effort." I grabbed Jim's hand. "In Bob's own way, I'm sure he appreciated the support of his friends."

"Lynda, I'm not so sure. On the drive home we discussed Bob. In all the years we've known him he's never shared anything personal. We've only heard him talk about his triathlons, his job, and the reserves. All of us agreed we just don't know the real Bob."

3

A Life Unravels

On the evening of Tuesday, April 10, 1984, I was dressed in real funeral attire. Jim and I pulled into the parking lot of the Proko-Wall Funeral Home next to the Buliks' van. Even though it had reportedly been impounded, it was obviously back in Bob's hands. The MacNeils pulled in alongside us. I gave Beezie a hug and said, "I'm having second thoughts about seeing Pam."

Yesterday, Beezie had called me at work. Per her request Bob had just met with her. "Lynda, he was overcome with grief. I certainly felt sorrier for him than I did for myself."

I leaned further into my desk cubicle and lowered my voice. "Did he give you any details about Pam's death?"

"No. He never brought that subject up, and I felt I couldn't ask. We just discussed Pam's funeral arrangements."

That certainly was a subject right up Beezie's alley. Her dad had owned a funeral home in Munising, Michigan, where she'd written obituaries and offered condolences to bereaved families. She'd even sewn up the head of a homeless man when his autopsy had ruled out a homicide.

"Bob told me he wanted a closed casket," Beezie said, "thinking it would be easier for the kids."

The only funeral I'd been to was my grandmother's. Following her death, I'd carried a remorseful burden for so many years. Even through my guilty tears, I still remembered that her casket had been closed. "Beezie, that's what I'd prefer," I said, my hand tightening around my coffee cup.

"I don't agree. That's what I told Bob. My dad encouraged families to see their departed loved one so they'd believe the individual was actually gone."

"So did Bob change his mind?"

"He did. There's going to be a private showing for just family and a few close friends before Pam's casket is closed for the public wake. In addition to me, Bob said I could invite you and Sylvia."

My stomach curdled. "I've never seen a dead person…I don't think I want to see Pam that way." But because Beezie definitely did, I finally agreed.

Tonight, as we entered the funeral home's vestibule, followed by our husbands, I couldn't believe Beezie could find the combination of floral arrangements, stale smoke, and tinge of embalming fluid comforting. To me it smelled like death.

Tom and Sylvia Madden had already arrived. During my four-month maternity leave Pam had encouraged me to join her ladies golf league. That's where I'd met Sylvia, who was as tall as Pam,

Sylvia Madden taught Special Education at Preble High School initially with Bob Bulik

vivacious, full of fun, and about as bad a golfer as Pam and me. Sylvia's son was the Buliks' babysitter, and her daughter was in the fifth grade with the Buliks' son. After the August incident, when Pam had given up her cane but still couldn't run, she'd started to walk with Sylvia. That's when she'd joined Beezie and me as a main confidant.

Bill and Bonnie Metzger approached. I knew Bonnie had been more like a sister than sister-in-law to Pam. After we expressed our condolences, Bill explained how he'd learned about Pam's death. On Saturday evening, Bob had called the Metzgers' home and said, "We had a terrible accident here. Pam's dead. She drowned." Bill had been blown over. His first thoughts had been for his parents. For six years they'd endured his unknown fate as a POW, and now had to deal with the tragic loss of their only other child.

The Metzgers excused themselves so Bill could accompany his parents into the viewing room. Bonnie would not be joining him. She couldn't bear to see Pam.

Moments later the funeral director asked Beezie, Sylvia, and me to follow him. Muffled crying could be heard as we entered the room. There was a noticeable division between the two families. To the left, Bob stood with his arms around his children. They were adjacent to Bob's father and brother. To the right, the Metzger family was stationed.

Beezie grabbed my arm as we stared into the open coffin. I could see Sylvia was shaken as well. How could this be Pam? The bruising near her left eye and forehead were unsuccessfully covered by makeup. Her swollen face barely resembled any woman, let alone my dear friend. I couldn't fathom why Bob had ever allowed us to see Pam like this.

People arrived at the funeral home in droves. Most wakes were celebrations commemorating a loved one's long and memorable life, but today there was only painful emotion over the horrific loss of Pam.

Part of the Fun Run group that attended Pam's funeral and luncheon. Karen & Larry Boehm, Bob Delong, Daryl Kapalin, Leroy Vogt, Lynda Drews, Sandy Johnsen, unknown, Per Johnsen, Pam Bulik, Jim Drews, Barb Delong, Dick Lytie, Bob Bulik, Kathy Kapalin

Because it had been inappropriate to talk with Bob at the private showing, Jim and I waited in a long line with the MacNeils and Maddens to do so. We discussed Pam's disturbing appearance with our husbands and also our friends who'd gathered after offering their condolences to Bob.

"This whole thing is so surreal," said Per Johnsen, a professor at UW-Green Bay and a fellow runner. "Everyone knows about the Buliks' earlier marital troubles, but friends are putting that aside today to express their sympathy, which Bob is graciously accepting."

Dick Lytie piped in, "The police stopped at the Jogger's Joynt to interview me."

"A detective talked to me, too," Per's wife, Sandy, said. Before Pam had lost her recent weight, the two women had often run races together toward the back of the pack. Sandy now looked at Beezie and me. "I recommended that the detective talk to the two of you."

We both cringed hearing that.

For more than an hour we'd been inching up toward Bob, who stood tall among the floral arrangements that engulfed Pam's casket. It was now our turn. He responded warmly to my sincere embrace and grasped Jim's hand. I waited for the MacNeils and Maddens to do as we had. Then we three women huddled to talk.

Sylvia was amazed that Bob's hand was so warm when hers was so cold and clammy. Even though the police were asking questions, she said he didn't appear to be the least bit concerned. Sylvia had been interviewed yesterday. In addition to being asked about the events in the Buliks' lives leading up to Pam's death, she'd told the detective that she was worried about the children, especially Alex, who frequently suffered migraines. Sylvia knew Abby hadn't attended school yesterday or today, but Alex had. Pam had always considered him to be her sensitive child, and Sylvia found it hard to believe, he was doing so well.

Sylvia then related some information secured from her daughter.

On the morning of Pam's death, a fifth grade classmate, Scott Burnham*, had stopped at the Buliks' to see if Alex wanted to go to Port Plaza Mall. Scott had told friends that he'd noticed Mrs. Bulik sitting at the kitchen counter. We each added this confusing fact to our growing list.

The funeral director meandered through the crowd, announcing that the prayer service would begin shortly. Sylvia excused herself to find her husband. Before Beezie and I did the same, a friend from our bridge club joined us. As Bob headed toward the designated area, he passed the three of us and said with a peculiar smile, "Looks like you gals are missing your fourth for bridge."

It seemed such an insensitive comment, but perhaps this was Bob's way of handling his grief.

I entwined my fingers with Jim's during Pam's prayer service. Even though comforting words were being said, my grief would only be prolonged by not knowing what had caused my friend's death.

Near the top of the hour, as we bowed our heads for the final prayer, a chorus of running watches beeped—a fitting tribute to our lost running mate.

Sylvia caught me as we were leaving and asked if I'd noticed Kevin VandenLangenberg*. She was shocked that he'd actually come to the wake. Under his sport coat, Sylvia said he'd been flaunting a screen-printed California T-shirt. He'd smirked and told her—it had been a special gift from Linda.

◇◇◇◇◇◇◇◇◇◇◇◇◇◇◇◇◇◇◇

Because Bruce MacNeil advertised the Fun Runs in the newspaper, it wasn't unusual to have new runners show up. Back in July 1983, Jim pointed Linda VandenLangenberg out to me. She worked at Anne Sullivan Elementary School as a multi-handicapped and early childhood teacher. That spring, Jim had helped Bob Bulik run a school sponsored jogging and fitness clinic, which Linda had attended.

"Lynda, I never brought this up, but something about the clinic bugged me. Bob was supposed to be in charge. Each week I ran with a group and expected him to do the same, but that didn't always happen. At least a couple times he just took off with Linda."

At tonight's Fun Run, I envied her long toned legs as she glided across the parking lot in her snug-fitting running shorts and singlet. No matter how thin I was, I'd always hated my legs, especially my fat knees. This was something Pam and I commiserated about together. Even though she'd had surgery to improve her very obvious varicose veins, I knew she would've gladly exchanged her thick legs for Linda's slender ones.

Tonight, I noticed a number of the guys tracking Linda with their eyes. She appeared to enjoy the attention. With olive skin, high cheekbones, thick chestnut curls, and a cute turned up nose, she was quite striking. I found Pam and asked if she knew Linda, not mentioning Jim's comments. Pam said, "Slightly." Linda had once worked in the same department as Bob at Edison Junior High. When the Buliks hosted a few staff parties, Pam said she'd been introduced to Linda and her husband Kevin.

**Edison Junior High Special Education
Department. Linda VandenLangenberg is
far left and Bob Bulik is far right.**

We walked over to the larger group where Linda was currently stealing the spotlight. In a flirtatious voice she was giggling with a group of guys that included our husbands. I put my arm through

Jim's waiting for an introduction. He complied. "Linda, I don't believe you've met my wife, Lynda."

I held out my hand, smiling. "Nice to meet another namesake, but I bet you're a Linda with an 'i' not a 'y'?"

She nodded, returning my smile and handshake.

I asked what pace she ran. Before she could answer, my husband butted in. "Bob, you probably know, since you two have run together."

I elbowed Jim. It was just like him to be so obvious.

"Well…" Bob hesitated as he eyed Pam's questioning glance. Linda interrupted, quickly announcing a pace close to mine.

"Why don't you run with Pam and me?" I offered. "We'll speed up or slow down, whatever works for you."

When Bruce kicked off the five-miler, we three women took to the street running side by side. Curiosity about Linda was foremost, especially since she knew our husbands. Questions were exchanged and information shared freely. Linda was bubbly, definitely an extrovert. Actually, she wouldn't shut up.

I figured Pam might bring up my husband's comment, and eventually she did. "So Linda, you've run with Bob?"

"Just a few times," Linda said. On the runs he'd been a great sounding board, helping her sort through some issues related to her students and family.

I peeked at Pam, whose eyebrows had shot up. She'd complained that Bob found it difficult to talk about serious matters. It appeared he had no problem with Linda.

≈

July turned into August and the Buliks' home assault occurred. By mid-September Pam's neuro-surgeon referred her to a psychiatrist, Dr. Michael O'Neill. He was to help her cope with the aftermath of the attack. Because the assault had occurred within the home, Pam was now fearful inside her previous safe haven. This was making her overly anxious and very stressed. In addition, Pam was disturbed about Bob's baffling reaction. Initially he'd been wonderful, providing support through her physical and mental distress, but that had changed. Bob had begun rehashing old marital problems he'd shelved, and had turned cold toward Pam.

Close friends felt Pam's pain. In the past Bob had doted on her. He'd frequently given Pam flowers for no reason, and gifts of expensive jewelry. He'd run errands for her without complaint, encouraged her running, and shared her enjoyment of their beautiful home. So Pam was pleased when Bob scheduled an appointment to see his own psychiatrist, Dr. Gerald Wellens.

Just days later, however, Pam called me at work with new concern in her voice. While checking Bob's pants' pockets before doing laundry, she'd discovered a receipt from Zale's Jewelers in a pair of his jeans. Her birthday was next month, and she did love surprises, but because she was still on disability she felt it wasn't the right time to be spending so much money. At one point she'd worked part-time at Rummele's Jewelers. Since they still honored her discount she also questioned why Bob hadn't used it. "I then checked his calendar to see if he'd be in town for my birthday and another entry caught my eye." On October 4, Pam said that Bob had written "Birthday Linda." Pam knew my birthday was September 29. She thought Bob had gotten the date mixed up, but thought he should've known I spelled my name with a "y." "What's more, Lynda, I'm surprised he'd think to record your birthday in the first place."

So was I.

≈

Weekly, I visited IBM clients in Wisconsin and the Upper Peninsula of Michigan, covering a radius of about 300 miles. In mid-October I arrived home after a three-day trip. Like Fletcher, Collin wiggled all over when I walked in the door and immediately wanted his mommy's attention. That's when Pam called in tears. My son's started, too, his tiny arms clinging to my legs.

Guilt gushed through me as I managed to pull Collin off, collapsed in a chair, and then lifted him into my lap. He kept trying to yank the phone away as I attempted to talk to Pam. Something had to change.

She'd just returned from a counseling session with Dr. O'Neill where her husband had been asked to attend. "I listened to Bob say that he was losing his identity in our marriage," Pam sobbed. "That he was sick and tired of my dependency, and I needed to have my own goals. That he couldn't go on like this...Lynda, how can he say that?"

On today's long drive home I'd contemplated my own life. Pam's problems were consuming too much of the precious time I had available to spend with Collin. If I didn't give him priority over Pam, he would hardly know his mother. Even though Pam's crisis was escalating, it was impossible for me to support her needs the way I should. After I hung up, I called Beezie. As a substitute grade-school teacher, with her three children all in school, Beezie could devote time to Pam when I felt I couldn't. Over the next four weeks, I was grateful when Beezie became Pam's crutch.

≈

Our untraditional Halloween Party was a much-anticipated event. Instead of spooky costumes guests arrived at our Jackson Street home dressed as a song. In turn, they secretly handed me their tune, designated on a record or a tape. For hours we'd mingle trying to guess each other's title.

This year I'd chosen *Natural Woman* by Carol King and purchased a cheap doll to cut off its wavy hair. With plastic flowers tucked behind my ears, I'd dressed in a gunnysack shift over a T-shirt, and pinned the hanks of curls into the armpits. Très natural!

It had been two weeks since I'd last talked to Pam. The Buliks had received an invitation with a regrets only RSVP. By 10 p.m. they still hadn't arrived. I couldn't wait any longer. Our living room furniture was pushed to the edges, and with Bruce as my assistant, we began to play each song as the owner took center stage. Friends either cheered at their creativity or booed at the song's obscurity. Bruce then continued as the DJ while the nonstop dancing began.

Born to Run was eventually unleashed. The entire group created

**Our Halloween Party's non-stop dancing.
Buliks didn't show up.**

a circle as Jim, mirroring college days, performed forward rolls on our hardwood floor. Other years, Pam might even have joined him, or, at least, been one of the first on the dance floor. She'd sway to the music enticing guys to participate or accompany the women in our own rendition of the Rockettes, kicking in line to *Sherry Darling*. With all the alcohol flowing, even Bob might have loosened up—but not this year.

I pulled Beezie aside and asked, "Do you know why Pam and Bob never showed up?"

"Lynda, I have no idea," she said, while avoiding my eyes.

≈

The Buliks' absence at the Fun Runs and Friday night fish fries continued to be noticeable, too, but on the second Wednesday in November, Pam finally came to the Fun Run alone. She immediately found Beezie, and the two began whispering, only quieting when others approached.

I tried to talk with Pam. Because I'd been out of town for her birthday I asked what surprise she'd received from Bob. There was a deep sadness in her voice, something she wasn't telling me. I listened to her mention flowers and another gift that wasn't related to the jewelry receipt she'd discovered. I figured that she'd probably returned whatever Bob had bought.

Pam then hesitated, her eyes catching mine, like something important was on the tip of her tongue. But her words tripped over themselves as she moved on to some mundane matter instead.

Later, I cornered Beezie. I knew she was also hiding some secret. She would only say, "The Buliks' counselors are still helping them work through their issues."

A terrible sense of rejection overwhelmed me. I felt that my best friends wouldn't trust me with their confidences when we'd shared absolutely everything in the past.

≈

A week later, Kathleen Leadley called our home. She and her husband, Rod, were in the Fun Run group and both taught physical education. Within the Green Bay Schools, Jim and I'd affectionately dubbed Kathleen the redheaded gossip queen. If you needed the scoop on anyone, you'd give her a call. If she hadn't heard it, she'd hunt it down. If she was the one who'd discovered the dirt, the culprit better beware—it'd be out on the "wire" before the end of the day. So my stomach flip-flopped when Kathleen asked, "Hey, Lynda, what's going on between Bob Bulik and Linda VandenLangenberg?"

In the basement of Anne Sullivan Elementary School, Kathleen said, they had a little hovel where the PE teachers stored equipment and held meetings. It had a *Laverne and Shirley*-type window, allowing a good view of a parking lot that was rarely used except for big school events. While waiting for others to arrive for a lunchtime meeting, Kathleen, along with Joe Hanson, another PE teacher in our Fun Run group, saw the Buliks' distinctive van drive in and park far off to the side. They then watched Linda VandenLangenberg scurry over to it, climb right in, and remain inside for nearly half an hour. "I told Joe that Bob should've posted a sign on the van saying: DON'T COME A'KNOCKIN' WHEN THIS VAN'S A'ROCKIN'."

Sickened, I hung up the phone. Could Kathleen be right? Was Bob actually cheating on Pam? The couples in our running group always prided themselves on their secure and loving relationships. Had I naively ignored the hints that had been out there? Had Pam done the same? Or did she already know about Bob's deceitful extracurricular activities? Based on her recent behavior, she must. That's why she'd seemed so down. That's why Bob had been missing in action. That's why Pam and Beezie had been whispering—Beezie must know too. I again picked up the phone. After relating Kathleen's information, I demanded, "Now Beezie, tell me what's going on!"

≈

Sunshine poured through the windows of the Terrace Room Restaurant located on the top floor of Pranges Department Store. Because it was a few blocks from IBM it was one of my favorite places for lunch. Rarely on the other end of a late arrival, I waited for Beezie. Last night, after admitting that Bob's infidelity was depressingly correct, she'd agreed to meet.

Waitresses in starched uniforms hustled between tables covered in white linens. Holiday music played while the scent of a gigantic spruce mingled with the aroma of fresh-baked rolls and the Terrace Room's famous chicken potpie. My stomach churned, but not from hunger. How devastating for Pam—this was normally her favorite time of year.

I spotted Beezie and waved.

She wove through the lunch crowd, dodging shopping bags stuffed under diners' chairs to reach me. "My, weren't you lucky to get a table by the window," she said touching my hand.

Once the waitress had taken our order, Beezie took a deep breath. "On Pam's birthday is when everything fell apart."

"My God!" I shook my head. "What awful timing."

Nodding, she grimaced. "Pam was putting a thoughtful card in Bob's travel bag just before he was to leave for a week of active duty in Texas. That's when she discovered a massage book she'd never seen before. She showed it to Bob and an envelope from Linda fell to the floor from inside the pages. Pam accused him of having an affair with her and he didn't deny it. Then Bob still left."

"Wow!" I leaned back in my chair, wondering what visual images had traveled through Pam's mind? If I could picture Linda's long slim legs wrapped around Bob's sleek back, while she massaged his muscular shoulders, as the prelude to their ultimate "act," what must Pam have thought? This certainly had to have dug a deeper crater into her already struggling self-image and emotional insecurity.

"I don't think Pam slept a wink Friday night," Beezie was saying. "She called me the next morning and I drove right over. She was sobbing uncontrollably, though it didn't take long before her tears were replaced by every explicative I've ever heard—all aimed at Linda."

"I can just imagine."

We were silent as the waitress poured our coffee.

Beezie took a cautious sip and continued. "That Saturday, Pam was already trying to figure out how to fix her marriage. She called Bob's doctor and told him about the affair. Dr. Wellens agreed to jointly counsel the Buliks if Pam got Bob's permission. Before I left, I made Pam take a sleeping pill so she could attempt to rest. Fortunately, it worked."

"How long has Bob's affair been going on?" I asked, adding a bit more cream to my coffee.

"Pam thinks about a year."

I cringed. "A year?" If this were Jim, the idea of him having sex with someone and then climbing back in our bed was so repulsive. But knowing how Pam idolized Bob, she'd probably convinced herself that the affair was all Linda's fault.

I let everything sink in as the waitress brought our lunch.

As we both spooned our chicken potpies onto our plates to cool, Beezie said, "Lynda, I wanted to tell you, but Pam swore me to secrecy. She hoped they'd work things out before anyone else needed to know."

"I definitely understand." My eyes met my friend's. "Do you think Bob went to Texas with Linda?"

"Pam wondered the same thing. When I was there, she located Linda's address and phone number in Bob's teachers' directory."

"Where does she live?" I blew on a forkful and took my first bite.

"Only about a mile and a half from their home. Because Pam frequently runs near it, she wondered if Bob had been doing the same, but stopping. Pam actually drove over to Linda's duplex the day after I was there, but Linda's mother answered the door and said she'd have her daughter call Pam."

"Linda must've been with Bob, then."

"I'm not sure," she said buttering a roll. "Pam isn't either. Linda called her back soon after, but refused to discuss the situation in person until Bob returned from Texas. When Linda didn't follow through, though, Pam called her again. Linda told her to discuss the situation with Bob and hung up."

While we ate, Beezie explained that Bob had agreed to joint marriage counseling. Their third appointment was actually scheduled for today. Dr. Wellens had made Bob pick from three choices: He could say goodbye to Pam and live with Linda to determine if divorce was the solution. He could say goodbye to Linda and Pam and see which one he missed the most. Or, he could say goodbye to Linda and continue to live with Pam, while working on their marriage. "Bob picked the last option," Beezie said, "and signed a contract not to see or communicate with Linda for six months."

"It certainly appears he's reneged!"

She nodded. "I told Kathleen's news to Bruce last night. He couldn't believe that Bob had actually parked his 'rolling lovemobile' inside a grade school lot."

We both couldn't help but laugh, before Beezie said, "I know, though, that Pam already had her doubts. I admonished her when she told me that she'd been tailing Linda's car."

I shook my head. "It looks like she picked the wrong vehicle."

"You're right, but Lynda," Beezie's mouth quirked with reproach, "there's also been other infractions."

"What do you mean?"

"You know how Pam doesn't like to attend church alone."

I nodded.

"So when Bob's out of town, she often drops her kids off for Sunday school and then stops at my house for coffee. Anyway, even though Bob was in town yesterday, he stayed home because he didn't feel well. That's when Pam drove over and told me she'd discovered some recent cards from Linda. They'd been sent to a PO box that Pam assumed the two were still sharing."

"Unbelievable!"

"Pam was going to bring that issue up in this morning's session with Dr. Wellens. She and I'd arranged to meet here for lunch so I assume we'll hear the outcome."

Since Pam already had enough to worry about, Beezie and I decided to keep Bob's van escapade to ourselves.

Moments later, I noticed Pam entering the dining room. Her face fell seeing me. As she reached our table I stood, accepting the blame for forcing Beezie to tell all.

Pam's cheeks took on a deep hue. "Lynda, I should have told you."

I hugged her, whispering how sorry I was, that she was strong, that she'd get through this.

Close to tears, she returned the hug. After ordering only coffee, Pam explained the emotion-filled therapy session she'd just attended. "Dr. Wellens was supposed to dismiss us, but Bob asked for another chance." Pam's voice held hope when she said, "Thankfully, Dr. Wellens agreed."

◇◇◇◇◇◇◇◇◇◇◇◇◇◇◇◇◇◇◇◇◇◇

The investigation of a death that might lead to an arrest and trial required the team effort among three departments: The Brown County District Attorney's Office, the Green Bay Police Department, and the Brown County Coroner's Office.

While Sergeant Taylor's responsibility was to get closer to Pam's life, Assistant DA Royce Finne's job was a paper case. He reviewed prior court decisions, prepared and participated in hearings, and dealt with motions—all leading up to a potential trial. A bit of a renegade, Finne had started college at the University of Miami. After falling grades proved to his parents that he enjoyed the beach more than studying, he transferred to the University of Wisconsin Milwaukee to finish his undergraduate degree. In 1977 he earned his law degree from the University of Wisconsin Madison, then bummed around Europe for two months before accepting a position under William Appel, the Brown County District Attorney at the time.

As one of the four Brown County Deputy Coroners, Genie Williams's job was to work with the medical experts and labs to determine the victim's cause of death. In Pam Bulik's case, in addition to the pathologist who had performed her autopsy, Genie had contacted Dr. Helen Young to review Dr. Skarphol's autopsy results and provide her expert opinion. Highly respected throughout the Midwest, Young had been Genie's professor at Marquette University. The Brown County Deputy Coroner always made sure she locked in the best experts before the defense got hold of them. That way, she'd ensure they'd be testifying for her side if the case went to trial.

The detectives called Genie the Duchess of Death. She called a spade a spade and never let the doctors give her any crap. In the station Genie would often lounge in one of the detectives' chairs with her feet up on a desk. They'd ribbed her once by pointing out the holes in her shoes. "Yeah, I guess I do," she said, wagging a cigarette their way. "This job doesn't pay enough." That week Genie received a gift certificate from a local shoe store signed, "The Boys."

Genie Williams and Sergeant Taylor had been meeting daily with Assistant DA Finne to provide an update on the status of the Bulik case. Their three offices had reviewed the disturbing autopsy report provided by Dr. Darrell Skarphol. It revealed a considerable amount of trauma to Pamela Bulik's body, particularly to the head area. Her left eye showed bruising that extended up the forehead. This had been caused by blunt trauma—either her head had struck something or had been struck by something relatively flat. Blunt trauma had also caused two bruises on the top of Pam's head and three located in the right occipital region, located just above the back hairline. Additionally, Skarphol had discovered a recent hemorrhage in the right cerebral peduncle, one of the structures that attached the brain to the spinal cord. A rotational twist of the head most frequently caused this area to tear. Bruises had also been found on Pam's right index finger, right wrist, and the backside of her left elbow.

Further drug tests were yet to be completed, but Dr. Skarphol had received confirmation that a contamination level of 48 percent carbon monoxide was present in Pam's blood. In some individuals, this percent could prove fatal. But in Pam's case, her cause of death was drowning. When she entered the bathwater, she was still alive.

4

Present Meshed with Past

On Bay Settlement Road, high on the bluff overlooking the sparkling expanse of Green Bay, a crowd gathered on Wednesday, April 11, 1984 for Pam's funeral. Jim and I entered the Shrine of the Good Shepherd Mausoleum with the MacNeils. A detective had called Beezie this morning. She was to meet with him tomorrow.

We descended steps to reach the chapel, hearing the depressing music Bob had selected. We agreed that he should've considered picking something by Neil Diamond, Pam's absolute favorite. In front of the congregation, a twenty-foot statue of the Good Shepherd was stationed over Pam's casket, draped in white cloth. We slid into a pew a few rows behind the Metzger family. A broad-shouldered man seated behind Pam's father leaned forward to whisper into Mr. Metzger's ear. I later confirmed he was Bob Whitrock.

At the age of fifteen, he and Pam had met at a Wisconsin Rapids's Y dance and dated through high school. Whitrock had played football and Pam had been a baton twirler in the band. The two had loads of fun, but he admitted that Pam could also be a troublemaker. He'd purchased Pam's brother's old Corvette and used all his money to fix it up. The Metzgers had a fuel pump installed on their property and secured with a key. On the sly, Pam routinely filled Whitrock's gas tank. Her dad thought their underground tank had a leak until Whitrock helped Mr. Metzger install basement drywall. For payment he was told to use the pump a few times to fill up his car. When the two teens doubled over with laughter, Pam's dad finally caught on to their scheme. After Pam and Whitrock broke up, the two Bobs had met. Bob Whitrock had felt that Bob Bulik was cold and not right for Pam, though he'd realized there'd been no changing her mind. Whitrock was immensely saddened by Pam's death. She'd been a good girl—a great girl—and a great friend. She'd always seemed happy and her problems were few. He wondered how things had changed so drastically.

Now, following a quick succession of chords, Bob and the Bulik children walked down the center aisle and took seats in the pew with Bob's father and brother. Alex and Abby took after their mom in facial features, bone struc-ture, and her great smile—obviously missing today.

Reverend Lewellyn Thomas began with a prayer, just as two women rushed down the side aisle and slid into Bob Whitrock's pew. I later confirmed they were Sue (Christensen) Weimer, Pam's best friend from Wisconsin Rapids, and Sue's mother.

From the age of five Pam and Sue had spent nearly every moment together. The two tomboys had biked, climbed trees, and captured the horses of a neighboring farmer, riding them bareback while he'd yelled and chased them around his field. After they'd taught them-selves to swim at Lake Wazeecha, Pam had loved the sport so much that she'd tried out successfully for

Best Friends at 1962 Prom Sue (Christensen) Weimer and Pam

the Wisconsin Rapids swim team. Before Pam turned sixteen, the two friends had illegally tooled around town in the Metzgers' old Rambler.

The girls had always been there for each other. Prior to Pam's wedding, Sue had met Bob Bulik. "He was drop-dead gorgeous," she said. "For Pam's sake I hoped he wasn't too good to be true." In September, after hearing about the August assault, Sue had called her friend. "Pam said Bob was instrumental in saving her life. Without his help she could've died. Pam painted this picture of Bob as her salvation, her savior."

Now, nearing the end of Pam's funeral service, Reverend Thomas said that Bob wanted him to close by reading a beautiful poem by the 19th Century clergyman, Henry Van Dyke.

As the pastor began to read the *Parable of Immortality*, I froze, recognizing the words.

◇◇◇◇◇◇◇◇◇◇◇◇◇◇◇◇◇◇◇◇◇◇◇

Normally, the Bulik family painstakingly decorated their home together for the Christmas season, but in 1983 Pam did it with only the help of her children. The hope she'd expressed just a week earlier at the Terrace Room had already faltered. In addition to her constant worries about Linda, when a problem arose, Pam said, "Bob and I don't discuss it, so we can't settle it." Sylvia felt some of these issues were due to the Buliks' money problems. Recently, she'd purchased an old organ from Pam for $100 just so she'd have some extra cash for Christmas gifts. On top of this, Pam had skidded off their steep driveway. She admitted to friends that "Bob seemed more concerned about the damage to our van and the fencing, than about me."

Another Bulik therapist had been added to the mix. Along with Dr. Wellens's joint counseling, Bob had wanted his own therapist again. He was scheduled to meet with Jean Weidner, a psychiatric counselor in the same practice as Pam's individual therapist.

In addition to her weekly sessions with Dr. O'Neill, Pam was now calling Dr. Wellens on a regular basis, not waiting for their joint appointment. She told me that Dr. Wellens was frustrated with them. He wanted the Buliks to make some decision about their marriage. Were they serious about trying to keep it intact or should it be dissolved? I knew Pam didn't want a divorce. She still really loved Bob and didn't want to put her kids through what she'd experienced when her parents split. "Bob's also opposed," Pam insisted. "He knows how divorce has affected many of his students." The Buliks had told Dr. Wellens they wanted to get through Christmas and promised to make their decision by the time their tree came down.

I wanted to give Pam encouraging words, but I was beginning to think that fixing their marriage seemed hopeless.

≈

Our Fun Run group's annual Christmas party was fast approaching. Encouraged by Beezie and me, Pam finally convinced Bob to attend. By now, most of our friends knew about his affair, and both Buliks realized that Bob had to break the ice.

Festivities were in full swing in the backroom of the Knight's Lounge when the couple arrived. It was a rather grungy place, not the most appropriate venue to wear holiday attire, but with lights dimmed, decorations already in place, an ample dance floor, and cheap beverages—it was the perfect spot. In a slinky gold dress, Pam looked amazing. Everyone told her so. She was the thinnest I'd ever known her to be. With all her issues, plus her reduced sense of smell, Pam had lost nearly half the weight she'd set as her goal.

She whispered to me that she felt as if everyone was talking about them—like she and Bob had walked into a stranger's home and flopped down on the couch uninvited. Pam may have been right. What amazed our friends was that the Buliks, more than anyone else in the group, had appeared to be this well-adjusted and admired nuclear family of four. Now that others realized a troubled marriage was behind the perfect façade, many found it difficult to handle and to simply forgive Bob.

Tonight was the first time I'd seen Pam drink alcohol since the assault. Both Buliks were pouring cocktails from a silver thermos of old-fashioneds they'd brought along to share.

Even though Pam's marriage was undeniably struggling, she seemed so pleased when friends welcomed Bob. I went out of my way to include him, grabbing his hands and insisting he join me out on the dance floor.

≈

After spending Christmas with our families in Waukesha, Jim, Collin, and I returned to Green Bay on Wednesday, December 28. Because the Fun Runs were suspended over the holiday week, a couple from the group, Karen and Larry Boehm, had invited a few others over for dinner. Jim and I'd arrived and so had the Mac-Neils. We were waiting for the Buliks. Like Beezie and me, Karen didn't want to ostracize Pam for Bob's mistake.

The guys headed for the kitchen to sample a fresh batch of Larry's Cherry Bounce, while the women chatted in the living room, sharing holiday stories. Of course the conversation strayed to the Buliks' situation. The day after Christmas, Beezie had talked to Pam. She said, for the children's sake, they'd managed to make it festive.

Karen had lived near the Buliks before she'd married Larry. Even though she and Pam had frequently run together, Pam had always been guarded about her personal life. At the Fun Run's easier pace, Bob and Larry had often run together, too. He'd never felt as comfortable with Bob as with the other runners. Larry perceived a sense of aloofness, a feeling of separation. Now he wondered whether it was because Bob had been living his double life.

A light knock interrupted our conversation. Karen opened the door with a welcoming smile that quickly transformed into one of alarm. Bob and Pam entered, his arm around her. She appeared to have a hard time walking on her own and didn't acknowledge us. Incredibly, Bob didn't give the impression he even noticed. He left Pam seated on the couch and joined the guys in the kitchen.

I was unable to comprehend Bob's lack of concern for Pam. We all tried to talk with her, but it was difficult. She wasn't making any sense. Her eyes kept drifting shut as her head lolled to one side. Our distress at Pam's condition contrasted with Bob's inattentiveness. Beezie stayed with her while Karen and I cornered him in the kitchen. "What's going on?" we asked. "Did Pam have too much to drink? Is she taking medication?"

Bob seemed taken-aback by our questions. After checking on Pam, he apologized, and the two departed. Everyone in attendance wanted to pretend it had never happened.

≈

It was remarkable that the Buliks still held their annual "Run out the Old and Run in the New Year Party." Pam appeared normal, definitely back in her element as she showed off her lovely home, served beverages and snacks, and organized rotating stations for board games. All night long a teasing rivalry flowed as we competed for prizes. Then, around 11:30, the two-dozen inebriated partiers completed a three-mile jog. Over wind suits, many guys wore tuxedos with tails purchased from thrift stores for the occasion—my husband included.

The Buliks first held their party in 1979. Instead of joining us for the run, Pam had prepared the cul-de-sac for our return. She'd poured champagne into plastic glasses and provided hats and noisemakers for the group. A portable radio had played that year's number-one song: *Don't you think I'm sexy?* And, everyone was. As steam rose from our bodies, the swooshing sound of our running suits had accompanied the music. When *Auld Lang Syne* had begun, Jim and I had hugged and kissed. Pam's eyes had been radiant as she and Bob had done the same.

Recently, during the Buliks' marriage counseling sessions, Bob had revealed to Pam that he'd always hated these kinds of parties. As we welcomed in 1984, the Buliks did embrace, but when Bob pulled away, Pam's eyes held only tears.

≈

Bundled for near-zero weather, I watched for Pam through my foyer windows on New Year's Day. We'd resumed running back in early December, and though she claimed I hadn't been pushing her, I wasn't so sure—periodically she'd mentioned feeling some numbness in her extremities. Since Pam had been the hostess last night, we'd talked very little, and certainly not about the Boehms' dinner party. I hoped she'd bring it up today.

As her van pulled up, I stepped out into the frigid air and studied my friend's face. A tightly pinched line replaced her smile. Where color normally popped out on her cheeks, they were now sallow and sunken. It had been a late night, but this was something more. "So how are you doing?" I asked, worried.

"Not so good." She slammed the van door. "Before I swapped out my calendar I noticed we'd missed the Boehms' party. Karen was having such a small group. I feel terrible that I didn't call her or at least apologize last night."

I gaped at her. "Pam, you and Bob were at their party. Don't you remember? Didn't Bob mention it?"

"What are you talking about?"

"Everyone was worried about you. We thought you were drunk or maybe overmedicated. Bob took you home early."

"I don't understand." Bewildered, Pam leaned against her vehicle, trying to remember. "Wow, I can't believe I was at the Boehms'!" Her cheeks flushed. "I'm so embarrassed. What did everyone think?"

"Pam, we're your friends. We were just worried about you."

Stress lines formed on her brow. "I wonder if my occasional drinks are bothering me?"

"Are you on medication? It could be the combination of the two."

"I sometimes take a sleeping pill when Bob's out of town, but Lynda, the last time he was in Denver was weeks ago." She paused, her eyes now moist with fear and confusion. "You don't think Bob could be giving me sleeping pills, do you?"

"Oh Pam! I'm sure he isn't."

"What if he's putting them in my drinks so he can leave the house and go meet Linda?"

"I can't believe he'd ever do that!" I tried to think. "There could be issues from your skull fracture." I grabbed her arm. "Come inside. Let's call your doctor."

Blinking back tears, she shook her head. "I'll call later. I'm sorry, Lynda, but I'm going to skip our run."

≈

All week Pam's distress hovered in the back of my mind. I'd also shared Pam's drugging concerns with Beezie. On January 4, after Pam had tried to explain her missing hours to Dr. Bressler, she'd completed some tests for him. No residuals from her head injury had been found, so he'd deemed her physically fit to return to teaching on January 23. That definitely was good news, but Pam, understandably, continued to be distraught—the reason for her amnesia was still a mystery.

The afternoon of January 8, Beezie phoned me, sounding frazzled. This weekend Bob was again out of town for reserves, and Pam had made her traditional Sunday morning coffee stop at the MacNeils.

"Lynda, Pam found a poem in Bob's wallet."

My forehead creased. "What kind of poem?"

"It's the type that might be used at a wake or a funeral." Beezie had a copy that she recited to me:

I am standing upon the seashore.
A ship at my side spreads her white sails to the morning breeze and starts for the blue ocean.
She is an object of beauty and strength, and I stand and watch until at last she hangs like a speck of white cloud just where the sea and sky come down to mingle with each other.
Then someone at my side says, "There she goes!"
Gone where? Gone from my sight . . . that is all.
She is just as large in mast and hull and spar as she was when she left my side and just as able to bear her load of living freight to the place of destination.

Her diminished size is in me, not in her.
And just at the moment when someone at my side says,
"There she goes!" there are other eyes watching her coming
and other voices ready to take up the glad shouts
"Here she comes!"

Listening, I shivered. It was creepy. "Why would Bob ever have that?"

"That's what Pam wondered. She was physically shaking and asked me if she should be afraid? I told her that I still couldn't believe that Bob would do anything to harm her. But, I also told her that if she didn't feel safe, she and the kids could come to our house day or night."

≈

On Friday, January 13, arriving back from visiting an IBM client in Manitowoc, the route passed by my old neighborhood grocery store. To save time, I decided to stop. In the produce section, I ran into Sylvia Madden.

Her face filled with concern as she told me what had occurred today. "Lynda, you should've seen Pam. I nearly plowed into her with my van. She looked like a Zombie, staggering in the street—out of it."

"What happened?" My hands gripped the shopping cart.

"Pam had just found some crushed pills in one of Bob's coat pockets."

My eyes widened. "She's been wondering if Bob might be drugging her."

"I know … I certainly was alarmed and told her to call the police, but instead, Pam said she wanted to talk to a pharmacist."

"Did she follow through?"

"Yeah. Pam said he was vague. What she'd discovered might be some kind of sleeping pills, but he wasn't sure. Pam was beside herself thinking back through everything that's happened since August." Sylvia hesitated, her face tightening with worry. "She said she was afraid of Bob."

≈

As Collin clung to my leg crying, "Hungry mommy, hungry," I unpacked the groceries, while telling Jim about my disturbing encounter with Sylvia.

When the phone rang, he answered it, and then frowning, handed it to me. "It's Beezie."

I gave Jim a sheepish look as he found some Kraft singles in one of my bags and unwrapped a slice to appease our son. I knew this on-going saga was putting a strain on our marriage.

Beezie said that Pam had told her about the crushed pills, too. Apparently, Pam had called Dr. Wellens. He'd told her that she needed to confront Bob about her drugging suspicions, and based on his response, if she was still fearful of him, she had to make him move out.

"So did Pam confront Bob?"

"She did."

"I'm amazed!"

Beezie was too. She said that Bob had denied there was anything sinister. Pam had simply found some of his medication that had gotten damaged when he'd stepped on his prescription container, crushing it and the pills inside. He couldn't believe that Pam would ever think he was drugging her and advised her to follow up with Dr. O'Neill. "Lynda, that's what she's decided to do."

≈

On Wednesday night, an amazingly cheerful Pam showed up at the Fun Run. She grasped my arm. "Dr. O'Neill said my December memory lapse was caused by stress."

I let out a big sigh of relief. "Pam, I'm so glad you have an answer."

Since his words had calmed her fears, they'd done the same to mine and the rest of Pam's friends.

We'd filed away both her drugging concerns and the discovery of the poem, as meaningless memories.

◇◇◇◇◇◇◇◇◇◇◇◇◇◇◇◇◇◇◇◇◇

Pam's funeral luncheon was being hosted at the Buliks' home. I realized how uncomfortable this might be for everyone. The in-ground tub that Pam had drowned in was visible from the bathroom, often used by guests. On our way over from the Shrine of the Good Shepherd Mausoleum, Jim and I discussed our mounting confusion. Hearing the poem that Pam had discovered back in January was so unexpected. The implications were monopolizing my thoughts.

As we entered the Buliks' foyer, I carried in Pam's gift, the one I'd brought to the Jogger's Joynt run just four days ago. I quickly ran it upstairs, wanting Abby to unwrap it later. The louvered door to her room was closed. When the Buliks built their home, their children were very young. These doors allowed Bob and Pam to hear any possible cries from a nightmare or tummy ache while they lay in their master bedroom below.

I turned the knob and entered Abby's lovely room. Pam had made the bedspread and curtains from white percale sheets sprinkled with pink flowers, and had even stapled the patterned sheets to the walls. I gently laid the gift in the middle of Abby's four-poster bed and then headed back downstairs.

Pam's presence was everywhere. I kept expecting to see her as I turned a corner. Her book bag covered in bright butterflies still lay on the fireplace hearth. Near the family room couch was the quilt she'd been stitching. In the kitchen, Pam's navy blue shoulder-strapped purse was still perched on the kitchen desk next to some reminders scribbled in her distinctive script. I could picture Pam over a steaming wok, toweling perspiration off her face while preparing wontons for guests, or checking on a batch of her famous chocolate chip cookies, or ladling out macaroni and cheese while her children, with eager faces, waited at the counter. Pam loved to work inside her special home, but she especially loved being a mom.

As I filled my lunch plate from potluck dishes provided by the Fun Run group, Sylvia joined me to clear up some misinformation. Her daughter's classmate had been disturbed by Pam's death and now realized that he hadn't seen Pam at the kitchen counter Saturday morning. It had been Friday night when he'd come to the door for Alex. As I mentally extracted that piece from the puzzle of Pam's death, I meandered into the backyard to join Barb Delong. Her husband had already relocated to Illinois so she'd come alone. Quietly, we shared our memories and our escalating concerns. She looked at the Buliks' backyard, deck, and hot tub. "Lynda, Pam had everything, and she did it all. She even maneuvered a bobcat to finish this fantastic landscaping. Nothing was a big deal for Pam. She just did it! So why did this happen?"

It's what everyone wanted to know.

Friends started to disperse. Jim and I unsuccessfully searched for Bob to say our goodbyes. At the front door Kathleen Leadley told us that she'd just seen him walk up to the top of their drive. I was speechless when she said, "I'm pretty sure it was Linda's Pontiac he leaned down to talk into."

<hr />

The Buliks' tree had come down by the second weekend of January 1984, but no decision about their marriage had been made. Instead, Pam continued to call Beezie, Sylvia, or me daily, going over and over the same issues. I knew Jim tried to understand, but he was getting close to his limit.

Actually, so was I.

Tonight, while I slid a dollar out of Jim's wallet for my high stakes at bridge club, he asked, "Will Pam be there?"

Our club met once a month at alternating homes. Recently we'd been getting a sub for Pam. It wasn't that she couldn't play, but rather she'd worried about giving Bob the opportunity to see Linda.

When I told Jim, Pam would be there, he rolled his eyes. "Lynda, just try to have fun."

The eight women that made up our bridge club drew tallies, placing Beezie and me at Pam's table. While the first hand was being dealt she choked out, "Bob's seeing Linda again." Through her tears she explained that Dr. Wellens was privy to some information that had convinced him that Bob had broken his contract for the second time. The doctor had been firm. He'd refused to give the Buliks another chance and dismissed them.

Pam was a wreck blaming Linda and saying, "If she'd just leave Bob alone we could work our marriage out!"

Beezie finally asked, "Will Dr. Wellens still take your calls?"

Pam nodded and abruptly stood to find a phone.

For close to an hour she talked to him as the two table groups discussed the whole Bulik mess. Nobody could believe that Pam had allowed it to continue this long. She eventually returned with red eyes, yet with a new sense of determination. "I'm doing it—I'm kicking Bob out! He can't have both Linda and me. He needs to choose."

≈

On the weekend of February 4, a locksmith was packing up as I arrived near dusk at the Buliks' home to run with a newly separated Pam. The temperature was below freezing, the wind blustery, and the sky overcast. Our shoes crunched on the packed snow as we headed up her driveway. I beamed at Pam, telling her how proud I was that she'd been strong and had followed through.

With a shaky smile, she admitted, "I need all the encouragement I can get from friends."

Everything had moved rapidly. Pam's brother had loaned her $500 for attorney fees and a lock change. On January 27, Pam had served Bob divorce papers. In order to request a legal separation, this had been required.

"It had to have been scary," I said jogging beside her, still amazed at her gumption. "How did Bob take it?"

"He was incredulous. I literally watched the color drain from his face. He first begged me to reconsider before we went to court. Then he met with his therapist to get her opinion. Bob told me that Jean Weidner recommended that we continue living together if our ultimate goal was reconciliation."

I was confused. "Weren't you surprised?"

"I've never met her, Lynda, so I don't know how she does things. I called Dr. Wellens again and asked for his advice. He definitely didn't agree with Jean. He said if we wanted to attempt a reconciliation we'd need to go at it slowly." Pam's eyes found mine. "That's why I stayed on my current course."

"You know, I'm glad." I nudged her arm as oncoming headlights flashed across our faces. "I bet this week was difficult for you."

"Nearly unbearable. Bob refused to leave or get an attorney. I told him, if he didn't leave, the kids and I would be forced to move out. He finally realized that I was serious."

We skirted around a bad patch of ice, the sound of our running suits rhythmic with every stride.

"So Pam, how did the court hearing go?"

"I was pleased with the outcome, but Bob sure wasn't." She explained that he'd been ordered to vacate. She'd been given exclusive use of their home and furnishings while Bob would be responsible for their monthly house payment. "The kids are to live with me, but both of us were awarded custody."

"You definitely got the better deal, but Pam, after what Bob's put you through, you deserve it!"

"I do, don't I." She finally cracked a smile, as we paused at a busy corner to wait for cars to pass and then took off again.

"I stopped at Danz School after the hearing and talked to the kids' teachers. I wanted them to know I'd filed for divorce."

"Really?"

"Uh-huh, I told them that Bob was having an affair and I didn't want to be part of a 'package deal.'"

"Good for you! So I take it Bob moved out?"

She nodded. "Last night he found an apartment. " Pam hesitated. "Lynda, you should've seen his eyes. They were so cold." Her voice caught. "Guess what he told me when he left?"

"What, Pam?" My brow creased.

"'I'll be back.'" As she shivered, chills ran down my spine, too, and it wasn't from today's weather.

~

A brilliant sun glinted off the snow piled along the Buliks' shoveled front steps. It had now been ten days since Bob moved out. In my red and blue Bill Rodgers running suit, I knocked on the front door. Pam opened it wearing matching attire.

I smiled. "We look like twins." Since December Pam had lost another ten pounds. I'd convinced her to run a local marathon in May. By training for it, she'd lose even more.

Back in 1982, about twenty Green Bay runners had joined 6,000 others to tackle Grandma's Marathon in Duluth, Minnesota. Even bucking a strong headwind, many ran personal bests. Jim was among them, finishing fourth overall with a time of 2:18:54. But another crowning achievement went to Pam. That day she joined

Jim with Kathy and Daryl Kapalin at Grandma's Marathon. Kathy placed 2nd for the women with a time of 2:52:15. Behind, Pam is celebrating her own accomplishment.

an elite rank by completing her first marathon in 4:44:20.

This year's Green Bay Marathon would be her second. Because I also planned to run it, we'd created a duplicate training schedule and were tracking it in our running logs. I recorded only my distance and time, while Pam also noted how she felt physically, her mental attitude, and her weight. We both knew a thinner runner often experienced fewer injuries and ran faster. About a 3 percent decrease in body weight produced a 2 percent increase in speed. Pam was increasing her mileage and losing weight, so her times were improving immensely.

Today as we took off, I turned to Pam. "You sounded so mysterious on the phone. Tell me what's going on?"

Her eyes shone. "Bob and I are dating."

My jaw dropped. "You're doing what?" I stared at her in amazement. "Do you think that's a good idea?"

She took a deep breath. "I hope so. I haven't forgiven him, and I'm not sure I ever will, but you should see the kids. They want us to be a family again more than anything."

I frowned. "So you're doing this for the kids?"

"No, for all of us. When Bob and I went out last night, I had butterflies. It felt like our first dates in college. I don't even have an appetite, and Lynda, when have you ever heard me say that?" Wound up, Pam picked up the pace. "I know what you're thinking. I must be out of my mind and it's way too soon. Right?"

"Yes, I guess that's my first thought. What should I think? Since Bob moved out, you're a new person and I like the new you a whole lot better. You've started to focus on your positive qualities. The ones your friends have always seen in you. I just hope you're not jumping back into this too fast."

"It's different this time." Her eyes pleaded with mine. "Really, Lynda, it is."

I kept trying to reason with Pam, like my mother would've with me, but it was evident her emotions were prevailing over her rational thinking. She swatted away my words like pesky mosquitoes. Jogging beside me, her face was animated, her voice bubbling over with optimism. I could only pray that Bob wouldn't destroy her hopes—once again.

≈

At tonight's Fun Run, Jim's Valentine's gift of long-stemmed roses was centered on our family room table. Kathleen Leadley noticed them and flopped her arm around my shoulder, her voice oozing mock compassion. "I'm so ... sorry, Lynda."

I grinned, giving her a jab in the ribs, then checked to see if Pam had overheard. I didn't see her yet.

The running group completed a five-mile loop and began trickling back inside to line up for dinner. A subset then took seats in the living room to confirm plans for this weekend's Brule Mountain ski trip. Pam finally showed up in a buoyant mood. Her face flushed with happiness when we discussed which vehicles we'd take. "Bob will be driving our van. He moved back home on Monday."

There was an extremely awkward pause. My worried eyes strayed to others'. The Buliks had been separated for less than two weeks! How could they have reconciled so soon? I had this uneasy feeling realizing that Bob had already made good on his earlier threat—*He was back.*

Pam seemed oblivious to our concern as she excitedly mentioned her family's upcoming Easter vacation plans. They'd just locked in a week at their Bahamas timeshare.

Beezie and I were both upset at Pam's rash decision. Before she left, we cornered her.

Pam assured us that Bob and Linda's relationship was over for good. "He wrote her a letter, telling her so." In addition, Pam had already accompanied Bob to a joint counseling session with Jean Weidner to work on a full reconciliation. "But," Pam's eyes met ours, "I know there are no guarantees." She'd told her attorney to keep the divorce proceedings in place. A final decision would be made in sixty days.

After the group's departure, I turned to Jim while we cleaned up the kitchen. "For Pam's sake, I certainly hope their reconciliation works out, but I can't help but wonder what Linda thinks?"

Pam's glowing disposition had radically changed tonight when she'd told Beezie and me that Linda had already purchased a

Y membership for Bob, so the "new couple" could finally work out in public together. And when Pam had accompanied Bob to his apartment to help clean it out, she'd discovered a Valentine addressed to Bob from "that woman." It certainly appeared as if Linda hadn't known the Buliks' reconciliation was coming.

Following Pam's announcement tonight, Jim said he'd talked to Kathleen Leadley. "An acquaintance of hers, who works in the school business office, received something by mistake inside an interoffice envelope yesterday. I understand it was a note intended for Bob and sent by Linda after he'd moved back home." Wiping the counter, Jim chuckled. "I guess that Linda told Bob she was sorry and hoped he didn't think she was a nymphomaniac."

"She said that!" I gaped at Jim.

He nodded, lifting his brow. "Apparently the note was returned to Linda, along with a warning to be more discreet."

"Wow!" I leaned back on the counter. "Remember what Beezie told me last week?"

"Honestly, Lynda, I can't keep the gossip straight."

"It was about the report card that Bob had created to rate the Buliks' marriage."

"Oh, yeah, I remember." He smirked. "Didn't Pam boast that Bob had given her an 'A' in the sex category?"

With a wry smile, I nodded. "I *now* wonder how he rated Linda?"

I went to bed troubled, feeling sure that Linda wasn't ready to admit that Bob had chosen Pam over her.

5

Darkness to Dawning

Lieutenant Tom Hinz was the department's spokesperson addressing the impatient media. When asked if there were reasons to suspect foul play, he continued to reiterate, "We're in the preliminary stages of our investigation and it would be wrong to speculate." Away from the prying reporters, however, the investigation into Pam's death was in full press.

Taylor's prime focus was still on determining whether Pam's death was an accident, suicide, or homicide. When Bob had been interviewed at the station he'd admitted to having an affair with Linda VandenLangenberg. On the night of Friday, April 6, upon Bob's arrival home, he said that Pam had accused him of meeting Linda that day. The Buliks had briefly discussed it and then, according to Bob, gone to bed.

If Pam had believed that Bob had again been with his girlfriend, Taylor wondered whether that could have put Pam over the edge. Those of her family and friends interviewed so far thought she had too much to live for. Deputy Coroner Genie Williams said that young men were the demographic group most likely to commit suicide in response to a breakup with their significant other. "Girls don't do this. They're too smart, and they don't want to leave their chicks." Since Bob had signed a release for the Buliks' joint therapy records, Taylor could now receive the expert opinions from all of Pam's therapists.

While the jury was still out on the suicide issue, Taylor felt disappointed that he'd come to the end of his quest concerning his initial premise. It didn't appear the August incident had been a potential motive for Bob to murder Pam. She'd never accused him of being her assailant, even to her therapists. What had surfaced, though, in discussions with them and Pam's friends were comments about an unexplained event concerning Pam's memory loss in the December/January time frame. As Taylor completed additional research into that area, he was also examining more traditional motives.

Passion was often the prime reason for committing violent crime. Taylor reached Linda VandenLangenberg at Anne Sullivan School. At first she agreed to an interview, but then declined after consulting her attorney. Linda believed no crime had been committed, so she saw no reason to discuss her personal life. Since she wouldn't talk, alternate avenues were required.

Kevin VandenLangenberg was contacted. Detectives discovered he was now Linda's ex-husband. Shortly before the Buliks' August 1983 assault, Linda had filed for divorce and it had been finalized in November of that same year. In trying to analyze when Linda's affair with Bob might have begun, Kevin recalled that around October 1982, Linda had completed a Red Cross CPR course that Bob Bulik had also participated in. Then, when she'd gotten into jogging, she'd run with Bob when the opportunity had arisen. This past Christmas, Kevin said he'd entered a florist's shop and noticed an arrangement on the counter addressed to his ex-wife. He hadn't opened the card, but felt sure it had been from Bob Bulik.

Teaching associates of Linda's were also contacted. They considered Linda a perfectionist, competitive, driven to succeed—a classic type-A personality. She was, however, also viewed as being overly sensitive, worried about what others thought of her. She might say, "Me? How could they say this about me?" Linda was intelligent and charismatic, and guys thought she was "hot stuff." She was considered a caring teacher, extremely attentive to her students' needs.

**Linda VandenLangenberg and Sylvia Madden were
both in the special education department at Edison
Junior High before Sylvia moved to Preble High.**

Pam's teaching colleagues at Freedom provided their own insight. Pam had claimed that Linda had frequently driven by the Buliks' home. Pam believed Linda had been incapable of leaving Bob alone.

Linda had grown up in Milwaukee, Wisconsin. Before earning her undergraduate degree from the University of Wisconsin Milwaukee, she'd attended St. Matthias grade school and Pius XI High School. The 1965 Pius XI yearbook documented Linda's extensive involvement with the school's newspaper. She'd written a poem entitled "a time that we own." It expressed her feelings about leaving high school and moving forward into her new future. It ended with these lines:

> *How suddenly*
> *we are betrayed*
> *by a time*
> *that we own no longer.*
> *So let us dare to BE.*

Another motive for murder was frequently life-insurance money. When questioned by Lieutenant Langan on April 7, Bob had stated that Pam had a $10,000 policy, plus whatever her school contract called for.

Detectives met with Vice President Richard Beverstein from Murphy Insurance. He said the $10,000 figure was incorrect. The previous year, the individual policy coverage for both Buliks had been increased, but Beverstein would not reveal the amounts. Even though he wanted to help, he was uncertain whether he could provide that information. He was told that a subpoena for his records would be issued if need be.

A representative from the Green Bay Board of Education was also interviewed about Bob's school life-insurance policy. Bob had selected the family plan, but the amount he'd receive in the event of Pam's death was yet undetermined. Detectives were still tracking down Pam's insurance information from Freedom High School.

According to friends, Bob had handled all the money in the Bulik household. Sylvia Madden related that after Pam found out about the affair, she'd looked at their bankbooks, realized they were in deep financial trouble, and didn't know how they'd get out. When the Buliks were separated, Pam's fellow teachers said she'd complained that Bob had used their charge cards almost like he couldn't control his spending. For instance, he'd just gone out and bought a small color TV without considering their money issues.

On April 7, Bob had provided Langan an estimate of the Buliks' financial status. Their monthly income included Pam's take-home pay of $1,250 and $1,600 for Bob. He also received $200-$300 a month in Marine Corps Reserve pay. Along with their expenses for food, clothing, utilities, insurance, car, entertainment, travel, etc., the Buliks' monthly mortgage payment was $1,300. They also owed $6000 for furniture, credit cards, credit union, and their timeshare condo in the Bahamas. After completing an analysis of the Buliks' debt structure, Taylor realized, there certainly could be some money problems.

≈

Detectives seldom interviewed children without a parent present, but on Friday, April 13, before returning to Florida, the Bulik children's grandmother, Myrtle Metzger, accompanied Taylor to Danz Elementary School. The sergeant had heard conflicting stories about how her grandchildren were doing, and he wanted to know if they needed assistance—had everybody been treating them okay? Rather than being purely investigative, the meeting was to deal with the human factor.

Taylor first talked to their teachers, who reported that Abby and Alex were acting as if nothing had changed in their lives. Neither teacher felt this was a normal reaction to their mother's death.

Taylor wondered if Bob might have prepared himself to deal with their loss. The department had received a call from an unidentified female teacher who'd asked whether the police had searched Bob's school desk and locker. She had keys to his office and a reason to be there. Inside, she'd found a paper back book purchased in February 1984 titled *How to Survive the Loss of a Loved One*.

Police also received a call at the station from a Peggy Fuller*, who had lived in the Buliks' old neighborhood. Both families had taken their children to Mayflower Daycare Center in the basement of Union Congregational Church. At that time, Peggy felt the Bulik children had been mentally abused. Their hair had been kept short, and Bob had treated them in a military fashion. She described him as a loner, tough and rough, strange and very soldierly.

Taylor agreed that Bob ran the house. Even though he'd heard from family and friends that Bob cared for his children, Taylor felt they needed to fit nicely into his life. He believed Bob to be a cold, calculating, emotionless individual who had no concern for anyone but himself.

Taylor had immersed himself in Pam's life. He'd talked to her family, friends, fellow teachers, and therapists. He'd relived Pam's earlier happiness, Bob's heartbreaking affair, Pam's ongoing turmoil, her strength to separate, her newfound hope in reconciliation, and finally her untimely death in this awful way. Taylor had broken the cardinal rule. He was personally involved. Maybe it was due to his initial investigation into the Buliks' August incident. Maybe it was because there were defenseless children in the equation. Whatever the reason, Taylor was beginning to feel like he knew Pam better than his own wife. Even though he'd never talked to Pam, he'd find himself thinking she might like something done this or that way. He pictured her as this outgoing gal, joyful to see you.

Taylor's wife told him she was jealous. While standing in front of Grace Lutheran's congregation, waiting to be installed as a church officer, Judy had turned to connect with her husband's proud eyes. Instead, she'd caught him scribbling an investigation reminder about Pam in his pocket notebook, oblivious to his wife's landmark event. The department's psychologist told Taylor that he was too involved and should watch the movie *Laura,* about a detective who fell in love with the victim of the homicide he was investigating without ever having met her.

Taylor couldn't help himself. Everything he'd uncovered was leading him to believe that Pam's death was senseless. In the court of law, proving motive was not required, if, however, one was evident, it could only help put a defendant away. Shortly before Pam's death, she'd confided to an associate at work that Bob was living in a fantasy world most of the time. Taylor wondered whether Bob had achieved his fantasy? He was still living in the home he took pride in, had sole control of his children, and had easily replaced Pam with his new lover. That could certainly be enough motive.

<hr />

In late February, Jim and I had purchased six tickets to attend a Milwaukee theater performance of *Evita* planning to attend with the Buliks and MacNeils. At Pam's funeral, Beezie and I'd discussed it. Even though we weren't mentally ready to have "fun," we couldn't see throwing our money away. Instead of mentioning it to Bob, we split the cost of the Buliks' tickets.

On Saturday, April 14, during the two-hour drive to Milwaukee, Beezie and I talked in the rear seats of our van while our husbands did the same in the front.

"How did your police interview go yesterday?" I asked, as both of us sipped from travel mugs of coffee—hers decaf, mine hightest.

"It was hard trying not to volunteer any information to Detective Parins. Even though things have been bothering me about Bob's actions, like you, Lynda, I still want to consider him a friend. I just can't believe he could've physically harmed Pam."

I nodded. "Did you ask the detective if Pam was naked when she drowned?"

"I did, but he couldn't tell me."

I frowned. This was something I needed to know.

As we passed the communities of Two Rivers, Manitowoc, and Sheboygan, Beezie also told me about her lunch with Bonnie Metzger. They'd met before she and Bill had flown back to Washington State. "Bonnie said it was difficult being around Bob. She and Bill were civil, but there was this hostility festering because of Bob's earlier affair and the pain it had caused Pam. Back in January, Pam was calling Bill almost daily, too. It was frustrating for him to be 2,000 miles away when Pam seemed so desperate and was making illogical decisions."

"It sounds familiar, doesn't it?"

"Sure does."

Beezie explained that the Metzgers and Bill's mother had met with a Sergeant Taylor and Assistant DA Royce Finne. Bonnie flatly told them, "The whole suicide theory doesn't hold!" She felt there was no way that Pam would have taken her own life and left her children behind. Bonnie and Bill considered his mother, Myrtle, to be a very intellectual lady, who was processing Pam's death in her own manner. Up to this point, she'd kept her feelings to herself, but at this meeting, Myrtle was also adamant that her daughter would never have committed suicide.

When Bill had first heard about Pam's death, Beezie said he hadn't linked it to her previous August assault, but the Metzgers had told the authorities, they were now reconsidering. "Bonnie remembered hearing about Pam's head injury through Bill's mom." Beezie eyes found mine. "I guess Pam informed her only after being discharged from the hospital. Bonnie didn't believe that Bob had ever called any of the family back in August."

I sat back, stunned. At that time, I knew Bob had been in terrible shape, blaming himself for not stopping the intruder. Maybe he'd been too embarrassed to let them know. Yet it sounded so wrong. Pam had been in the ICU for days. She could've died ... then.

I gazed out at the rolling miles of farmland dotted with cows and then turned back. "Did Bonnie tell you why Bob was home the night before Pam died rather than in Denver?"

She nodded, brushing dark bangs out of her eyes. "Apparently, he'd had car trouble and missed his flight out of the Illinois naval base."

"That makes sense. What about the Buliks' van? Did she explain why it was impounded?"

My eyes widened when Beezie said, "Lynda, the police believe Pam was in it."

Our seats for the play were exceptionally good. As the lights dimmed, a smoky movie theater full of patrons was revealed onstage. A voice resonated through both theaters: "Eva Peron has entered immortality."

It was simply too much.

≈

At the Green Bay Police Department's front desk, I asked for Lieutenant Robert Langan. I was told he was on his way back from the courthouse, and he'd see me shortly. It was Wednesday, April 18. Yesterday the detective had finally contacted me at IBM. I wondered when someone would.

Over the past ten days many emotions had consumed me, but I'd kept returning to my initial thought: Why had I considered that Pam might have committed suicide? Sure, there had been her marriage turmoil, but had it possibly been triggered because I'd obsessed for years over my own grandmother's death?

When my dad had been admitted into his month-long alcoholic treatment program, my mother's mother had come for a visit. Over supper one night I related how some guys had cornered me between two garages on the way home from high school that day. I probably exaggerated, making it sound worse than it was.

My grandmother reacted badly. "Lynda, you were molested!"

Of course I wasn't, and I tried to convince her, but it only got worse. Irrationally, she left in a cab for the train station.

Our phone rang early the next morning. My grandmother was dead. She'd been discovered in her home along with a letter written to my mother. I felt that I alone had driven my grandmother to suicide.

My father's treatment staff told my mother it would be disastrous if he left at this stage, so while my dad remained in Minnesota, my mother drove my brother, sister and me to East Chicago, Indiana. My mother, who was my grandmother's only child, somehow got through the funeral, cleaned out her mother's home, and sold it. I wallowed in my guilt all the while. Remarkably, my mother didn't blame me. Feeling that I was so pathetic, I could only admire her strength.

She had long refused to discuss that painful period in her life, and had only recently allowed me to broach the subject. When I attempted to apologize for causing my grandmother's death, my mother was astounded. "Sweetheart, you had nothing to do with it! An aneurysm killed your grandmother."

I was so confused. "But what about the suicide letter?"

"It was no such thing. Before the aneurysm burst, your grandmother had some lucid moments. She wrote that letter explaining that she had no idea what had gotten into her."

During my run on April 7, had I also jumped to the wrong conclusion about Pam's death? I hoped to get my answer today.

The approaching detective certainly didn't resemble the ones

I watched on *Cagney and Lacey*. With his silver hair, bushy eyebrows, and wide brown tie, Lieutenant Langan looked fatherly. When he expressed his condolences for the loss of my friend, his kind words made me look away.

I was escorted into a bare-bones room where he questioned me about the August incident, Bob's affair, and any situations in which I'd been concerned for Pam's safety. Finally, he asked, "Since the Buliks' Valentine's Day reconciliation, do you believe that Bob might have contacted Linda again?"

I flushed, remembering one situation I'd never shared with Pam...

On Friday, March 16, 1984, I'd arrived home from an IBM Systems Engineering Symposium. That evening Jim insisted on going out for dinner—alone.

At Café Espresso, surrounded by hand painted Turkish murals and the chatter from the crowded bar, the air was filled with the scent of spices and flavored coffee beans. Jim waited until we'd ordered drinks and gyros, and then took a deep breath. "Lynda, I need to tell you something."

My heart sped up, seeing his concerned face. "What is it?"

"Last night, Pam invited Collin and me over for dinner—"

"Well, that sounds nice." I gave him a questioning look.

"Let me finish." Jim started drumming his fingers on the table. "Beforehand I went out for a run, taking the route that follows the East River. After crossing Mason Street, I eventually reached the footbridge near Anne Sullivan School and started up the incline." His voice and fingers paused to make sure he had my attention. "As I came down the other side, guess who was walking hand-and-hand toward me?"

"Oh, no..." My body deflated. The earlier van sighting had been at the same grade school. It had to be Bob and Linda.

Jim confirmed that it was and looked grim, watching the misery appear in my eyes. "Lynda, it was impossible to turn back without looking more conspicuous, so I just kept my head down as I ran by."

"How could Bob do this to Pam again?" I said near tears. "He's not to have any contact with Linda."

"I know," Jim said, as the waitress delivered our food.

No longer hungry, I pushed my plate back. "Did you still go to dinner?"

"I felt I had to, but honestly, I would rather have eaten a TV dinner with our drooling dog."

"Was Bob there?"

"Yeah. He seemed normal, like he hadn't seen me or was trying hard to pretend he hadn't. Pam seemed excited about their summer travel plans. Bob has an opportunity to make a military pentathlon team. If he does, the family might attend the event in Italy. Even if he doesn't qualify, Pam said they'd be flying to Hawaii for his Marine Corps active duty week."

"So Pam must not know he's seeing Linda."

"It sure didn't seem like it unless she's an excellent actress."

Throughout the rest of March, a heaviness sat in my belly as I wrestled with my options. Should I tell Pam or keep it to myself? I'd tried to convince myself that Bob and Linda's meeting had been totally innocent. Maybe she'd just called him to talk. Yet I knew that was prohibited. And their handholding was undeniably an intimate gesture.

Then, the week before Pam's death, Pam told me that she'd suspended her divorce action. For another ninety days she and Bob would continue to work toward a full reconciliation.

I just couldn't see dampening their good intentions, so I never told Pam.

Today, as Lieutenant Langan waited for my answer, I worriedly turned his question back on him. "Was Bob involved with Linda again?"

Langan didn't respond. Instead, he asked, "If Bob was seeing Linda, and Pam found out, what do you think her reaction would be?"

Since the Buliks' reconciliation, I knew Pam's optimism had been precariously balanced against her concern that Linda might again lure Bob away. I hesitated, before telling the detective, "In March, Pam admitted to me that she didn't know whether she could handle that situation again."

He finally asked me about the suicide comment I'd mentioned to others at the Jogger's Joynt race. After I tried to explain my thoughts, I was ready to ask him the same question Beezie had attempted. I needed to know if Pam had been naked in the tub. This was very important to me. I still remembered what Pam had told me the week after Collin was born.

Because he was nearly nine pounds, I tore during delivery and had to be stitched up. My mother was staying the week to help out, so the first night home she suggested I soak in the bath to relieve my soreness. Being a shower gal, this was unusual for me. Getting in was easy, but in the process of getting out I dislocated my previously injured shoulder. I fell back into the tub and cried for help. My mother and Jim tried to lift me out, but it was too painful. Jim finally called 911. Minutes later he escorted four rescue-squad guys into our bathroom. They carefully extracted my naked, stretched-marked body from the tub, while the rugged-looking guy, in charge of my legs, chatted away, saying how much he and his wife loved their home. He understood from their realtor and neighbors that Jim and I had been the previous owners.

The whole ordeal was quite an experience! At the hospital they gave me a sedative before popping my shoulder back in place. I was a mess. I had a newborn baby, stitches in my bottom, and a stabilizer securing my shoulder, which left me with one mobile arm. My breasts were engorged with milk, but I couldn't nurse Collin because of the painkiller.

Over the next few days, friends stopped over to help, especially Pam. She cooed at Collin, nestling him in her capable arms, gently rubbing his soft cheeks with her finger, saying what a handsome boy he was.

My tears still welled up at the memory of that moment. Back then I'd watched Pam's immediate connection with my son, just as she'd connected with me. That same day I'd also shared my bathtub rescue adventure with Pam and watched her blush through her laughter.

"Lynda, how awful for you! Weren't you embarrassed? Before I'd ever call 911 and let the medics see me naked, I'd grit my teeth and deal with the pain!"

That was why I needed to know.

In response to my question, Lieutenant Langan watched

Pam had a special connection with Collin.

my face as he said, "Mrs. Drews, Pam was naked."

I started to cry. I couldn't help it. In my heart, I now absolutely believed—Pam did not commit suicide.

∞∞∞∞∞∞∞∞∞∞∞∞∞∞∞

Inside the courtroom of Judge William J. Duffy, a closed John Doe hearing was in process. The Brown County District Attorney's office had initiated this investigative proceeding into the Bulik case. It was a rarity for Green Bay. Like a trial, witnesses would be subpoenaed and questioned under oath, though after the presiding judge heard the testimony, he alone would decide whether there was probable cause to move forward with an arrest.

Lieutenant Langan reentered the courtroom and took a seat next to Sergeant Taylor. Before he'd left to conduct an interview with Lynda Drews, Linda VandenLangenberg had been subpoenaed at Anne Sullivan Elementary and had testified while consulting with her attorney.

Now Bob was escorted into the courtroom. He'd been subpoenaed at Edison Junior High School around noon. In addition to

Linda and Bob, the Bulik children, police personnel, the deputy coroner, and two pathologists would be called to the stand.

The detective delivering Bob to the courthouse told Taylor that Bob was upset. He hoped this proceeding wouldn't impact his family's scheduled departure for the Bahamas, just two days away. If he canceled his timeshare week he'd lose the option for another year.

The judge first turned to Bob to ask whether he'd like counsel. After responding in the negative, Bob was sworn in.

With light brown hair worn fashionably long, Assistant DA Royce Finne had an angular face, sleepy eyes, lanky limbs, and a clever brain. Over six feet tall, and wearing a tailored suit, he now stood. Finne echoed the judge: "Mr. Bulik, you understand that you do have a right to have an attorney present, here, before you answer any questions?"

"I understand that," Bob said. "But I guess I don't understand John Does...is it normally done that an attorney ought to be present?"

"That's entirely up to you...Do you wish to proceed here now or do you wish to secure an attorney to advise you at this time?"

Possibly considering the time it would take, and the impact it might have on his Bahamas trip, Bob hesitated before saying, "I guess we can go on."

"All right," Finne said. "I'd like to direct your attention initially, Mr. Bulik, to August of 1983." In the prosecutor's hand, he held the police incident report that began with the 10:30 p.m. call on August 18, initiated by Cindy Mitchell, an RN from St. Vincent Hospital. She'd reported that a Robert Bulik had brought his wife, Pamela, into the ER. He'd told Cindy someone had entered their house and struck his wife on the head with some object. That night, Sergeant Taylor had checked the Buliks' home and found one garage door up, and the rear patio door unlocked and opened approximately one inch. The interior had appeared normal with nothing tipped over from a struggle, and no sign of forced entry.

Today in court, after Finne asked Bob to explain his recollection of the attack, Bob began:

"...We had come home, eaten dinner...We were going to go out for a run later. I recall the TV was on and perhaps one other light in the family room...We were doing some stretching exercises on the floor prior to getting our running gear on. I heard a noise out toward the front of the house. I thought it was perhaps the dog that wanted to go outside...so I just got up while Pam continued to do her stretching. As I walked around the corner I was hit in the abdomen with something. It was other than a fist, perhaps a rod or a stick...I blacked out momentarily...I recall hitting the ground. I also came to...I saw that Pam was lying on the floor and groaning. I thought that she was also hit in the stomach. As it turned out she was hit on the back of the head. And following that, I drove her to the hospital."

"How would you describe the person that you viewed in your home that night?" Finne asked.

"It was just a brief image that appeared out of the dark, and I was just taken aback." The only thing, Bob said he could remember had been a blondish-haired individual, about the same size as him, and older than the kids he worked with at the junior high level.

The police report related that, four days after the August assault, Sergeant Anderson had met Bob at his residence to step through the event again. The detective had noted that after Bob had been hit, the subject merely needed to take five good-sized steps and he would've been out the front door. Instead, he'd gone into the middle of the family room, struck Pam, and exited through the patio door. Anderson had also noted that Bob appeared to be in good shape and could take a pretty good hit.

Finne now asked Bob, "When did you first become aware that your wife had received a head injury?"

"...I don't recall if she said something or if I felt a little bit of blood on the back of her head, but she was coherent. She talked with me after she settled down. She got up and walked around."

At that time, Bob said he hadn't known how many stitches Pam would've needed or if any would have been required. "But she was functioning fine, so instead of calling an ambulance we drove to the hospital."

"Did you do anything between the time you discovered Pamela on the floor and the time that you got into the car to drive to the hospital?"

"I can't recall—we had some towels on the floor, and I guess I wiped up—there was a blood spot there, and I poured some water on it, because she told me to, and wiped that up...that was the only other thing that I can recall."

Finne had watched Bob as he answered that question. Earlier he'd told Sergeant Anderson that before taking Pam to the hospital, he'd cleaned up Pam's vomit from the rug. "Why didn't you call the police?" the detective had asked Bob, back in August.

"I was too excited," he'd replied.

'Not enough to clean the vomit up first!' Anderson had noted.

Finne now asked, "What type of dog did you have then?"

"Scottish terrier." Bob explained that the family kept Misty in one of three places: tied up out front, in the back laundry room, or down in the basement.

"Do you remember where the dog was that evening?"

"No."

"Do you recall hearing the dog barking?" Finne asked.

"The dog does not bark at strangers."

The prosecutor looked intently at Bob before switching gears. "I'd like to talk to you, now, about April sixth and April seventh of 1984...You were planning to attend your reserve meeting in Colorado that Friday, is that right?"

"Yes."

The questions and answers continued until 4:30. Bob was then told he was free to travel to the Bahamas.

◇◇◇◇◇◇◇◇◇◇◇◇◇◇◇◇◇◇◇◇◇◇◇◇

Now that I believed Pam's death was not a suicide, I considered the remaining choices. Was it an accident? Or was Bob somehow responsible?

Right before Beezie's departure for tonight's Fun Run, Bob had called her. After much consideration, he said he and his family had decided to leave for the Bahamas on Good Friday. In the aftermath of Pam's death, we'd assumed he'd scrapped those plans.

"You know Beezie, I bet Pam would've wanted the kids to go. It might help them to get out of that house."

She sighed, "You're probably right." But that hadn't been the only reason Bob had called her. He'd asked whether she'd pack up Pam's things while he was gone. "I don't like the idea, but I told him I would. I'm afraid he'd throw away items the children should keep to remember their mom by."

"You know we're going to Waukesha for Easter and Collin's second birthday. If you can hold off for those few days, I'll help."

"I appreciate your offer, Lynda, but I want to get it over with."

On my return, I called Beezie, who said that Sylvia had helped. "I kept thinking that Bob was vacationing in the Bahamas while we were doing this miserable job. Something was wrong with this picture!"

Beezie said she'd boxed up Pam's gold dress. "It was so hard. I kept remembering how special she'd felt and looked wearing it at the Christmas party." In the Buliks' bedroom, they'd also discovered a small bag containing a necklace with the letter "P" charm attached, and a sentimental plaque. The enclosed mall receipts were dated the day of Pam's death.

"But Lynda, listen to this—in one of the large closets, just off the master bedroom, there was a cardboard box filled with books, cards, and documents."

"Were they Pam's?"

"Far from it! Most of them were intimate communications between Linda and Bob."

"Wow! What would make him think that you wouldn't find them?"

"I have no idea. Among the cards and letters was also a copy of Linda's will."

Neither Beezie nor I had known that Pam had discovered its draft back in the January timeframe, but Sylvia had. "She said Pam was understandably distraught since Linda had willed the care of her son to Bob if something should happen to her ex."

"I can't imagine," I said, blinking at the absurdity of the idea. "Pam would never have agreed to that!"

"I know, but, Lynda, the most disturbing thing we found was a journal Pam was keeping. The last entry was written the Sunday before her death." She hesitated. "It was titled, 'I Am Afraid.'"

My heart started to pound. "Did it say why?"

Even though Beezie said that she and Sylvia had both studied the entire entry, neither knew what to make of it. They'd left the journal and the other documents where they'd found them, but when Beezie got home, she'd called Dr. Wellens. "He said I should contact the police. I didn't need to protect Bob. If he weren't guilty, the things we discovered wouldn't hurt him."

"Did you call?"

"I did."

~

For the past five years, Pam had maneuvered her nine-passenger van to our women's only Bonne Bell Race weekend in Chicago, Milwaukee, or Minneapolis. At each hotel we'd cart in our own luggage, snacks, and coolers. Then Pam would often disappear to the gift shop and return with a *Playgirl* magazine to get our adrenaline flowing before the next morning's race. Giggling, we'd flop down on beds while she'd turn the pages to our exclamations of "ooh" and "aah" and "oh, my God!" After changing into loungewear, she'd always make herself an old-fashioned and offer to make more. The nights would then be filled with rounds of bridge accompanied by girl talk and gossip.

On race mornings, we'd complain about lack of sleep and either rotate for showers or go without. Then we'd clamber into Pam's van, and with Neil Diamond blasting, we'd rev up while driving to the run. After check-in, Pam would lead the charge, as we'd hijack the men's bathrooms. Once the gun went off, she would relish sweating and even spitting during the race.

Like the rest us, Pam loved the Bonne Bells. They celebrated the gains women had made in the sport of running. In 1984, of the 25 million US runners, nearly half were now women. Each of the Green Bay gals had been an early adopter, breaking the social constraints decreeing that exercise was unseemly for us, but appropriate for our husbands.

For Pam it had been exciting to be at the cusp of the changes for women in the physical world. She'd taken delight in what had been hers all along. At this year's Bonne Bell Race, the weekend of May 5 had a gigantic hole in it without Pam's special exuberance.

≈

On Saturday, May 26, 1984, a member of our running group was celebrating a momentous occasion. Back in the sixties, at the mere age of nineteen, Kathy Kapalin, with the feistiness of her Irish heritage, had married her match, devilish Daryl. Now at thirty-seven she'd graduated from the University of Wisconsin Green Bay with a business degree.

Today the Kapalins, with their three daughters and son, were entertaining family and friends around their backyard pool, while Kathy's dad was in charge of the drinks. Until the Kapalins third child, Melissa, came along, he'd found it difficult to show affection to his children and grandchildren. But early on, "Little Red" had taken him by surprise by climbing into her unapproachable grandfather's lap. Out of character, he'd succumbed, outwardly loving her back.

Today, with the knobby, coltish look of a preteen, freckle-faced Melissa was all jaunty and bright, parading around with her mother's graduation cap perched on her chlorine-shiny red head.

This party's atmosphere was beginning to revive feelings we'd buried since the loss of Pam—that was, until the backyard gate swung open and Bob Bulik entered.

It had been six weeks since Pam's death, and we were still in the dark. Brown County Coroner Timothy Blaney refused to comment on its cause, even though Deputy Police Chief Richard Rice said their investigation was concluded. The police said they were awaiting a meeting with District Attorney Peter Naze. The DA, too, declined to comment on the case, but said the next move belonged to Judge William J. Duffy who'd presided over a John Doe hearing into Pam's death.

One of Jim's former East High cross country runners was now Officer James Arts. My husband had asked him whether he knew what was going on. Arts said he was sorry, but he couldn't help out his old coach. It was still all hush-hush.

After the Kapalins made a point of welcoming Bob, he stood around the pool in the midst of things, but not really included. Other than his call to Beezie about packing up Pam's things, which he'd never even thanked her for, nobody had seen or talked to him since the funeral luncheon. I tried to converse with Bob, though I wasn't quite sure what to say. For the past month, we'd all continued to speculate about Pam's death and his behavior. Then on top of this was Pam's disturbing journal entry. In the final week of her life, we wondered if she'd been afraid of Bob like she'd been last winter? But what mainly bothered me, and the rest of the Fun Run group was that Bob had never told anyone what had really happened.

∞∞∞∞∞∞∞∞∞∞∞∞∞∞∞∞∞∞∞∞∞∞

Robert Langan had recently received a promotion to captain, and now, like Sergeant Taylor, was assigned full-time to the Bulik case. In 1966, after marrying a local girl, Langan had left his career as a New York City patrolman to join the Green Bay Police Department. Jim Taylor had been one of the guys who had broken him in. "It'd be twenty below, and you'd be the only one on the street, walking your midnight-to-eight beat, and you'd be thinking *why am I doing this? Maybe I should've been a fireman.* In the firehouse they get to sleep in their nice warm beds."

Langan had eventually moved into a squad, and for six years patrolled East Broadway. At that time, the chief of police had run a testing procedure. Fortunately, Langan had come out number one, so at twenty-eight he'd advanced to detective sergeant with a bunch of "old guys." He loved the job and liked playing cops and robbers. "Kickin' down doors and all that kinda stuff."

At the John Doe hearing, the testimony provided by Dr. Helen Young, the pathologist secured by Deputy Coroner Genie Williams, had cemented Langan's initial feelings about Bob. Young had reviewed Dr. Skarphol's postmortem examination notes and autopsy photos of Pam. In her expert opinion, the trauma to Pamela Bulik's head, and other bruising, particularly to her extremities, indicated that, in the several hours prior to her death, Pamela had been in a fight. Langan felt Young's testimony also validated why the August incident had just happened to the Buliks and nobody else in the neighborhood.

The detective believed that there were just too many circumstances surrounding Pam's death that were too bizarre for a major in the Marine Corps Reserve and a schoolteacher. "The things Bob said and did were poor choices. They stuck out like sore thumbs. People don't do that."

Langan had worked with the district attorney's office to author Bob's criminal complaint, addressing the five W's: who did what, when, where, and according to whom.

It was still in Judge Duffy's hands.

≈

On the morning of May 29, 1984, the department received the call. A warrant for Bob's arrest had been signed. Jim Taylor was given the honor. He wanted to read it to Bob face-to-face and see his reaction at being accused of Pam's brutal death.

About a block from the Buliks' home, Taylor and his partner waited in a squad. The detectives had been instructed not to make the arrest until a SWAT team was in place. Because Bob was a marine, they felt he might have access to a weapon.

In shorts and a T-shirt, Bob coasted down the hill toward the detectives on his ten-speed bike. Taylor felt he couldn't wait. He moved his squad forward and cut Bob off. At that same moment, the Emergency Response Unit pulled up. As Bob was cuffed, Taylor smugly stated, "Mr. Bulik, you're under arrest for the first-degree intentional homicide of Pam."

For nearly two months, Taylor had kept his emotions in check. Today punching Bob in the mouth would've felt good, but Taylor knew that impulsive act wouldn't accomplish much. Hopefully the evidence they'd gathered would instead put Bob away for life. That would then be as good as punching him in the mouth every day for the rest of his life.

Now as Bob's calm, emotionless eyes met Taylor's, Bob claimed, "I didn't do it." With neighbors looking on, he was then helped into Taylor's squad as his bike was loaded into the Emergency Response Unit. Meanwhile, a representative from Brown County Social Services was en route to Danz School to place the Bulik children temporarily with the Maddens.

At the station, Bob was read his rights. This time, he refused to waive them and requested an attorney. Bob was then fingerprinted, three photos were taken, and he was placed in the Brown County Jail.

Per Bob's request, Linda VandenLangenberg was asked to pick up his athletic bag along with his bike.

Bob's Arrest May 29 1984

6

Media Madness

The media took full advantage of Bob's arrest for first-degree murder. All TV channels and radio stations interrupted their scheduled programming for Deputy Chief of Detective Richard Rice's news release:

> At approximately 11:45 a.m., May 29, 1984, Robert J. Bulik, thirty-six, was arrested a short distance from his home. An arrest warrant was signed by Judge William Duffy for first-degree murder this morning. The arrest was made after a lengthy investigation by the Green Bay Police Department, Coroner's Office, and the District Attorney's Office.

Ever since I'd begun to believe Pam's death had not been a suicide I'd tried to stay open-minded about Bob's involvement. But after stopping home over my lunch hour, and listening to the awful details on Channel 5's news, I felt physically ill. The announcer was saying, "According to Naze and the Green Bay police, a report from the state crime lab proves Pamela Bulik's death was no accident. The autopsy report shows, shortly before her death, Pam was severely beaten and probably knocked unconscious. She was then exposed to fatal levels of carbon monoxide in the family van. Police conjecture, that's where her husband dumped her body. Later that day she ended up in her bathtub where she drowned."

I tried not to visualize what had happened to Pam, but it was impossible. How could Bob have planned to kill her in this monstrous way?

The announcer finished "…neighbors say Bulik had a history of beating up his wife, and they wonder why it took so long for the police to make the arrest."

≈

To reach the Fun Run on Wednesday, May 30, our family crossed the Fox River using the Hwy-172 Bridge, one of the five that connected the east to the west side, and part of the twenty-two-mile beltway around metropolitan Green Bay.

After the night's running events, everyone stayed late. Nobody could get over that one member of our running group could actually be arrested for murdering another. Opinions varied as to whether Bob was guilty or not. Most people simply needed more facts.

The front page of today's *Press-Gazette* had featured Bob in handcuffs, an orange jail jumpsuit, and his blue Nikes. If convicted, he would face a possible maximum sentence of life in prison. At Bob's initial appearance Judge Charles Kuehn had accepted Assistant DA Royce Finne's request that bond be set at $100,000 cash—the largest amount the judge had ever ordered. Former DA William Appel was now Bob's lawyer. Appel had served two terms before moving into private practice to perform civil and criminal work. He stated that he planned to challenge the criminal complaint issued against his client.

Both Jim and Bruce MacNeil had taught with Bill Appel's wife, Kathy, at East High School. In the past we'd also attended school functions and political fundraisers with the couple. We'd heard good things about Bill: if, for example, we ever needed a lawyer, we should put him at the top of our list. Ironically, Bill, like Pam, had been raised in Wisconsin Rapids. But leave it to Kathleen Leadley to have some story about the Appels. A few years back, when she and Rod had taken disco-dancing lessons, Bill had then been district attorney, and he and his wife had been in the class. "Bill was a terrible dancer!" Kathleen said, her green eyes twinkling. "And his wife would hit him on the shoulder and nag at him, 'Bill, you're doing it wrong!' Rod and I would chuckle on the way home saying Kathy Appel was beating up on the DA—and what's more, she led!"

**Bruce and Beezie MacNeil standing by "Scout"
at a Wednesday night Fun Run**

In the newspaper, Deputy Chief Rice had praised Sergeant Taylor and Captain Langan for sorting through the evidence to make Bob's arrest. Rice stated that from the start "we had a strong suspicion we had a homicide." It had been based, he said, on Sergeant Taylor's knowledge about the August incident. "We didn't really buy the first story—even less so the second."

The newspaper also included statements from Linda Vanden-Langenberg's John Doe testimony used to secure Bob's warrant for arrest. On the evening of Saturday, April 7, she said that Bob had called her and related that Pam was dead. When he'd returned home Friday night, he said she'd accused him of being with Linda and they'd argued. Later that night, he'd found Pam in their van with the engine running and the garage doors closed. He'd then carried Pam into the house, where he'd drawn a bath for her. Bob told Linda that Pam must have gone to soak her legs, slipped in the tub, and drowned.

Deputy Chief Rice made an interesting comment. While the police were at the home, he said Bob had never mentioned finding Pam in the van. To the running group, this seemed rather suspect, but we weren't the only ones weighing in on Bob's guilt or innocence.

Rachel Metzger, Pam's stepmother, was quoted as saying that Bob's arrest hadn't surprised her or Pam's father. "Pam had too much to live for to try to commit suicide." At Pam's funeral, Rachel said Bob had been a cool unemotional man who hadn't shed a tear. Pam's dad described him as cold, but he also admitted that he'd never seen Bob lose his temper.

At Edison Junior High School, Bob's principal, Michael Hermans, was taking a "wait and see" approach. Pam's fellow Freedom teachers said they weren't surprised by Bob's arrest. Nancy Gloudeman's response was: "What about the children? Where are they going to go? What are they going to do?"

The Fun Run group wondered how Bob would come up with $100,000 in cash. To us this was an exorbitant amount. When Jim and I'd purchased our home we'd paid $76,000 and assumed a thirty-year mortgage that we didn't see paying off any sooner. Pam had told a number of us, that their home was worth more than $100,000 and mortgaged to the hilt. I hoped, for the Bulik children's sake, Bob would find a way to make bail. No matter what he'd done to Pam, I believed he really loved his children.

On the drive home, after checking on Collin who'd nodded off in his car seat, I turned back to Jim. "I miss Pam so much more on Fun Run nights." Aimlessly, I looked out at the Fox River that paralleled Riverside Drive. "I keep wondering whether any of this would've happened if I'd told her that you'd seen Bob with Linda back in March."

Jim slid his hand under my hair and began rubbing the nape. "Lynda, we both could've told her. Don't agonize over things you can't change."

I knew he was right, but I couldn't help feeling the way I did.

≈

Because the Delongs had moved to Illinois, I realized that Barb probably didn't know that Bob had been arrested and gave her a call.

She was shocked by the news. Back on Friday, April 13, the evening before Barb and her children had left Green Bay for good, Bob had invited them over for dinner. He'd also driven them to the airport the next morning. On the way Barb had finally blurted out, "Bob tell me, what happened to Pam?"

I admired Barb. Her question was what everyone else had wanted to know, but had never asked.

"Lynda, he told me that Pam had gone into a fugue state and drowned in the bathtub."

"Bob said that?"

"He did." She hesitated. "Bob also said that this had happened twice before, and he'd been told, if it happened again, Pam would need to be placed in the Brown County Mental Hospital."

I was confused by Bob's response. I told Barb that she should call the police. The papers hadn't mentioned anything about fugue states.

≈

For Green Bay teachers, their 1984 summer vacation had officially begun. Jim would get to spend three months with Collin, while I continued in my same routine.

The morning of Tuesday, June 6, before I headed to IBM, Jim was completing his run. With Fletcher at my heels, I took Collin's hand, and with his favorite Richard Scarry book, we strolled out to the front porch to use its swing. On the way, I picked up the morning paper from the step. Once settled, Collin's pudgy legs helped me pump as we both started to "read."

"I Am Afraid" jumped out from the *News-Chronicle's* front page like it had in last evening's *Press-Gazette*. Because of Sylvia Madden, the authorities now had Pam's journal in their hands.

Sylvia had been going through an ordeal since Bob's arrest last Tuesday. Because the Maddens had temporarily agreed to care for the Bulik children, an officer had provided Sylvia the Buliks' house key after Bill Appel received Bob's okay. Though, by Saturday, Abby and Alex had moved back home with their grandpa. Since Sylvia had offered to assist John Bulik with their summer activities, she'd stopped by to retrieve the schedules for swimming lessons, summer school, and choir practice. Some of the information had been on the Buliks' calendar, but the choir information had been inside the West Moravian church bulletin stuck to their refrigerator door. Bob's dad had told Sylvia to take it.

At her house, she'd been distressed to find some hand-written words on the back of the bulletin and delivered it to the police station. Once there, Sylvia had also asked a detective why they'd never retrieved Pam's journal? "I still saw it at the Buliks' home," she'd told him with a bit of reproach in her voice.

We'd all wondered whether the police had taken any action following Beezie's call on Good Friday. Obviously, they hadn't.

On Sunday June 4, with a search warrant now in hand, the police had Sylvia accompany them to the Bulik home. Under both Bill Appel's and Linda VandenLangenberg's watchful eyes, a number of items had been removed from the master bedroom. These included Pam's journal, a loose-leaf binder, and some folders containing insurance policies, bank documents, and a loan payment book. In the large closet, just off the master bedroom, Bob and Linda's personal cards, letters, and Linda's will had been secured from the cardboard box that Sylvia and Beezie had previously discovered. "I was not allowed to speak while the search was conducted," Sylvia told me, "but I used my eyes to help direct the detectives."

Last night, when the *Press-Gazette* stated: "Pamela Bulik had expressed fear in her diary a week before she drowned," I got that same sick feeling again. It appeared as if the newspapers were, indeed, inferring that Pam had been afraid of Bob. Like Beezie, Sylvia hadn't been sure what the journal entry meant, but was thankful that it was now in the authorities' hands. They could figure it out.

I looked up as Jim opened the front gate and Fletcher bounded toward him. As Jim joined Collin and me, I showed him the latest article. "I was thinking ... it took the police six weeks to get a search warrant. What if Bob had thrown out the stuff that Beezie and Sylvia had found?"

"Good question," Jim said, raising his sweaty brow.

As Collin continued to find "Goldbug" on each page of his book, Jim and I agreed that Bob apparently felt he had nothing to hide. Could he be an innocent man who'd been unjustly arrested? We just didn't know.

I folded the *News-Chronicle* to another spot. "Check this out."

Jim bent over my shoulder to look.

"It's spoofing how Sylvia found evidence on the refrigerator that the police overlooked. Notice," I said, pointing, "this guy's proposing an episode for a TV show where the cops arrest a guy for his wife's murder ... They search the house for evidence ... The suspect gives a house key to a friend who is taking care of his children ... The friend finds an incriminating will and journal, and turns them over to the police who haven't been able to find them ... So in the end his boss doesn't go for the idea. He thinks it's too unbelievable!"

"Lynda, everything about this mess is unbelievable!" Jim said, tousling my hair.

≈

College friends had asked us to attend the 1984 Olympic track and field trials in Los Angeles. After another running couple graciously offered to host our annual Bellin Run Party, Jim and I decided to go.

Considered one of the premier road races in Wisconsin, the Bellin Run drew thousands each year. Back in 1977, George Kerwin, who headed up Bellin Hospital's purchasing department and was a good running buddy of my husband's, had participated in a Milwaukee 10K race in which Olympic gold and silver medallist Frank Shorter had been featured. George thought a similar event might work in Green Bay and would get the community involved in some sport other than football. When Shorter agreed to come, the Bellin Run's rich history had begun. Part of that ongoing tradition was the post-race party hosted by our family. Each year the hospital provided the beer and soft drinks, while the Fun Run Group provided the food. After the race, George would escort the elite runners to our home, giving everyone an opportunity to rub shoulders with the celebrities. In my eyes Jim was one himself. During the early Bellins he'd clocked a time of 29:54 and placed second to the likes of Frank Shorter and Bill Rodgers.

Last year's Bellin Party had been held on our veranda and front lawn. Amid the heady scent of lilacs and shaded by red maples, competitive runners, easygoing ones, first-timers, even walkers, had chatted while amply replenishing their fluids. Pam and her children had arrived alone. Abby had run the race with her mom, finishing with a time of 63:54. Pam had proudly announced that Alex had finished nearly seven minutes ahead of them. She'd been disappointed that Bob had been unable to participate. After fulfilling a week of active Marine Corps duty, he'd been on his way home from California.

At Pam's wake, when Kevin VandenLangenberg had paraded his California T-shirt around, he'd told Sylvia that Linda had actually been with Bob.

Now, while packing for LA, I heard on the news that after five hours of testimony at Bob's preliminary hearing, Judge Alexander Grant had found probable cause to bind Bob over for trial. Bill Appel had tried to argue that his client's only action had been to save his wife from the Buliks' running van.

Since my police interview, I'd definitely believed that Pam had not committed suicide in the bathtub. But, now knowing that Bob had found her in the van, had she possibly attempted suicide there? But why hadn't Bob called 911 then? And what about Pam's bruises? And why had she eventually drowned in the bathtub? At this point I just didn't know enough to determine if Bob was guilty as charged.

≈

The Olympic trials gave us a brief respite from the Bulik situation. They were exciting, yet bittersweet for Jim. Back in February of this year he'd hung up his competitive running shoes. At that night's Fun Run friends had reminisced about Jim's running career. Among them were the Johnsens. Before the individual local runners had coalesced into the Fun Run group, Per said he and Sandy had been sitting by a window at the Big Boy restaurant. "We watched Jim Drews run by shirtless, with his long blond hair streaming behind him. Sandy nearly choked on her dinner. She thought he was a 'Running God.'"

Always modest about his accomplishments, Jim had been surprised when TV 11 had arrived at that February's Fun Run and filmed the occasion. Newspaper articles had also included Jim's career highlights. In addition to earning all-American status in cross country and track, he'd been pleased when he'd qualified for the 1980 Olympic trials and had been named Green Bay's Athlete of the Year, beating out Packers' coach Bart Starr. Then, following a local controversy, school-board policy had finally been changed to allow Jim to take an unpaid leave to participate in the Olympic trials. But when Soviet tanks had rolled into Afghanistan, President Carter had asked the US team to boycott the 1980 Moscow Olympics, so Jim had decided not to try out. After 1982, though, it would be hard for any Midwest collegiate runner to ever forget his name. Despite the practice of naming events for the deceased, Jim had been very much alive when his former UWL cross country coach, Phil Esten, had done just that. Now the Jim Drews Cross Country Invitational was one of the largest in our state.

While we were in LA, Bob had entered his plea of not guilty in Judge Richard Greenwood's courtroom. Bill Appel had asked that Bob's bail be reduced to $50,000, claiming that unless Bob's name was DeLorean, he'd never be able to come up with $100,000 in cash.

Judge Greenwood hadn't budged on the amount, but did rescind the cash-only requirement, noting that Bob had two children, a steady teaching job in Green Bay, and no prior criminal record. The newspapers stated that Bob's father was providing more than half of the bond by signing over his $62,000 Kenosha home. The remainder would come from Bob's motorcycle and van, the $18,000 equity in his $120,000 home, and the $25,000 cash he'd managed to raise.

It appeared Bob was close to making bail.

≈

Our family was seated on blankets near the Bay Beach Park pavilion. Tonight, the Green Bay City Band was playing its Fourth of July concert in this historic venue. Even though the dance hall had fizzled out, and swimming had been banned due to pollution, the ten-cent amusement rides and the picnic grounds remained.

Every summer this park attracted thousands of people who shared a common belief that the stranger at an adjacent picnic table, or standing behind you in the Ferris-wheel line could be trusted to watch your belongings, or hold your spot while your family searched for popcorn or a bathroom or even a lost child. This made Green Bay what it was. That's why the ongoing press coverage surrounding the Buliks' situation was stealing the imaginations of these law-abiding souls.

As the crowd celebrated our country's independence with patriotic music accompanying the fireworks exploding over the bay, Jim and I assumed that Bob Bulik might be celebrating his own. He'd been released from the Brown County Jail six days ago.

◇◇◇◇◇◇◇◇◇◇◇◇◇◇◇◇◇◇◇◇◇

Until a trial verdict was reached the investigation never stopped. The goal of the Brown County DA's office was to strengthen their case against Bob by clarifying any confusing details.

Assistant DA Lawrence Lasee had recently been assigned to work jointly with Assistant DA Royce Finne on the Bulik case and to aid the police with their field investigative footwork. At thirty-three, Lasee had been an assistant DA in Green Bay for three years. He'd completed his undergraduate studies at St. Norbert

College in De Pere, Wisconsin, and received his law degree from Marquette University before first accepting a position as a Milwaukee County assistant DA. After five years, he and his wife had decided to return to Brown County. Lasee still missed the faster pace of the larger metropolis where something was always happening, so he was excited to assist on the challenging Bulik case. "Most murders are crimes of passion that happen on the spur of the moment. I'd never seen anything like this."

Assistant DA Lasee and Sergeant Taylor were meeting with the Buliks' three therapists in their offices all located in the Bellin Building adjacent to the Walnut Street bridge. Prior to Bob's arrest, Taylor had briefly talked to each of them. The purpose today was to delve deeper into Bob and Pam's emotional states and their marital issues leading up to her death. Even if Bob hadn't given the authorities access to his therapy records, the charge of first-degree murder now rescinded patient/doctor confidentially restrictions.

The detective and the assistant DA were escorted into Dr. Wellens office and got right down to business. He confirmed that Bob's first experience with any psychiatric treatment had started with him. Wellens initially hadn't known that Bob was having an affair, but found out accidentally while supervising Dr. Bertrand, another therapist in his office. She'd been working on the VandenLangenbergs' case and had mentioned Linda's involvement with another teacher, a Bob Bulik.

When Pam also found out about Bob's affair in October '83, the Buliks had begun joint marriage counseling. Wellens said he'd met with the couple for twenty hours over ten sessions. "The clinic has definite conditions. If a third person is involved, there must be no contact with that person whatsoever." The doctor explained why the Buliks' counseling had been terminated. As managing partner, Wellens said he opened all mail. When Dr. Bertrand had been out of town, Linda had dropped off an envelope for her. Inside was a letter from Bob to Linda, dated January 2, 1984. Today the doctor provided a copy of it to Assistant DA Lasee.

Wellens said he'd been treating Pam for dependent personality disorder. The characteristics included an excessive need to be taken care of and fear of separation. "Pam was a very dependent person, certainly, in the beginning of our therapy, although I think she was getting stronger as therapy went on. She was much in love with Bob and I felt, wanted the marriage to work out, almost at any cost. I never felt Bob was genuinely sincere in being there. He told me he was very much in love with Linda. I told him that the dignified thing to do would be to separate from Pam, rather than having a relationship with Linda while staying married."

Wellens believed that Bob suffered from psychopathic personality disorder. This was characterized by such traits as lack of remorse or empathy, shallow emotions, manipulativeness, lying, egocentricity, glibness, low frustration tolerance, episodic relationships, and persistent violation of social norms. Psychopaths were also more likely to commit a crime and be more violent. Wellens said that Bob, as a voluntary client, had lied to him more than any patient he'd counseled in seventeen years.

From the onset of Bob's treatment, Wellens said he had no doubt that Bob had been involved in the August incident and tried to harm Pam. Fearing for her safety, Wellens had persistently encouraged Pam to move out. "I was surprised she couldn't see him as a rat. I thought that once I got her to kick him out, I'd saved her!"

Down one flight of stairs were the Green Bay Psychiatric Services offices. Assistant DA Lasee and Taylor were first meeting with Pam's individual therapist, Dr. Michael O'Neill. Like Wellens, the doctor said he believed the potential for domestic abuse had existed in the Buliks' relationship. He'd based this on Pam's initial referral by Dr. Bruce Bressler following the August incident. It had never been satisfactorily explained, the marriage had deteriorated, the affair had been discovered, and due to Bob's continued involvement with Linda, their problems had not been resolved. "To me it was an explosive situation. I did advise Pam of that."

O'Neill said he'd conducted seventeen therapy sessions with Pam from September 1983 through March '84. Another had been scheduled for April 12. Much of Pam's self-esteem, the doctor said, had been based on the family unit, so Pam's therapy had been to focus on her individual accomplishments. Early in her treatment, she'd placed Bob on a pedestal. She'd idolized this perfect image of her husband. Then, when the affair occurred, all of that had been shattered.

The doctor discussed Pam's anger and outrage at Linda VandenLangenberg's behavior. Pam had felt she'd been aggressively pursuing Bob and he'd been vulnerable and taken in by her. Pam's therapy had been intended to help her see Bob's part in the affair rather than placing all the blame on Linda—to reach a more realistic view of Bob, their marriage, and herself. O'Neill felt this had changed Pam dramatically. She'd been able to see the problems rather than denying them and could recognize her husband's faults.

Taylor asked O'Neill about Pam's December/January paranoia reported by her friends.

The doctor referred to his notes to discuss that episode and also handed the detective a letter from Dr. Bressler concerning the subject.

Lasee and Taylor's last stop was the office of Jean Weidner, Bob's psychiatric counselor. In December of 1983, she said Bob's first of seven individual sessions had begun with her. He'd wanted to make some decision—to continue in his marriage or to separate. "Bob felt his wife emotionally drained him. He felt like her caretaker." Although, when Pam filed for divorce in January 1984, Weidner said Bob had been quite depressed and still wanted to consider reconciliation.

After the Buliks did reconcile, Weidner explained that she'd jointly counseled the pair for three sessions. At their last meeting, on March 23, "The Buliks seemed to be getting along fairly well. They were looking forward to the summer, making plans."

During the three interviews, Lasee and Taylor had asked each of the therapists whether they'd felt Pam had been suicidal. Their expert opinions, along with Pam's family and friends', were key to the prosecution's case. Hopefully they'd rule out any doubt that Pam had entered the family's van of her own accord.

"I don't think Pam was suicidal," Weidner said. "Generally, when I see depression in a patient, I ask them if they are considering suicide. And I did not see the depression." She confirmed, though, that her judgment had been based on only three appointments. "I saw some anxiety, but I did not see depression."

In the course of Pam's therapy, Dr. O'Neill said, he'd never found any suggestion that Pam might be suicidal. "I saw no risk or urge that she was feeling toward suicide."

Finally, Dr. Wellens stated that he'd last seen Pam on March 30. "She came to make a payment on her account. We talked for five minutes. At that time, she was in good spirits. I never saw any indication that Pam was suicidal or had suicidal tendencies. I'm convinced she did not."

≈

Substantial investigative work still needed to be completed in Illinois, too. In Bob's police statement, he'd said that on his way to the Glenview Naval Airbase, on Friday, April 6, he'd had car trouble at I-94 and Waukegan Road due to some loose wiring. This had caused him to arrive late and consequently miss his plane to Denver. At first, Bob said he'd intended to take a commercial flight from O'Hare the next morning, but then had changed his mind and returned to Green Bay.

Taylor had just touched on these areas before the arrest. Now they were to be a focus.

On Wednesday, June 20, he and Assistant DA Lasee drove down to Illinois to investigate Bob's claims. Back on June 1, Taylor had phoned the Illinois State Police headquarters. A Sergeant Bolda had checked their records but couldn't find any trooper that had assisted Bob on Friday, April 6. Today, Taylor and Lasee wanted to review this again with Gerald Smith, who worked with the tollway patrol.

When an officer stopped to help a motorist, Smith said that a Record of Call form was filled out and then turned in at the end of the day. The department also maintained a radio log that recorded the troopers' motorist assistant calls and their requests for tow trucks. Even though Taylor and Lasee confirmed there was still no log of Bob's car trouble, they'd asked Smith to run a hand check of the Illinois State Police computer records just to make sure.

Next, Taylor and Lasee traveled to the I-94 and Waukegan Road area where they stopped at five service stations. At each they flashed Bob's photo and talked to employees that had worked on April 6. None of them recalled Bob, and none of the stations had any record of work performed on the Buliks' car.

Taylor and Lasee then proceeded to the naval air station in Glenview, Illinois, approximately eighteen miles north of Chicago. This base, originally known as Curtiss Field, had been one of the hubs for Chicago's commercial air service. In 1940 the US Navy had purchased it and changed its name. Now it was the host to the Coast Guard Air/Sea rescue helicopter service for Lake Michigan. It was also used as a staging point for East Coast antisubmarine warfare.

At the security check-in, Taylor and Lasee were directed to the BOQ (Bachelor Officers Quarters) to meet with Special Agent Richard Edmonds from Naval Investigative Services, and Michael Clark, the clerk for the BOQ.

Clark said Major Bob Bulik had checked into a BOQ room on April 6. The standard operating procedure was that all officers were assigned a single unless the BOQ was crowded. Because of a military exercise that weekend, doubling up had become a necessity, and a Captain David Haralson had later been assigned to Bob's room. Before driving down to Glenview, Taylor had called Haralson. He'd confirmed that he'd signed in around 8:30 on the evening of April 6, but had never seen Bob or any sign he'd been in the room or the bathroom.

From the BOQ, the group next traveled to the base airstrip to check the passenger manifest lists. Agent Edmonds stated that the flight Bob had missed took off at 2:28 p.m. If he'd then decided to take a commercial flight, he would've made his own arrangements, which would not have been reimbursed. Back in April, detectives had contacted the airlines that flew out of O'Hare to Denver. They were told that if the party had not purchased a ticket, as Bob had not done, the original reservation record would have been deleted. According to Pam's friends and brother, the weekend before Pam's death, Bob had supposedly flown to Denver and then onto Yuma. Taylor noted that Bob's name did not appear on that manifest list.

Driving back to Green Bay, Taylor and Lasee discussed their findings. Had they possibly caught Bob in some major lies?

∞∞∞∞∞∞∞∞∞∞∞∞∞∞∞∞∞∞

Rain, rain, and more rain. That word had branded this northeastern Wisconsin summer. Our snowfall had been below average, and now like a former teetotaler at a bar, the bay and other surrounding bodies of water were bellying up for one refill after another. During the first week of August, while our windows continued to be pelted, Jim and I watched the Los Angeles Olympics live. For me, the highlight was seeing America's Joan Benoit win the first ever women's marathon event. Her time of 2:22:43 would've won thirteen of the previous twenty men's Olympic marathons. Since organizers had considered the race too strenuous for women, it had been a long battle to get the women's marathon included. So, watching the petite lady, in the white painter's cap, enter the stadium had given me goose bumps. Her last lap was certainly a victory lap for all women marathoners.

Over the second weekend in August, Dick and Bernice Lytie staged their own triathlon. For the event, about eight couples, along with their children and dogs camped out or squeezed into the Lyties' cottage in Townsend, Wisconsin. That Saturday morning we finally awakened to sunshine. Loons floated on the pristine lake and the air was scented with pine. It was already hot, and our shirts stuck to our skin. While our husbands were out on the course, swimming, biking, and running specific distances consecutively, Bernice was in charge of the dogs. "I'd rather have ten kids than these damn dogs!" she said, while chasing after the misbehaving mutts.

Since Pam's death and Barb's departure, Bernice and Sandy Johnsen had become some of my new weekend running mates. I'd found it surprising how they'd perceived Pam. Sandy, a slender blond, said, "I didn't feel Pam had the right chemistry to call her a best friend. She had inferiority issues—an image problem with herself. She always thought she was heavy and not worthy of Bob. I wondered if, perhaps, because I was thinner and smaller, that hurt us from having a closer relationship. A smaller person reminds a larger one that they're bigger." Bernice startlingly felt the same way about Pam. With long slim legs, Bernice looked ten years younger than her forty-three years. In spite of raising seven children, she had a great figure. She wondered if this was the reason Pam had kept her at arm's length, too.

1980 Green Bay Pentathlon. Jim Drews, Pam and Bob Bulik, Larry Boehm, Daryl Kapalin, Lynda Drews, Kathy Kapalin, Sandy Johnsen kneeling.

Today I laughed when my exhausted husband finally crossed the finish line, definitely not in first place. I knew if Bob Bulik had participated he would've won. Pam had always been so proud of his triathlon accomplishments. He'd never received the running accolades Jim had, but when Bob combined his swimming skill with his decent biking and running abilities, he'd excelled.

Per Johnsen had participated in the 1982 Menominee Tinman Triathlon with Bob. "I thought he was uptight and it made me uncomfortable. Bob seemed to follow military rules. Very regimented. I found him to be a strange person, all social skills and no depth. I never saw him upset. The impression Bob fostered was that everything was okay." Per had been raised as a pacifist and had a hard time dealing with the military mindset. "I saw that kind of stuff in the Buliks' relationship. Bob always knew where they were going and when they would get there."

Bob had now been out of jail for more than a month, but had been keeping his distance, not showing up for any of the Fun Runs or local races. Per said he'd passed Bob running hills in Baird's Creek, though the two had just said a quick hello and continued in opposite directions.

We all agreed, if we were Bob, we would be at every imaginable function, not only to gain the support of friends, but to also convince everyone that we had nothing to do with Pam's death.

After Bob had pled not guilty, the attorneys had entered into their discovery phase. To be constitutional, this had to be reciprocal, allowing both sides access to each other's police reports, medical records, photographs, diagrams, witness statements, physical evidence, and any expert analysis. Neither side was permitted to hide evidence and then surprise the other at trial.

Bob's attorney had filed a number of motions. One requested copies of the witness statements taken by detectives. We running group friends realized ours would be included. It was a little unnerving to know that Bob would be reading what we'd said. Bill Appel had also asked the State to disclose any previous crimes or wrongful acts that they planned to enter against Bob at trial—in other words, the August incident.

Additionally, Appel had filed a motion to suppress evidence seized by the police on the day of Pam's death. The defense attorney said it had been taken without a valid search warrant and was therefore inadmissible. On August 14, the *Press-Gazette* covered some highlights from the first motion hearing on that subject. It stated that a search of the Buliks' house and yard, by Sergeant James Taylor, had produced these findings: Drag marks through lawn grass, damp woman's sweat pants and underpants, a piece of a leaf in the sweat pants, and bits of leaves and dirt in the house.

This information had kicked off new community speculation. Had part of Pam's death scenario included some outdoor activity?

≈

This week marked the end of Jim's summer school session where he'd completed additional courses toward his master's degree. Last summer, Pam had finally completed her special education credits necessary for full certification. I still flushed remembering how we'd agreed to celebrate her achievement.

Beezie actually offered up her house. After Jim and I arrived with the Buliks, everyone uneasily joked about getting stiff drinks. Pam then led the group down to the MacNeils' lower level family room with Beezie bringing up the rear. "The kids are upstairs," she announced, locking the door behind her and giving a nervous laugh.

I nudged her, whispering, "I can't believe we let Pam talk us into this, especially in mixed company!"

Eager to begin, Pam loaded a videotape and dimmed the lights before joining a smiling Bob, and the rest of us, on the MacNeils' two large sofas.

The title flashed, *Is It Heaven Or Hell?*

We watched a sleazy man swagger through fluffy clouds. It appeared as if he'd died and ascended into heaven. A throng of huge breasted women greeted him, suggestively offering to perform his "heart's desires."

Initially we all giggled and sniggered, but as the plot unfolded, everyone became uncomfortably quiet as the "star" was fed engorged grapes, the juices spewing all over his body. Of course his voluptuous companions had to lick up the mess as the orgy shifted into high gear.

The video flickered in the dark. Overcome with embarrassment, we friends now averted our eyes from each other. When the animals arrived on the scene, Beezie leapt to her feet and forcefully turned off the set. "I'm sorry, but that's enough! If you want to watch the rest of this, it won't be in my house!"

Her action caused grateful laughter and released the awkward tension.

Even though we six had shared many personal moments, this video had definitely crossed a line. We quickly jumped back and returned to the wholesome world of the MacNeils' kitchen for Hansen's pizza and ice cream. That night I'd felt that none of us had wanted to wreck what we had.

Boy, was I wrong.

≈

Bob's trial date had finally been set for December 3 of this year. Bill Appel, however, had filed a motion asserting that there'd been too much pretrial publicity to guarantee a fair jury from Brown County residents. He'd also claimed that some of the publicity had been highly inaccurate.

More than 350,000 people were receiving coverage from our local media. Whenever I traveled to see my IBM clients they brought up the case. They knew I was a runner. The papers and television reported that the Buliks were, too. They wanted to know if there was any chance I knew this infamous pair and the girl-friend? When I said I did, my clients turned into paparazzi, excit-edly gathering any inside details of "the murder." They couldn't get enough. The subject simply stole the conversation and pushed our business discussions aside.

Like the community, Bob's closest friends were forgetting there was such a thing called presumption of innocence. The newspa-pers constantly reminded us of Bob's charge, reiterating over and over that Pam had suffered bruises from an apparent beating, been poisoned with carbon monoxide from her family van, and then drowned in her oversized bathtub. The police would not have arrested Bob if he weren't guilty, right? And surely, Bob would not have been held over for trial unless the judge had believed there'd been a good reason to doubt his innocence.

In the past, the city of Green Bay had taken special pride in being known as the "City of Churches." Now it was on a mission to convict this immoral schoolteacher and marine who'd diabolically planned his wife's death. The trial was still three months away, yet nearly everyone in the community already believed that Bob was guilty of murder in the first-degree.

7

Motion Maneuvers

The Brown County Courthouse complex was made up of three facilities: the jail, the courthouse with its annex, and the safety building. When the Beaux Arts style courthouse, constructed of Marquette raindrop stone with a limestone super-structure and granite base, was dedicated in 1911, it was described as being unsurpassed in the state. In the rotunda area, murals of Jean Nicolet's landing and Fort Howard highlighted Brown County's historic past. As the building rose, the detailing increased—the first floor columns were created in the simplistic Doric style, the second floor, Ionic, and the third floor, elaborate Corinthian. Over the years, however, modernizing had hidden much of its original beauty. Inside Circuit Court Branch I, the third floor courtroom of the Honorable Judge Richard Greenwood, the wall decorations had been painted over and the ornate ceiling was now covered with glued-on acoustic tile.

Unlike Milwaukee, where judges specialized in divorce, criminal, misdemeanor, juvenile, probate, etc., Brown County judges were assigned cases by lottery rotation. Here the judges tried to divvy up the caseload so everyone got a taste of everything. It was advantageous that Judge Greenwood had drawn the Bulik case. He had the largest courtroom. Officials knew the trial would attract heavy public attention since Bob was no run-of-the-mill criminal.

Judge Greenwood was considered extremely intelligent, but

quite a character. Over the noon hour, he and Captain Langan would work out at the YMCA. On their walk back toward the courthouse and police station, the judge, wearing a jaunty beret, would chat away like a commandant in the French Air Force. Assistant DA Royce Finne had nicknamed Greenwood the Dean of Judges, but agreed that with his great legal mind came a bit of eccentricity. He'd announce from the bench that he needed to see the attorneys in chambers, but once there, instead of discussing the trial, he was known to pull out a harmonica or escort the lawyers over to his photo-covered walls displaying navy memorabilia from 1949-1955. There he would point out his aircraft carrier and reminisce about flying VC-12s off of it, in the dark of night. Throughout his college years, then as a lawyer, and now as a judge, Greenwood remained in the US Navy Reserve. Ironically, he was attached to the fleet out of Glenview Naval Air Station.

On October 3, Judge Greenwood would be listening to final arguments on Bill Appel's motion to suppress evidence. At the earlier hearing, Appel had argued that the items seized from the Bulik home on April 7 had not been in "plain view." According to law, only such items could be taken without a search warrant. Finne had countered by saying that no warrant had been needed since the officers had been in the home at the invitation of Bob; the discovered items had been plainly visible to the officers trying to uncover the cause of Pam's death; and, because this had been a 911 emergency situation, the responding officers had not known if Pam had been dead or alive. Judge Greenwood had requested today's hearing because he'd felt those arguments were insufficient for him to make a ruling.

Under Finne's direction, detectives had been recreating the Bulik crime scene to test hypothesizes. It had been difficult when some evidence was yet unknown. Items requiring further analysis were still at the Wisconsin State Crime Lab. Finne had asked for verification of St. Vincent Hospital's lab results from the filter paper used to blot the van seat. He'd also wanted other substances collected from the van's seats and floors analyzed. Tests had been requested on the sweat suit and underwear found in the laundry room. Additionally, he'd wanted to know whether the grease-like substance found on the garage steps, the garage floor, the woman's and man's jogging shoes, the master bedroom floor, and Bob's bathrobe was all the same. Lastly, he'd wanted to know whether anything could be learned from the scrapings under Pam's fingernails.

If Judge Greenwood ruled in the defense's favor and suppressed the evidence gathered at the scene, any of the crime lab derivatives not discovered on or around Pam's body would also be eliminated before trial.

At today's hearing, Bob sat adjacent to Bill Appel, who wore a conservative suit—a contrast to his bushy sideburns and shock of wavy brown hair. Because Appel had previously been the Brown County DA, some interesting dynamics would be in play.

Years earlier, he and the Green Bay Police Department had been on the same team. When Appel was fresh out of law school, it was Sergeant Taylor who'd made the traffic arrest for the attorney's first jury trial. The defendant was charged with negligent homicide in the death of a local business owner. Taylor told Appel, "Bill, calm down, we're going to win this." But they hadn't. Nevertheless, lasting mutual respect had developed.

The same held true for Captain Langan. He and Appel had worked together on a lengthy case focused on the Drifter Motorcycle Club. Members would come into the police station, pound on the desk, and say, "You better lay off or we're going to deal with you." At any opportunity, Langan said, the police were impounding their motorcycles. It was like a war. Behind the police station, the bike club had torched four squad cars by punching holes in the gas tanks and lighting them up. Langan knew who had done it, but it took four years before the Drifters' president was convicted of arson. The detective admired Bill Appel's perseverance and patience and believed if he hadn't been the DA, they would never have won their moral victory.

In the courtroom today, however, Appel would be arguing that his former teammates had operated in error when they'd discovered and removed evidence from the Bulik home without a warrant. The defense attorney was clearly representing the opposing side and would handle the detectives seated behind him as adversaries.

Sergeant Taylor was sworn in. After admitting that he'd been inside the Bulik residence prior to April 7, 1984, he was asked to explain the incident of August 1983. Judge Greenwood followed his testimony intently. It was the first time he'd heard about the assault.

Even though Appel insinuated that Taylor's knowledge of that incident had made him suspect foul play on April 7, the detective insisted, "I was just investigating an unusual death." But when Appel showed Taylor his police report, the detective reluctantly confirmed he'd written the words: "I don't think this is an accident."

Captain Robert Langan next testified that while Bob had been at the station on April 7, he'd never objected to the earlier presence of police officers in his home. In addition, Bob had readily signed a consent form allowing detectives to search his van. Part of Langan's work was to teach a police science course at Northeast Wisconsin Technical Institute where students learned the investigative approach used by the Green Bay Police Department. The standard procedure was to treat any death as a potential homicide and to preserve the scene. "A loss of a life," Langan said, "is the most serious matter any policeman confronts."

At the testimony's completion, Appel addressed Judge Greenwood. "In spite of whatever good intention the police may have been operating under, what right do they have to invade Mr. Bulik's home—and I mean all over, the garage and the laundry room and the bathroom.... The answer is they have no right unless they have a search warrant... If they go in there and make an investigation, sure they're going to see things, and sure things will be in plain view. It's the question of invasion. Is that right or wrong or legitimate?"

∞∞∞∞∞∞∞∞∞∞∞∞∞∞∞

The strange hormonal sensations I was feeling brought back waves of excitement and pangs of fear. Come May, Jim and I were now expecting our second child, though this was actually my third pregnancy.

In 1980, after seven years of marriage, we were elated when I discovered I was expecting. But during my second trimester, I slipped and fell on some ice, dislocating my shoulder for the first time. A few days later I miscarried. We were devastated until, six months later, we were expecting again. This time Jim and I cautiously hid our secret until my expanding belly gave me away. Then on April 22, 1982, two weeks before my due date, I'd waddled out of work with back pain and infrequent contractions. Since the Buliks had previously team-taught Lamaze to other couples, I called Pam for her advice rather than pulling Jim away from a track meet. She insisted on coming over.

Within fifteen minutes, Pam entered my bedroom, her eyes bright as she knelt beside me. "Hey, girl, how are you doing?" She gently touched my sweaty face, while soothingly explaining that I was experiencing back labor. Once Pam had contacted Jim, she helped me turn onto my side and then climbed into bed behind me. With each contraction I felt her strong hands push against the small of my back, helping ease the

The Buliks at the Pictured Rock 11-mile run. I was impressed that the couple had team-taught Lamaze.

pain. Over my shoulder she reassured me, saying, "This will be a piece of cake compared to running the last six miles of a marathon!" We were giggling between contractions when my anxious husband arrived. He couldn't help but shake his head at the sight of the two crazy women lying on our bed.

Pam drove Jim and me to Bellin Hospital. As he got a wheel chair, Pam squeezed me tight and whispered, "The next time I see you, Lynda, you'll finally have that new life to hold."

She was so right. Now with Collin wiggling in my lap, I attempted to tie his shoes while trying to imagine handling two. Other than family, I'd shared our exciting news with just Beezie and a good neighborhood friend, Carol Schnaars. The other person I would've told was Pam.

≈

Always the romantic, Jim woke me on Saturday, October 13, and announced he'd planned a surprise weekend to celebrate our upcoming event. We'd have two days to do whatever we wanted in Door County, a scenic peninsula jutting out into Lake Michigan just north of Green Bay. The fall colors would be at their peak.

Two hours later the three of us parked by the shores of Eagle Harbor, before we crossed the road to Wilson's Restaurant. I picked up a newspaper from the outside box under the red and white candy striped awning. We were in luck and immediately got a booth that included a booster seat. Waiting for the waitress, Jim unwrapped saltines to keep Collin busy while I skimmed the paper's front page.

I looked up and smiled. "Jim, the judge ruled that the search of the Bulik home was legal. It was backed up by the fact that Bob signed a written consent to search his van."

"That's a relief!" His eyes found mine. "It would be a crime if it wasn't."

Since Judge Greenwood had also denied Appel's other motions to dismiss Bob's case, it appeared as if nothing should stop the trial from moving forward.

We unloaded our bicycles to enjoy a perfect Indian summer day. Collin was strapped into his seat behind Jim before we headed for Peninsula State Park. Once there we followed the winding roads to reach Eagle Tower, a seventy-five-foot observation platform orginally built to monitor forest fires. After we made our traditional climb to the top, Jim boosted Collin up on his shoulders to marvel at the stunning view of the outlying islands and the distant Michigan shoreline.

We laughed as he pointed out "boats, birds, and bikes."

Jim looked at my flushed cheeks and brushed the damp bangs out of my eyes. "I sure do love you."

I captured his hand, kissing the palm. "I've missed you this year. Other than the Olympic trials, we've had practically no time together. Everything's been about Pam...I feel guilty admitting it, Jim, but it's a relief to have our lives back. I know it sounds horrible, but for that to happen, it's like Pam had to lose hers."

"Lynda, don't feel guilty for thinking that," he frowned. "You certainly didn't wish for this to happen. But I disagree. We still don't have our lives back, and definitely won't, until Pam's death is resolved."

≈

The weather had cooled and on Sunday night we returned to a chilly house. I easily put Collin to bed and then joined Jim in the family room, now lit with an inviting fire. A dry log crackled and then shifted as I collapsed on the couch, snuggling into a wooly sweater I'd knit.

I turned on the TV while Jim read Sunday's paper. He soon set it down. "Lynda, there just seems to be only terrible news. I remember when Green Bay's biggest concern used to be only if the Packers won or lost."

Jim's comment was so true. On a daily basis, the community was being kept abreast of three pending first-degree murder trials. Back on September 23, a *Press-Gazette* article had discussed the cases and the good work attributed to the officers involved. The first was a man accused of leaving a woman to die outside a packing plant after he'd beaten her and then slashed her throat. The second focused on two grisly killings committed by one man. The last was Pam's death.

◇◇◇◇◇◇◇◇◇◇◇◇◇◇◇◇◇◇◇

By October 26, Judge Greenwood was ready to hear final arguments on the defense's motion to either change Bob Bulik's trial venue or to select a jury from a different jurisdiction. In Circuit Court I, the prosecutors and Bill Appel gathered with Bob seated at his attorney's side. For two months Appel had been feeding the judge photocopies of newspaper articles and transcripts from both television and radio.

The defense attorney began, speaking in a forthright manner with just a hint of a lisp. "I think this issue is the most important because it goes to whether or not Mr. Bulik will receive a fair trial." Appel then pointed out that the investigation into Pam's death had resulted in a great deal of media reportage, about 80 percent on the front page of the local papers and often the lead stories on TV and radio. "Any jury selected from this community … is bound to have misconceptions and preconceived notions coming into this case." Every person, Appel said he'd talked to, felt Bob had committed some kind of heinous crime of murdering his wife. "Looking at the articles as a whole, I don't think they allow for any presumption of innocence."

Appel addressed specific examples that cited the phrase: Bob Bulik severely beat his wife, poisoned her, and then drowned her. "That's used in the *Press-Gazette* seven or more times. I counted six or more times in the *News-Chronicle*. I found it in the TV and radio transcripts…I think it is absolutely prejudicial!"

Additionally, the statements the detectives had given to the press concerned Appel. He believed that the public assigned a great deal of credibility to what they said, and properly so. "But I think in this case, the police shouldn't have said those things."

Appel continued in this same vein, until he finally noted the article in which Bob's case was included among other gruesome local murders. "Judge, what this all comes down to is whether or not Mr. Bulik can get a fair trial in this community. And if this court denies my motion, the State isn't hurt, the defendant is. If this court grants my motion, the defendant isn't hurt. He isn't helped, and the State isn't hurt."

It was Royce Finne's turn. "Mr. Appel has not presented one iota of evidence to indicate that there is any prejudice against Mr. Bulik in this community." The only thing, Finne said, the defense attorney had cited had been rumors he'd heard from his acquaintances and social friends. "That proves only, perhaps, that Mr. Appel has a narrow-minded group of persons that he hangs around with." Finne added that Appel had taken twenty or thirty words, out of literally thousands, attempting to show there had been a grand conspiracy of prejudice against his client. "That is simply not the case!" The prosecutor then reviewed a number of similar cases and closed by stating that an extensive voir dire, to pick the jury from the Green Bay community, was the preferred method.

Judge Greenwood fixed his eyes on the attorneys. "It's kind of close, but it's my responsibility to balance the obligations between the competing people." He shifted his gaze to Bob's attentive face. "I have to consider the fact that the defendant is charged with first-degree murder." Since it was the highest liberty issue at stake, Greenwood ruled that going to another jurisdiction to select a jury, and returning to Green Bay to try the case in his courtroom, would ensure a neutral jury and guarantee Bob's constitutional protections.

◇◇◇◇◇◇◇◇◇◇◇◇◇◇◇◇◇◇◇◇◇◇

Halloween had come and gone, President Reagan had been reelected in a landslide, and the Bulik trial was now about a month away. As I entered the house after a short jog, I yanked up my running tights, yet again. It was difficult to keep them from sliding down over my expanding belly. I'd reached my first trimester, and at last week's Fun Run, Jim and I had finally announced our exciting secret to friends.

I now found my husband with his feet up, watching college football. Collin chattered away, grabbing my hand. Dressed in his Big Bird Halloween costume, which he refused to take off, he did an awkward somersault on the floor.

"Like father, like son!" I laughed, clapping at the sight.

Jim rolled his eyes. "Lynda, on the table there's an envelope for you from the district attorney's office."

"Uh-oh." I opened it and scanned the message before reading it to Jim:

> Dear Ms. Drews,
>
> As you know, Robert Bulik is charged with First-degree Murder in connection with the death of his wife. The Trial is scheduled to begin on December 4, 1984. A review of the file shows you will be needed as a witness for the State during the Trial. Enclosed is a subpoena. Please call when you receive this.
>
> Thank you for your cooperation.
>
> Royce A. Finne, Assistant District Attorney

I looked up over the edge of the letter. "I guess this isn't just a bad dream after all."

≈

At work on Monday, I called the DA's office. A secretary scheduled me for a meeting later in November. Then, after badging into the computer room, I heard my name paged for a call on line one. Next to a terminal, I picked up the receiver of the adjacent phone. When the caller said he was Bill Appel my heart started to race.

Bill was friendly, chatting briefly about the two of us being acquainted through our spouses. Then he cut to the chase. He said he understood the prosecution had subpoenaed me. To provide his client the best defense, he was interviewing each of the State's witnesses. Appel had read the statement I'd made to the police and wanted to discuss it with me.

◇◇◇◇◇◇◇◇◇◇◇◇◇◇◇◇◇◇◇

The Monday before Thanksgiving, Judge Richard Greenwood would listen to the attorneys' arguments on some final pretrial motions. His all-powerful decisions could produce major effects on the upcoming trial. Bill Appel was asked to begin.

"My motion is to obtain an Order to prohibit any testimony or evidence regarding an incident of an assault at the Bulik home in August of 1983." Appel said he'd made a written demand asking for disclosure of any prior wrongs, crimes, or evidence that the government might offer. But, as of this date, he'd not received any. "I'm suspicious, yet, that it's the intention of the prosecution to try to use this type of evidence."

"...Should there be evidence in the trial," Finne said, "that Pamela Bulik was injured, according to her husband, by an attack from an intruder...we'll produce no witness who will blame the defendant for that." But when he confirmed that the State might offer proof that there'd been an assault at the Buliks' home, Appel insisted they needed a ruling. He argued that Pam's physiological condition following the assault was a different issue than its cause.

"Your Honor," Finne's eyes flashed, "clearly to have evidence in this case that there were residual effects, because of this injury to Pamela's head in August of '83, but yet to keep silent about the circumstances under which she received it, invites the jury to speculate how she got it."

It wouldn't matter, Appel countered, if Pamela had been roller skating and fell on her head, if she'd been running, tripped and struck her head, if an intruder had hit her on the head, or, as the government wanted everyone to believe, her husband had done it. "They want to explain how it happened clearly for the prejudicial effect...And to say otherwise is being dishonest with the court."

Finne bristled at the rude remark. "I would like to think that I could refrain from calling Mr. Appel names. I would expect the same courtesy."

"What's the statute that talks about the prejudice weight?" Greenwood frowned as he paged through a guidebook to criminal law and then finding the spot, read aloud: "Although relevant, evidence may be excluded if its probative value is substantially

outweighed by the danger of unfair prejudice." He looked up.
"Mr. Finne says it has great probative value." The judge turned
to Appel. "You say it's highly prejudicial...Well it's prejudicial in
this sense—only Bulik and his wife were there—"

"The intruder was," Finne interjected.

"Maybe...I understand that. But the police didn't believe
Bulik."

Appel jumped in. "It doesn't matter whether it's in their case in
chief or on cross-examination of any of our witnesses..."

"I may agree with you," Greenwood said, "but I'm not 100 percent convinced that that's correct...I haven't heard live witnesses.
I haven't heard the case develop. I don't know where Pamela was
born. I don't know where she lived. I don't know where Bulik
comes from...I know very little about this case other than what
I've read in the preliminary examination and heard in the sup-
pression hearings. So it's difficult to rule on these things in a
vacuum." The judge paused, contemplating, and said he was not
ready to make any ruling on this important issue.

The arduous day continued as Appel stepped through the police
interviews of the State's witnesses to be called at trial. He and
Finne argued before Greenwood, reaching pretrial determina-
tions on the admissibility of specific evidence, particularly around
hearsay as it applied to Pam's fears.

≈

While the attorneys debated motions, Sergeant Taylor and Captain Langan reviewed their investigation notes in preparation for
trial. There were still numerous fuzzy areas, in particular—carbon monoxide. On the day of Pam's death, when Taylor had been
gathering evidence, there'd been no indication that carbon monoxide would be a factor in the case.

During Bob's testimony at the April 18, John Doe hearing, the
district attorney's office had realized that knowledge about the
level of carbon monoxide in the Buliks' house and garage on April
7 would have been extremely beneficial. Even though eleven days
had passed, Taylor had been asked to find a device that could

measure the atmospheric content of those areas and provide a printout for evidence. Wisconsin Public Service had no such device. The Green Bay Fire Department had a machine with a meter, but it couldn't print out the results. At the Milwaukee DNR office, Taylor had finally located a unit that fit the State's requirements, but by the time he'd fetched it, Bob Bulik had left for the Bahamas. The DA's office had realized they'd have to wait for Bob's return, and had acknowledged—it would have been far too late.

This week a Brown County Library employee had alerted detectives that the defense had been researching this area. She'd received a call from an adult male requesting a sixty-page report on carbon monoxide. After referring him to an inter-loan department, the caller had then asked that it be held for Linda VandenLangenberg.

Naturally, Linda's name kept coming up. The detectives believed she'd moved in with Bob. The owner of her duplex, Ed Burton*, lived on the property next to Linda's and had told them that one of her recent rent checks had been paid from Bob's account. At present, Burton didn't think that Linda was staying in the duplex. He'd contacted her a week ago and asked if he could check out the duplex's sump pump. Upon entering, he'd noticed that Linda's living room had been bare. Even though the mail and paper were being picked up each day, no one appeared to be residing there.

◇◇◇◇◇◇◇◇◇◇◇◇◇◇◇◇◇◇◇◇◇◇

The glass doors of IBM closed behind me. Sunshine warmed the sidewalk, melting stubborn ice and snow as I gingerly walked toward the district attorney's office. Tucked in the back of my mind was my earlier fall and the resulting miscarriage.

Since receiving my subpoena I'd wrestled with my thoughts. Considering everything I'd read, even if Pam had attempted suicide, the fact that Bob had never called 911, when he'd found her in the van, had convinced me—he must be guilty. I now hoped my testimony would help the prosecution.

Entering the safety building, I stamped my shoes on the mat and proceeded to the correct floor. A receptionist told me to take a seat. Unbuttoning my coat, I found a chair and smoothed my maternity dress in the process. I'd finally succumbed.

Two men entered bundled in winter coats and scarves. One was tall and thin, the other short and stocky—Mutt and Jeff. The taller man smiled at me. "You must be Lynda Drews." He introduced himself as Royce Finne and his cohort as Larry Lasee. The two assistant district attorneys then escorted me into an office.

After we were seated, Lasee's eyes glowed in his friendly boyish face. "I'll be the one questioning you on the stand." He explained that he'd be asking me about Pam's state of mind—if she'd been happy and looking forward to life, or sad and depressed. I would, however, not be allowed to mention anything Pam might have said about Bob, as that was considered hearsay.

Even though I was not, per se, an "expert" in the sport of running, the prosecutors wanted to know my credentials to better understand how my testimony would come across to the jurors.

I told them I'd been running for fifteen years. My best time in the five marathons I'd completed was 3:39:50, which had qualified me for the Boston Marathon. It was hard to estimate how many shorter races I'd run, but my personal record for a 10K was 42:57 at last year's Bellin Run, placing me within my age group's top ten.

My first marathon in Marquette, Michigan. Pam was very supportive of Bob, riding her bike the twenty-six miles next to him.

The prosecutors then brought up Bob's reason for drawing Pam's bath water on the morning of her death. He'd claimed that Pam had wanted to soak her sore legs before running the Jogger's Joynt race. They wanted to get my perspective on her training regimen. I explained the miles she'd been putting in. "It was just unbelievable how good Pam was running. She'd decreased her times by minutes in a 10K. She could never break fifty, and now could. She was a lot thinner, had more energy, and her legs weren't bothering her as they had prior years."

"Had she been having problems with her legs in the past?" Larry asked, lifting his brow.

"Mainly, because of her weight. When she lost her weight, she rarely complained to me about leg problems."

"Did you ever know Pam to soak her legs before she ran?"

"I know she never soaked them before any of the runs where we stayed in a hotel."

"Do you know any runners who soak before they run?"

I shook my head. "They may take a quick shower to feel clean beforehand, but I don't know anybody who soaks their legs prior to running. You would get too relaxed. If anything, people are drinking coffee and trying to psych-up for a race."

At the trial, Larry explained that I'd be asked similar questions and then warned me about Bill Appel. The prosecutors respected Bill. He was intelligent and would do a good job defending his client. But Bill could sometimes get tunnel vision—going after certain points and sticking with them until he got the answer he was looking for.

At the meeting's end, I asked Royce Finne what his thoughts were about having the trial so close to Christmas. "The jury must dread being away from home," I said, putting on my coat. "This is the busiest time of year, especially for women."

Royce agreed that it wasn't the best time for a trial. "Our hope is that the jury will be more upset at the defendant than at the State for hauling them to Green Bay." The trial would be very challenging, he said, by no means a slam-dunk. "What actually happened in the Buliks' home is still not crystal clear."

＝

On Saturday night, Jim and I invited five couples over to our house for a potluck dinner and a game of Trivial Pursuit. This week the *Fatal Vision* mini series, based on the best selling novel by Joe McGinniss, had aired. Beezie mentioned that when she and Sylvia had boxed up Pam's things, they'd noticed the library book in the Buliks' home. Since the true story coincidentally was about a marine accused of killing his family, Beezie had contacted Sergeant Taylor about it. Like Bob, the marine in the story still maintained his innocence. The detective had called the Brown County Library, but had been unable to discover which Bulik had checked it out.

In the series, we'd watched the grandparents agonize over the devastating murders of their only daughter and grandchildren. We thought there couldn't be anything worse and realized, since Pam's parents were convinced that Bob was responsible for Pam's death, that's what they must be going through.

Of course the impending trial came up. The prosecution team had subpoenaed Beezie, Sylvia, Dick, and me. The defense had subpoenaed Daryl Kapalin. He told me that I was the culprit. In my police statement, I'd mentioned an incident concerning Pam that Daryl had told me about. For some reason, Bill Appel believed Daryl's testimony would be important to Bob's case.

Unlike nearly everyone in the running group, Daryl and Kathy had remained unbiased about Bob's involvement in Pam's death. He'd been their friend and Kathy's frequent running mate. Daryl gently reprimanded us, "Maybe Bob is guilty. Maybe he's not. How do we know until we've heard all the facts?"

My face flushed. Daryl knew I'd taken a stand, and that once I did, I never wanted to back down, never wanted to be wrong or declare defeat.

Though, admittedly, I knew he was right.

◇◇◇◇◇◇◇◇◇◇◇◇◇◇◇◇◇◇◇◇◇◇

On November 28, the public seating area inside Brown County Circuit Court Branch I was nearly full, an indication that Bob Bulik's trial would more than likely be packed. Today's motion would switch focus. Judge Greenwood's eyes roamed his courtroom, passing by the defendant, his defense attorney, the State attorneys, to finally land on Linda VandenLangenberg alongside her attorney, John Evans.

"My client," Evans said, "has signed an attached affidavit to this motion in which she alleges that certain questions that she was asked at the John Doe hearing, subjected her to humiliation and further delved into her private, personal life." Evans was requesting that the court disallow questions about Linda's sexual activities. "My client feels it's nobody's business but her own."

Greenwood turned to Assistant DA Royce Finne. "Can you tell me what questions you're going to be asking?"

"We're not interested in Linda VandenLangenberg's sexual preferences or practices. We're simply interested in the nature of her relationship with this particular defendant. The theory is it formed part of the motive for the crime."

"I see. That's relevant. Very."

"Now, we're prepared, of course, to offer her immunity in open court for any acts that may be prosecutable under the old statutes: adultery, fornication, or what have you."

Greenwood's eyes found Bill Appel's. "You're representing Mr. Bulik and it bears on your case ... Do you want to make any statement on this point?"

"...I understand what the prosecution is claiming shows a motive for the murder." Appel felt, though, that the State could establish that without going into Linda and Bob's real intimate personal life. "They don't have to ask if they had sexual intercourse or how many times, when and why."

The judge leaned forward, palms flat on the bench. "Well, I respectfully disagree." If he were a lawyer, charged with murdering his wife, and taking his secretary out to a clandestine dinner at the Carriage Inn, Greenwood said, that would be one thing. If after dinner, the two of them went to the Ramada Inn West and had sexual intercourse—that would be bigger yet. "Obviously," he said, "there is passion and hot blood involved." He ruled that the State could go into explicit detail between the accused and a prospective paramour. However, as the presiding judge, Greenwood said he could prohibit the press from taking Linda's photo. Before she testified, he would make that ruling.

Within the courtroom, as Linda and John Evans took their leave, the members of the media whispered about the judge's last comment.

Greenwood now addressed the remaining attorneys. He said he was prepared to make his ruling concerning the Buliks' assault.

"I have really thought about the motion...Maybe what happened at Mr. Bulik's house on August eighteenth, 1983 should be admitted. It's a situation about eight months before the death of Mrs. Bulik. In both incidents she was the person assaulted. There are head blows...Both times they were done at the house and were quite unexplained and mysterious events. They might go to show plan and modus operandi. Because of all those similarities there's a certain coupling to the August incident and the April incident. They go to reinforce each other."

In hopeful anticipation the prosecutors held their breath.

"But I'm still not going to let it in," Greenwood said. "I realize this is a very close question, but there is no real strong evidence as to what happened...The best we've got is Mrs. Bulik's statement saying, 'I don't know what happened.' Mr. Bulik said an intruder did it. Mr. Bulik hasn't been prosecuted. Mrs. Bulik never filed a complaint. We never found the intruder. It's all very speculative, and I don't think the jury should be permitted to indulge in conjecture or speculation. I'm going to be the first to admit that maybe some trial judges would let it in. Maybe they wouldn't. I don't know. It's a close question. But I'm deciding the question. It's a case involving first-degree murder and I'm giving the accused the benefit of the doubt.

"However," Greenwood looked at each attorney in turn, "if that incident becomes relevant, I'm going to be listening very carefully as to what would be admissible in rebuttal or cross-examination. I think that's the better view." Finne and Lasee tried to hide their extreme disappointment. They knew pretrial rulings could be disputed in the Wisconsin Appellate Court, but because the court only reviewed whether the judge had performed a reasonable exercise to make his ruling, the prosecutors had no alternative but to live with Greenwood's decision. The defense had decisively won this round.

◇◇◇◇◇◇◇◇◇◇◇◇◇◇◇◇◇◇◇◇◇◇◇◇◇◇

In the Lambeau Field parking lot, Jim and I maneuvered through the animated tailgaters stopping periodically to chat with friends. The beer was flowing freely, and the air was thick with smoke from grills loaded with sizzling Wisconsin bratwurst.

Bundled up for the elements, we found our seats near the north end zone. Awaiting kickoff, we talked about the judge's disappointing ruling concerning the Buliks' assault.

Back on August 31, 1983, when Pam had signed her polygraph release, Bob had not. According to Pam, he'd told the detectives that he had no faith in the lie detector.

This had sounded suspect to Bob's friends. That was until his affair had been revealed. Then we'd believed that his refusal had arisen from fear that his involvement with Linda would've been exposed to Pam. But Sergeant Taylor had recently shed some light on that assumption. We now understood that Bob would only have been questioned about the assault. Based on that information, friends now believed Bob's refusal probably meant that he'd hit Pam in August. To us, disallowing this testimony was a travesty.

Tomorrow, the jury would be selected from Washington County residents. Royce Finne was quoted in today's *Press-Gazette* as saying that he'd be calling up to thirty witnesses and expected the State's case to take most of the week.

It was scary realizing I'd soon be testifying. Today's game was a nice diversion. It teetered back and forth, but ended on a high note, Pack-27, Bucs-14. I wondered if the looming trial would end with the same results.

8

Tale of Two Stories

Brown County Courthouse

New York City's Rockefeller Center came alive this week as its seventy-five-foot Christmas tree was lit. On Tuesday, December 4, the holiday season was in full swing, though in the copper domed Brown County Courthouse it was taking a backseat to day one of Bob Bulik's trial.

I climbed three flights of stairs, slightly winded after reaching the corridor outside Circuit Court Branch I. Unable to find Beezie in the noisy throng, I peered over the circular balcony and spotted her. She was standing nearly dead center in the inlaid star of the entrance level's terrazzo floor. "Beezie, up here," I shouted. A powerful echo embarrassed me as she waved.

The presence of camera crews and media personnel contributed to the zoo-like atmosphere. The executive director for the Family Violence Center was being interviewed, I supposed, due to the abuse allegations. This wasn't just a trial—it was a full-on Green Bay happening.

As the doors opened, the frenzied crowd pushed forward to secure the best seats in the courtroom. Furnished in quarter-sawn oak and lit by hanging chandeliers, its massive bench and witness stand were intimidating. Beezie and I secured spots in the public seating area with writing materials in hand, planning to take notes to share with our husbands. We also saved a seat for Marcy Prato, Beezie's sister-in-law. Marcy lived in Appleton, a city thirty miles south, and planned to drive up each day.

One long wooden table housed both the prosecution and defense teams. On the left side Bill Appel took his seat next to Bob. It seemed amazing that we'd reached this point. The last time I'd seen Bob was at Kathy Kapalin's graduation party. He looked thinner and wore a navy sport coat over a crisp white shirt and red tie. I couldn't help but picture Linda ironing the shirt for him last night, instead of Pam. I didn't see Linda, but noticed Bob's father and younger brother Ken.

Pam's sister-in-law had called Beezie. Bonnie and Bill Metzger had decided not to attend the trial, but asked her to mail any newspaper articles. If Bill were present, Bonnie said he might do something crazy, denying them the pleasure of seeing Bob behind bars. Because Pam's mother's health was poor, she was also not attending, so seated behind the prosecution team of Royce Finne and Larry Lasee were Pam's father and stepmother. They would represent the small Metzger family. Alongside them was Pam's first sweetheart, Bob Whitrock, accompanied by his wife. Because he owned a car dealership in Wisconsin Rapids, he'd arranged his schedule to be there to support Pam's father who'd "lost his little girl."

Marcy entered the courtroom, combing fingers through her short brown hair. Seeing us, she grinned and held up her own pad of paper. As she slid in next to Beezie, Royce Finne approached. He explained that the judge had just granted Bill Appel's motion to sequester witnesses outside the courtroom. Beezie and I could remain for the opening arguments, but would then need to leave until we had testified. We were disappointed, but Marcy promised to take good notes.

≈

At 9:45, Judge Greenwood took his seat at the bench, his salt and pepper hair neatly combed. Austere in black robe and wire-rimmed glasses, he surveyed his courtroom packed with approximately 150 spectators. He then nodded to the bailiff. The time had arrived to bring in the fourteen-member jury, including two alternates.

Their ages spanned from the early twenties to the late sixties. First among them were two of the four women, one a newlywed bartender and the second a homemaker. During jury selection, the defense attorney had asked them questions about the *Fatal Vision* mini-series, which the two had watched. They'd told Appel "it would not overpoweringly influence them in deciding the evidence in the case." The remaining women were a farm worker and a teacher's aid. Two of the men were athletically inclined. First was a tool and die maker, who'd participated in a few Wisconsin triathlons and second was a sporting goods storeowner, who was both a runner and a rescue squad volunteer. Two men had military experience. One was a minister, who'd served in the navy, and the second was a carpenter, who was currently an army reservist. Within the remaining jurors were a vehicle body shop technician and the owner of a popular restaurant. For the trial's duration, the Washington County residents would be sequestered at the Downtowner Motel, which once housed the office of Packer coach Vince Lombardi.

When the jurors were in place, Judge Greenwood announced, "This is the case of State of Wisconsin against Robert J. Bulik." He tipped his head toward the prosecutors. "You can make your opening statement whenever you're ready, Mr. Finne."

The State had talked to the witnesses, studied the evidence, anticipated problems, and developed a strategy. In his light gray suit and red tie, Assistant DA Royce Finne looked confident as he stood to address the jury. He carried a legal pad to the lectern and then faced the panel with a somber smile. After explaining that the opening statements would not be evidence in this case, but rather a road map of what each side felt the evidence would show, Finne began.

≈

I listened as he reiterated what I'd read in the newspapers for months. He talked about the morning of April 7 when Bob's 911 call had come in, how the police had arrived and found nothing to explain Pam's drowning, how evidence had been discovered in the van and garage, and how Bob had accompanied them to the station.

I knew that Bob had missed his flight to Denver and returned to Green Bay, but as I followed Finne's dialog, I couldn't understand Bob's explanation for why or where he'd parked his car before arriving home on Friday night.

The prosecutor proceeded to review the rest of Bob's statement. Apparently, Pam had accused Bob of seeing Linda, the Buliks had argued, and shortly thereafter, both gone to bed. Sometime during the night, Bob had realized that Pam hadn't been next to him. He'd heard an engine running, discovered her in the van and then managed to bring her back inside where they'd both returned to bed.

In the morning when Bob had awakened, he'd told detectives that Pam had still been asleep. Remembering that she'd been planning to run the Jogger's Joynt half-marathon, and that she'd been having trouble with her legs, Bob said he'd decided to fill their in-ground tub so she could soak them beforehand. Somehow he'd brought Pam alongside it, saying something like "I'm going to throw you in," although she hadn't responded.

I looked at Beezie. That was bizarre, but it only got worse.

Bob had told the authorities that he'd thought Pam had been ignoring him, so he'd leaned her naked body up against a hamper by the tub's edge before he'd left her to complete household chores, feed the kids, and deal with his car. Eventually, Bob had returned to the bathroom and discovered Pam facedown in the water. Until he'd touched her, he said he'd thought that she'd been giving him a hard time. According to Bob, he'd then pulled her out and administered CPR without achieving any beneficial effect. Based on his therapist's instructions, he'd gotten his children out of the house before finally calling 911.

"That's the story he told the police on April seventh, 1984." However, Finne said, it soon became apparent that there were things about Bob's story that didn't check out. "Things were not quite as they appeared."

I looked over at the jurors. Like me, they were on the edge of their seats, waiting for the rest of the story.

Finne took a deep breath and continued. "At about the same time the defendant was explaining to the police what he says happened, an autopsy was being performed on the body of his wife." Finne explained that the pathologist had discovered Pam's near fatal level of carbon monoxide. Eyes flashing, the prosecutor then detailed her numerous bruises and scrapes. "These were serious injuries. Of course none of those were accounted for or mentioned in the statement the defendant gave to the police, all of which were indicative of a struggle."

Finne explained that the police had uncovered the Buliks' serious financial difficulties and Bob's involvement in a significant affair. A divorce would leave little for Bob, but he stood to gain substantial money from Pam's life insurance. He had motive! And, Finne said, Bob had the exclusive opportunity. Other than his children, he'd been the only one in the home.

The prosecutor paused, leaning toward the jurors and said that at the time of Pam's death, she'd been an emotionally well and stable person. There'd been nothing to suggest that she'd been in any frame of mind to take her own life. "All of that, ladies and gentlemen, prove that the defendant," Finne pointed a long finger at Bob, "in fact killed his wife and intentionally did so."

Everyone in the courtroom sat absolutely still as Finne took his seat next to Lasee. He gave Finne an approving nod. The prosecutor had accomplished what he'd set out to do: laid the groundwork for a verdict of first-degree murder.

≈

On familiar turf, Bill Appel, dressed in a charcoal gray suit and a maroon dotted tie, walked deliberately up to the lectern to address the expectant jury. "The charge in this case … is first-degree murder. It is not my first, first-degree murder case, but I'll frankly tell you, I have never had one weigh more heavily on me. Mr. Bulik," he nodded at Bob, "my client, is charged with intentionally murdering his wife. Our government can bring no more serious charge than that." He paused to let that statement sink in. "Mr. Bulik has pled to this court and has pled to you his innocence, not guilty. I did not murder my wife."

Appel explained that the police had turned Bob's statement upside down and inside out. "And I'm pleased they did … It is not challenged, other than by speculation. But the government has had that massive investigative resource here," he gestured toward Sergeant Taylor and Captain Langan, sitting behind the prosecutors, "the Green Bay Police Department. And I don't fault them for that. That's their job. But that investigation pointed toward one thing, proving guilt not proving innocence … Mr. Bulik's protections are three: me, you, and the law." Until the government could convince the jury, beyond a reasonable doubt of Bob's guilt, Appel said, they must presume Bob innocent.

He next explained the jury's job. If they had a loved one about to undergo a serious operation, wouldn't they want the surgeon to have his instruments antiseptically clean, not contaminated? Appel searched out the jurors' eyes. "We all would!" For Bob's operation, it would be the jurors' judgment and thinking that would be the surgeon's tool. He asked them to keep it "antiseptically clean of conjecture and speculation."

As the defense attorney, Appel said his job would be to cross-examine each of the State's witnesses, call his own to prove that their "farfetched theory" was false, and show that the statement Bob had given to the police was absolutely true. "It's his story. It's his defense."

The attorney then began to humanize Bob to the jury, explaining his background, his job, his thirteen years of marriage to Pam, and his love for their children. Appel also brought up the Buliks' marital problems. "I don't want to try that issue. We recognize some of them are ours, but please don't say they're all ours." He reviewed Bob's affair, the Buliks' marriage counseling, and Pam's divorce action. "They made a decision afterwards to attempt reconciliation…Mr. Bulik came home at his wife's invitation and request."

The defense attorney said he'd show that Finne's comments about Pam's emotional state were incorrect. Everything had not been coming up roses. "I expect the evidence to show, Mrs. Bulik had a severe depression problem. That she was in tremendous emotional stress and turmoil…there were physiological consequences to that emotional stress that her husband saw, that others became aware of."

Next, Appel mentioned the autopsy and Finne's claim that Pam's bruises had been deliberately inflicted. "That's what is at issue here, because we say they were not inflicted." The evidence would show, Appel said, that those bruises had occurred as Bob rescued Pam from the van. The attorney also suggested that the carbon monoxide that had affected her, had affected Bob, too.

Appel swiveled toward Greenwood. "If the court has no objection, your Honor, I would like to have Mr. Bulik talk to the jury…"

Finne sprang to his feet with a swift glance at the judge. "I do object. This defendant is a party to this case and any statement from him has to be under oath."

"The objection is sustained," Greenwood said. "I don't think that's proper."

Appel turned back to the jury. "Mr. Bulik would like to participate, ladies and gentlemen. Mr. Finne won't let him."

"I object to that characterization. I have a right to cross-examine a party to this case. That's just improper and unfair and Mr. Appel knows it."

"Well, I don' t know if he knows it or not," the judge said dryly.

Appel seemed unfazed, even though he'd obviously lost the dispute. He said the evidence would show that the police had intentionally interrogated Bob. He'd been advised of his right to counsel, but had never asked for an attorney, either at the police station or at the John Doe hearing eleven days later. Bob had allowed the police to take whatever evidence they wanted. "He did all he could and could do no more."

The jury was with Appel. He was asking them to trust him, to trust Bob, asking for their help to get Bob through his horrible nightmare.

"Now, Mr. Finne told you their theory of the case. They have got to prove it!" Appel's eyes sparked passionately as he pounded his fist on the lectern. "Hold them to it! And remember that presumption of innocence."

The judge called for a noon recess. We three women slipped on our coats, knowing that only Marcy would return. I looked over at Bob's handsome profile. Appel had certainly wanted him to tell the jury he didn't kill Pam. I frowned. It just seemed to me that Bob should've tried to convince his friends first.

<hr />

In Finne's opening statement he'd claimed that Bob had intentionally murdered Pam. This afternoon the prosecution team was ready to begin proving it. First up would be the authorities that had gathered the critical evidence on April 7, 1984, eventually leading to Bob's arrest. In turn, Appel would be challenging their testimony to continually sweeten the "pot" of reasonable doubt.

Finne played the taped call the 911 emergency operator, Eunice Hanley, had received at 11:16 a.m. An unidentified male voice reported a possible drowning at 251 Traders Court and hung up. Hanley then reviewed the emergency system's operation. Even though the caller had disconnected, his phone line was still locked into the system. This had prevented her from losing his call. Once she'd dispatched the rescue squad, which had automatically alerted the police, she'd been about to reconnect to the caller's line to secure his name and phone number. Just before she had, the line had buzzed, alerting her that the caller had picked up the phone for his own use. At that time she'd taken the opportunity to obtain Bob's name and number.

Bill Appel asked Hanley if Bob had sounded upset and excited when he'd talked to her?

"He appeared okay, not overly excited," she said.

"The tape indicates he stammered over his phone number," Appel frowned, "talking in short, rapid responses?"

"Correct," Hanley admitted and stepped down.

As the first official on the Bulik scene, Officer Charles Peterson testified that Bob had answered the door at 11:21 a.m. and said, "She's in here." Within the area holding a sunken tub, Peterson had discovered Pam's naked body lying beside it, on her back, her left foot over the right, and the left arm bent, its hand lying on her left hip. The right arm had been extended and lay behind a brown

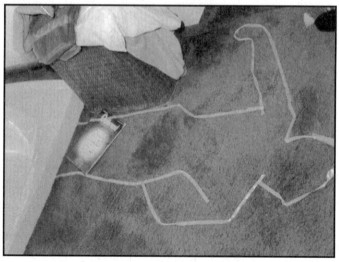

**Outline of Pam's body showing its position when
Officer Chuck Peterson arrived.**

hamper. At that point the rescue squad team had arrived.

Peterson said he'd located Bob in the master bedroom at the foot of the bed on his knees, "sort of like you would be praying."

The defense attorney looked at the officer's report and asked whether there'd been any particular reason that Peterson hadn't mentioned that Bob had been crying and sobbing?

"I wasn't asked the question."

"I appreciate that." Appel shot a quick glance at the prosecutors.

Peterson said he'd then helped Bob move into the living room. "I asked him if there were any family or friends that should be called ... Mr. Bulik told me, 'No.'"

"Did you notice if any windows were open?" Finne asked.

"I noticed one or two living room windows were open and also the one above the kitchen sink."

The prosecutor nodded, now ready to highlight the evidence discovered within the Buliks' garage.

Peterson said that a van had been located in the opened left stall. If the garage door had been closed, he believed that the area between the rear of the van and the door would've been quite small, but probably enough to get around the vehicle.

"Did there come a time when you opened the door of the van?"

"Yes, sir..."

"Did you notice anything about the front passenger seat?"

"Yes, sir. I was feeling the firewall ... and as I was pulling my way out, I put my hand on the seat..."

"What did you notice?"

"The seat on the van's passenger side was wet."

With raised eyebrows, Finne found the jurors' attentive faces.

Bill Appel stated that he wanted to clarify Officer Peterson's testimony about the wet passenger seat. "You didn't see it, didn't smell it. You touched it?"

Peterson concurred.

The day of Pam's death Sergeant Donald Baenen testified that his primary responsibility had been to keep an eye on the defendant. After Sergeant Taylor had questioned Bob, Baenen said he'd soon followed Bob's lead and moved from the living room to the family room.

"On the way to the family room, was the defendant doing anything with his eyes?" Finne asked, his face intent.

"Well, he was rubbing them."

Direct exams were more difficult than cross-examinations. For attorneys, there were limitations on the type of questions that they could ask. Leading questions weren't allowed, only open-ended ones that didn't suggest an answer. It was sometimes frustrating when a witness wouldn't give you what you were looking for. In this case, Finne had wanted Sergeant Baenen to say, that while Bob had been entering the family room, his eyes had looked down the short hallway toward the garage entrance. That's where a double hung window covered nearly half of the door leading into it. At that stage, Sergeant Taylor and Officer Peterson had still been checking for evidence in the garage. This was why the police believed during Bob's questioning at the station, he'd told them Pam was in the van, but hadn't done so earlier in the home.

Since Finne didn't get the desired answer, he tried to recover by asking, "Did you observe tears on his face?"

"Not actual tears, no." Though, Baenen said, Bob's eyes had been red.

Appel's goal was to counter the State's constant insinuation that Bob's grief was a sham. "Sergeant Baenen, isn't it a fact that Mr. Bulik was emotionally upset...crying and sobbing so badly that he visibly appeared to be trembling?"

Baenen confirmed that Bob had been in that condition for nearly forty-five minutes. "I put my arms on him and tried to console him and he was shaking."

On the drive to the police station, Baenen said he'd sat next to Bob in the squad's backseat.

"Didn't he talk to you about his children at that time?" Appel eyed him, holding up his report.

"Yes."

"He was concerned about their safety and welfare ... about not wanting them to come to the house?"

Baenen concurred.

Richard Katers, the lieutenant in charge of the Green Bay Fire and Rescue squad testified, that upon his arrival on April 7, he had done a personal inspection of Pam's body and noticed some dryness to both sides of her face and part of her upper chest.

"Lieutenant," the defense attorney said, reviewing Katers's report, "when you first came into the bathroom and looked at Mrs. Bulik, you indicated that you did not notice any physical marks on the body?"

Appel's eyes brightened when Katers said, "That is correct." Though, he added that his squad hadn't disturbed the body, so they'd only observed Pam's frontal portion.

The attorney also looked pleased when Katers agreed that Pam's body had been in the correct position to perform resuscitation. She'd been on her back, on a hard surface, with her left arm placed close to her body. The rescuer could've knelt to her left to blow air into her mouth.

That morning, the lieutenant said he'd asked Bob for the name and age of the deceased, but received no response. Next, like Peterson, Katers had inquired if Bob wanted him to phone relatives or friends. Again Bob hadn't answered. "Then I asked him if he had any children and he said he had dropped them off downtown around 9:30 at the mall."

"About 9:30?" Finne repeated.

He nodded. "That was the last question I asked."

Appel leveled his eyes on Katers. "Your attempts to communicate with him were unsuccessful because of his emotional condition?"

"In the beginning, yes ... the question about the children, I got from Mr. Bulik," the lieutenant said, refusing to back down.

The witnesses had been filing up, being sworn in, testifying under the scrutiny of Bob's intense eyes and being dismissed. Other than their voices and those of the attorneys, the courtroom had been hushed. Just an occasional cough, a sneeze, or the squeak of the courtroom door intermingled with the dialogue. The jurors and spectators, alike, were utterly engrossed.

Most of the information leading to Bob's arrest had been gathered and investigated by Sergeant Jim Taylor. He believed the State had prepared well for trial and had all their ducks in a row to get a conviction. It was now up to the prosecutors to get the last kick at their cat.

Taylor had been assigned full-time to the trial and like other witnesses, would be sequestered until he'd finished testifying. He'd stationed himself on a chair right outside the courtroom in case Finne or Lasee needed him to check on something that the defense might raise. It was now time for the detective to make his first appearance on the stand.

Finne had Taylor step through the morning of April 7, eventually reaching the point at which he'd talked to Bob. "He said about 8:30 he drew her bath water and she appeared groggy."

Next Taylor identified some photographs that had been taken inside the garage. One showed the backrest of the van's front passenger chair, stained with what was later determined to be mucus. Another was of the garage floor, on which were two parallel drag marks leading from the van to the house and running through some lawn clippings and a grease spot. Even though the press had given the public the impression that drag marks had been found in the Buliks' lawn, Taylor clarified, that was not so.

The next photos, Royce Finne felt, were some of the most damning evidence in the case. He had Taylor identify Pam's left-footed Saucony running shoe. This white shoe had grease on its top and heel, and was piled among Pam's other shoes inside her master bedroom closet. A subsequent photo showed the right-footed mate. It was located in the hallway that led from the kitchen to the foyer and was smudged only with dirt.

**Locations of Pam's
running shoes**

The last two photos showed Pam's bare feet. There was a grease-type material on the top of her right big toe and the toe next to it. The same substance was on the bottom of her right foot, by the side and toward the heel. Pam's left foot had no evidence of grease.

At this point, Judge Greenwood announced a brief recess and asked the attorneys to join him in chambers to discuss the State's motion for a view.

≈

At 2:52, Sergeant Taylor settled back into the witness stand pleased that the State's motion had been granted. Tonight's road trip was a go.

Royce Finne had questioned the detective for about an hour. It was now Bill Appel's turn.

Whenever Taylor was cross-examined by the defense, he used an old trick. Unlike TV programs, in which the defense attorney asked a question and the witness immediately answered, Taylor first looked at the prosecutor to allow him a fraction of a second to object. By answering too quickly, the detective knew he could wreck the entire case. At one trial the defense attorney had asked Taylor if he'd set up a signal with the district attorney. The detective had looked at the DA before answering. When he didn't object, Taylor had turned back to the defense attorney and politely said, no.

Bill Appel now smiled at his former teammate and began, "When you tried to ask Mr. Bulik what happened, he said that his wife was groggy... Is that a direct quote?"

It was.

Very slowly and methodically, Appel then stepped through every photo that Finne had presented and added some of his own. Taylor verified that many of the pictures had no bearing on the case. These included the various locations of leaves within the van and the house, the dirt-covered men's running shoes, and the man's jacket discovered on the dining room floor.

Within a photo from inside the van, Taylor next identified a used tissue lying on the floor by the front passenger seat. Then, in the photos of the garage floor, Taylor confirmed that only the right-hand drag mark went through the grease spot, but both were somewhat wavy. One drag mark even had a sort of loop to it. Taylor also agreed that there was evidence of grease on the six, rather steep, garage steps, leading into the house.

The detective next addressed a photo showing the underwear wrapped inside the green sweat suit pants. Both were wet and found on top of the washing machine. He said that the state crime lab had confirmed that the panties were streaked with outside dirt, rather than human waste.

Appel selected the green running suit from the evidence table. If Pam had been wearing this, he said, and had been dragged, because of the floor friction, "the underclothing could easily pick up that floor soil, could it not?"

Before answering, Taylor looked at Finne.

"Objection. That calls for speculation on the part of the witness."

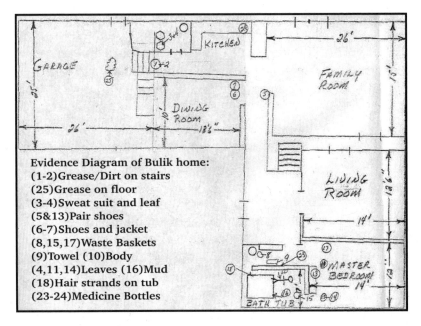

Evidence Diagram of Bulik home:
(1-2) Grease/Dirt on stairs
(25) Grease on floor
(3-4) Sweat suit and leaf
(5&13) Pair shoes
(6-7) Shoes and jacket
(8,15,17) Waste Baskets
(9) Towel (10) Body
(4,11,14) Leaves (16) Mud
(18) Hair strands on tub
(23-24) Medicine Bottles

"Sustained," Greenwood said.

Nevertheless, Appel had made his point. He next reviewed photos of the children's louvered bedroom doors. Even if they were closed, Taylor agreed that air or noise could still be exchanged through the slat openings.

While the detective had looked for evidence around the bathtub and master bedroom areas, Appel asked, "Did you find any drag marks?"

"Nothing that could stand out."

The attorney nodded. He then had Taylor identify two photos from the master bath. First were the contents of the wastebasket, including an empty prescription bottle with Bob's name on it. The second showed a towel rack on the north wall. Now making sure he had the jurors' full attention, Appel had Taylor concur that if either Bulik child had used the master bathroom sink, and afterward reached for the towel, the bathtub would've been in their line of sight.

Towel used to wipe hands is on the wall leading into the tub area.

At close to five o'clock, Taylor seemed to be getting more frustrated by the minute as Appel's never-ending questions about specific photos and evidence continued. The prosecutors looked peeved as well. Today they'd expected to complete Deputy Coroner Genie William's testimony before ending with a portion of Captain Robert Langan's. Finne had wanted the detective to read Bob's statement to the jury, just prior to tonight's road trip, so the accused man's own words would have been fresh in the jurors' minds.

Appel was smart. After losing the motion in chambers, it appeared he was deliberately dragging out Taylor's testimony to sabotage his adversary's plan.

Greenwood looked at his watch and informed the attorneys, they'd continue with Sergeant Taylor's testimony in the morning. The judge then addressed the jurors. "We're going to have, what in Wisconsin law is called 'a view.' Get your coats. The bailiffs will escort you to the bus located between the safety building and the courthouse. I'll join you there with the clerk. The attorneys and Mr. Bulik will rendezvous with us at the Preble High School parking lot."

Greenwood looked sternly at the lawyers. "Don't dilly-dally. I want you there. I'm not planning to wait."

"We'll be there," Finne promised.

$\approx$

Civil cases often entailed field trips, but Clerk of Courts Mabel Tuttle couldn't recall a criminal case requesting one in over five years. Bob led the caravan, with Bill Appel in the passenger seat of the Buliks' blue Monza. The bus transporting the judge, court reporter, and jury followed. Last came the car carrying the two prosecutors.

In Bob's statement to the police, he'd noted that after missing his flight on Friday, April 6, because of his marital problems, he'd decided to drive back home and surprise his wife. Upon his 10:30 p.m. arrival in Green Bay, Bob said he'd believed that Pam might see his approaching car and thus wreck his surprise, so instead of parking his car in their driveway, or in the cul-de-sac in front of the house, he'd parked at Preble High School.

At tonight's view, the jurors were taken to that spot, where they paused several minutes, and then were driven the half-mile that Bob would've walked to the Bulik home on the evening of April 6. This was to give the Washington County jurors a look at reference points under conditions similar to those on that night. Under legal rules, the view of the scene could not be offered as evidence in the trial, but could be allowed if the judge felt it would help the jury understand other evidence presented. Arguing for the road trip, Finne had told Greenwood that because the Buliks' house was located in a ravine below a tree-covered hill rising to their cul-de-sac, it was unlikely Pam could've seen Bob's car pull up near the home. "Mr. Bulik meant to hide his car from his neighbors."

Even though the jury never left the bus, the prosecutors hoped that this thirty-minute tour would help convince them that this part of Bob Bulik's defense made no sense at all.

≈

On day two of the trial the anxious mass of spectators nattered outside the closed courtroom doors. It was like waiting for the gates to open at Packer stadium on game day. When the bailiff finally appeared, the crowd pushed, pulled, and squeezed their way in, excitedly shouting when they'd secured a seat. It would be a standing-room-only session.

Sergeant Taylor was recalled so that the defense attorney could complete his cross-examination. Not surprisingly, in less than fifteen minutes, Appel posed his last question. He had the detective confirm that on the morning of Pam's death, even though seven policemen had been in the Bulik home, Bob had never objected to "any of the looking around or poking around that was going on."

On redirect Finne innocently asked one last question. "Sergeant Taylor, were there any telephones in the home?"

Taylor nodded decisively and said there were three on the main level. The first was inside the garage next to the stairway leading into the house proper, the second was on the kitchen desk, and the third was on the nightstand in the Buliks' bedroom.

As the detective stepped down from the stand, Bill Appel caught Taylor's eyes and said, "I wasn't too hard on you, Jim, was I?"

"No, Bill." Taylor grinned amiably. "It's never hard when you tell the truth."

≈

The intended witnesses from yesterday's lineup would now take the stand, first would be Deputy Coroner Genie Williams. Seated in the witness chair, she leaned forward, her hands clasped between her knees. Genie testified that she'd arrived at the Bulik scene around 11:25 a.m. on April 7 and checked for rigor mortis to establish Pam's time of death. "Basically, you check the jaw, the flexibility of the arms, elbows, shoulders, fingers, hips, knees, and toes to see if they are rigid or if they are relaxed."

"That would require, I take it, grabbing hold of those various parts of the body to move them around?" Finne asked.

As Genie responded in the affirmative, the prosecutor's eyes swept the jury.

The deputy coroner confirmed that she'd checked the temperature of the bathtub water at about noon. It had been 83 degrees Fahrenheit and was eight inches deep. After the wet passenger seat's discovery, she'd blotted it with filter paper. In addition, from the crotch area of both the green sweat suit and underwear, she'd

cut samples. This evidence had been submitted to St. Vincent Hospital's lab for testing. Only the filter paper collected from the wet van seat had tested positive for urine.

When Genie had checked the wet area on the van's seat, like Officer Peterson, she confirmed that she'd detected no urine odor.

"The only way this wetness could be detected was by feeling it?" Appel's confident voice asked.

"No," Genie shook her head with conviction, "you could see an outline of wetness. The area was saturated enough so you could see it in the fabric."

Captain Langan next walked up to the witness stand, his wavy silver hair neatly combed. He always hoped the State attorneys would ask the right questions of him. Even though there might be something valuable the jury should know, Langan couldn't simply volunteer it.

In response to Finne's direct question, Langan said that once Bob had been Mirandized on April 7, he and Lieutenant Hintz had first talked with Bob and then taken his written statement. Bob had not complained of any sort of illness and hadn't appeared to be under the influence of alcohol or drugs. The detectives also had no difficulty understanding his responses to their questions.

Finne handed Captain Langan Bob's statement and asked the detective to read it to the jury.

A bated silence fell over the courtroom. It's what everyone had been waiting for, the defendant's own words:

I Robert Bulik give the following voluntary statement to Lieutenant Hinz.

Pam and I have been married for going on 14 years. We have two children: Alex, age 11, and Abby, age 9. For the past five years we have lived at 251 Traders Court. Both of us are employed. Pam taught special-ed in the Freedom School system. I teach at Edison Jr. High and am a major in the Marine Reserve.

We have been seeing a marriage counselor, Jean Weidner, since last October, and one of the reasons was because of an affair I had with

Linda VandenLangenberg, who is a teacher at Sullivan School. Yesterday morning, I left school about 11:30 a.m. and drove to Glenview, Illinois, where I was supposed to fly out with the Naval Air, who was to take me to Denver. I did check into the BOQ about 4:30 or 5:00 p.m. I had car trouble at I-94 and Waukegan Road on the way down with some loose wiring problems, and this caused me to arrive late, and I missed my plane to Denver. The car I had problems with was my 1976 Chevy Monza.

At first I intended to take a commercial flight from O'Hare, but because we have had marital problems, I decided to drive back to Green Bay and surprise my wife.

I arrived back in Green Bay about 10:30 p.m. and parked the car at Preble High School. The reason was, I wanted to surprise Pam and if I drove down our driveway she would be able to see me. When I walked in the house Pam was in the kitchen, my daughter was asleep, and my son was playing with the computer. Pam was surprised to see me initially. Then she became suspicious of where I might have been. I think she was wearing her green jumpsuit. We argued a little bit. Our counselors tell us we don't argue well, we shut up and turn each other off.

I went to bed within an hour of when I came home. Pam came to bed about the same time. The kids were already in bed upstairs. We normally sleep in the nude.

Sometime during the night, I woke up and noticed Pam was not in bed, and I could hear an engine running. I looked outside and there wasn't any car in the driveway. Then I grabbed my robe and went to the garage, which is attached off the kitchen. I turned the garage light on and saw Pam in the van we own, with the engine running. I don't recall how the windows were. She was sitting in the passenger's side, which would be closest to me. After opening the door where Pam was sitting, I reached across to turn off the ignition.

Pam's head was resting against the doorjamb and she appeared to be passed out or asleep. I talked to her, but she didn't respond. I guess I must have put my arms under her and pulled her across the floor into the house. I might have carried her up the step, then pulled her into the bedroom. For some reason, I don't remember this particular segment very well. When I got her in our bed I undressed Pam, then went to bed myself. I can't remember what she was wearing or what I did with her clothes after I undressed her. She might have had running shoes on.

The only medication Pam has been taking is a sleeping pill prescribed by Dr. O'Neill. I gave Pam one of my sleeping pills before we went to bed. This was when we were brushing our teeth. My pills are Halcion from Dr. Reinhardt. It was the last one I had.

Today Pam was going to run the Joggers Joynt half marathon. I believe she was pre-registered. Last Wednesday we did a hard ten-mile run so I knew her legs were sore. This morning I woke, and Pam was still sleeping. She was breathing loudly. I filled our floor level tub with bathtub-temperature water. Then I went back to our bedroom, which is connected, and dragged Pam into the tub area. I said something to the effect "I'm going to throw you in," or whatever, but she never responded. I can't explain why I did this, but once in the tub area I set her against the brown hamper.

I felt Pam was ignoring me. When I left the tub area, Pam had her back resting against the hamper. So was her head. I left the area and checked on the kids, who said they had headaches. I remembered the van had been running so I opened some windows and gave Alex some aspirin.

I made breakfast and folded some clothes. Abby ate in bed because she didn't feel good. I didn't do any washing. I took the van over to Preble to get the Monza. The Monza has a history of not starting. That's why I took the van. First I took the Monza home then walked back to get the van.

After I had both vehicles back I picked up a little bit, then went to check on Pam. I found her face down in the tub with her head toward the windows and her legs out behind her like the little diagram I drew. Until I reached over to touch her I thought she was giving me a hard time. But when I grabbed her arm I felt it wasn't natural and she was dead. I pulled her out and laid her on her back, then gave her mouth-to-mouth till I could see it wasn't doing any good. I never yelled to the kids. I knew she was dead, and I didn't want the kids to see her so I called our counselor, Jean Weidner. But I couldn't get her the first time. I went back and stared at Pam for a while before I contacted Jean Weidner again. I told her Pam was dead and asked her, what should I do with the kids before I call an ambulance. She advised me to get the kids out of there first. They were already dressed so I took them to the mall and said I'd pick them up at 3:30 p.m. As fast as I could, I returned home and called 911, telling them something about a drowning victim. When the rescue squad was on its way, I broke down and was crying when they arrived...

    R. J. Bulik

Captain Langan handed the statement back to Finne and then identified the small stick-figure diagram Bob had drawn. It showed how he'd discovered Pam—face down in the bathtub, her right arm at her side and her left arm up.

During questioning, Langan said Bob had first stated that he'd carried Pam into the house. But when he'd been asked about the drag marks on the garage floor, Bob had changed his mind and said, "Maybe I dragged her." When Bob had been asked how he'd gotten Pam into the bathtub area, he'd again said he'd carried her. Lieutenant Hinz had then asked Bob how he could've carried her through the narrow passageway. Bob had considered this before saying that maybe he'd dragged her by putting his arms under her armpits. "Lieutenant Hinz then asked...wouldn't that hurt? Did Pamela complain or make any comment? And Mr. Bulik said no, not that he could remember at the time."

Toward the end of the interview, Langan said they'd asked Bob if he wanted to tell them what had really happened. "He thought about it a minute and then said, 'Yes,' and Lieutenant Hinz told him, I think that when you carried her into the bathroom you set her down in the tub water."

Finne leaned back, crossing his arms. "What was his response to that accusation?"

"Mr. Bulik thought about it for a few minutes, and turned to Lieutenant Hinz and said simply, 'Sorry.'"

"Was he visibly upset at the accusation?"

"No, sir."

"Captain Langan," the defense attorney's brow creased as he approached him, "you and Lieutenant Hinz told him you didn't believe him, didn't you?" He showed Langan the report.

The captain checked it before admitting, "That's what it says." He also concurred that he'd asked Bob to take off his shirt to look for some sign of a struggle or a fight.

"And you didn't see anything, did you?" Appel's lips tightened.

"Examining his upper torso, we didn't see any injuries, no, sir."

Both attorneys then took turns questioning Langan about the Buliks' finance and insurance information provided to detectives during Bob's April 7 interview, before the prosecutor asked Langan, "Did Mr. Bulik say what he thought was going to happen in his marriage?"

"He said that he thought he was going to make his marriage good and that he was going to go back with his wife."

"Did he say anything about ending the affair?" Finne asked, arching his eyebrows.

"Mr. Bulik said he believed in ending an affair the way it started, winding it down slowly."

The spectators murmured.

Finne switched gears and next asked Langan to tell the jury what the Green Bay Police Department's policy was for patrolling schools like Preble High.

Langan said that schools were checked each evening to protect against vandalism and break-ins. If patrol officers saw an automobile parked in a school lot, they were instructed to cautiously approach it, check for occupants, and search the surrounding area. They might run the license plate number to see if it was a stolen vehicle.

"Would running the license plate number give out the registered owner of that vehicle...the owner's address?"

"Yes, sir, it would."

Lastly, the prosecutor asked the detective to explain the test Lieutenant Hinz had completed on the Buliks' van while it had been in police custody.

In repeated attempts to start it, Langan said that Hinz had needed to pump the gas pedal while turning the key. Langan had later made his own attempt to start the van while seated in the passenger seat. Since he'd been unable to reach the accelerator with his foot, he'd been unsuccessful.

Appel selected a photo showing the detective sitting in that seat. "Now, you're not trying to suggest to this jury...that Mrs. Bulik could not have started the van from the passenger's portion of the vehicle, are you?"

"I don't believe she could have..."

Test Captain Robert Langan performed on Bulik van.

"Are you trying to suggest...that someone else had to have started the van?"

"I think the picture intends to show that if Mrs. Bulik was seated in the passenger seat, she could not have started the van. I'll concede that. Yes, sir."

"But I wonder what relevancy that has?" Appel looked perplexed. "There's no obstruction between the passenger's portion of the front of the cab and the accelerator and ignition, is there?"

Langan said there was. In the photo, he pointed out the engine housing, which was connected to the dash and extended back to where the seats started. Though, he agreed, albeit reluctantly, that if Pam had stepped into the open area between the passenger and driver seats, just in front of the housing, she could have gotten close enough to the accelerator to touch it while turning the ignition key.

"That van's seat also swivels," Appel stated, scrutinizing the photo, "left toward the driver's compartment?"

There was a beat of silence. Frowning, Langan said, "Yes, sir," his voice falling flat.

9

Pathology/Physiology/
Chronology

The means by which Pam had sustained her injuries were at the core of the prosecution's efforts to prove that Bob Bulik had murdered his wife. Since scientific experts, employed by the State, often carried great weight with juries, Finne and Lasee hoped that would be the case today as they called their next two witnesses.

First was Dr. Darrel Skarphol who had performed hundreds of autopsies, including Pam's. He was a soft-spoken man with a neatly trimmed beard and since 1963, had been a pathologist at St. Vincent Hospital. Second was Genie Williams's former professor, Dr. Helen Young. Her curly blond hair, sprinkled with silver, surrounded a matronly face. Over the last ten years she'd worked as a medical examiner for Milwaukee County, Lake County, and Cook County. As an expert witness, she'd testified hundreds of times. In preparation for today she'd reviewed Dr. Skarphol's materials.

The pathologists' testimony would focus on three areas. First was the carbon monoxide's effect on Pam. Second were her injuries. Third was how the carbon monoxide affected Bob.

In the autopsy report, Skarphol had noted Pam's height as five feet seven inches tall and weight as 146 pounds. Her toxicology screen included the prescription drug found in Bob's empty container, recovered from the bathroom wastebasket. When Skarphol stated that the lab's finding was of a therapeutic level or less, many in the courtroom seemed startled.

Bob's empty prescription container exposed on top of trash in bathroom wastebasket.

The doctor also confirmed that no other drugs were found in the hemoglobin extracted from Pam's heart other than the 48 percent level of carbon monoxide. The average fatal level depended on the condition of the person. For someone with severe vascular disease, bad blood vessels, and a bad heart, somewhere around 30 could be fatal. Someone with a good cardiovascular system could tolerate levels up to 70, though these were averages. "Each individual is different," Dr. Young said. "I have seen people with a ninety-percent carbon monoxide level at the time of death."

Both doctors agreed that urinary incontinence was uncommon in carbon monoxide poisoning. When it did occur, it was usually associated with a comatose state, unconsciousness, or convulsions.

Finne asked Dr. Skarphol, if an individual were removed from the toxic environment, "how much carbon monoxide would be expelled in, say, three to five hours prior to the point of death at a level of forty-eight?"

"Approximately half the amount of carbon monoxide that you absorb is breathed off in four to five hours."

"To make sure I have my math correct here," Finne paused, waiting until he had each juror's full attention, "Pamela Bulik was forty-eight percent at death. Does your answer mean that four or five hours earlier she would have been at ninety-six percent?"

"That's correct. But I'm not aware of anybody ever reaching ninety-six percent."

Finne crossed his arms and nodded.

Skarphol estimated Pam's time of death to be somewhere between 5:00 a.m. and 9:30 a.m. He said she'd died from lack of oxygen due to both carbon monoxide poisoning and drowning, but drowning had been the terminal event. When Pam went into the water, she'd been alive.

"Doctor, if medical intervention had been secured at the time Pamela was removed from the van, would she have lived?"

"Well, I would need more information as to what her carbon monoxide level was and whether she had already suffered irreversible brain damage." Although Skarphol hadn't seen any, given time, it still might have occurred. If there had been no irreversible changes in Pam's brain, he concurred that medical therapy should've given her a full recovery. "At a carbon-monoxide level of forty-eight, most people recover."

Skarphol, however, also agreed with the defense attorney, that even though medical treatment was the preferred method, a person could recover by simply breathing nontoxic air.

"A person recovering...might appear groggy?" Appel asked, emphasizing the last word for the jury's benefit.

"Certainly, especially if they were semi-comatose."

Appel seemed pleased.

Pam's injuries were the next focus. Skarphol explained that on the left side of Pam's chin were several areas of slight reddish discoloration. Rather than being elevated, like bruises, these were depressed. He believed those marks had been made postmortem. They were straight and quite long. Since there was no fingernail mark, he didn't believe a finger caused them. "I think they were produced by contact with some relatively flat object."

Neither attorney chose to delve further.

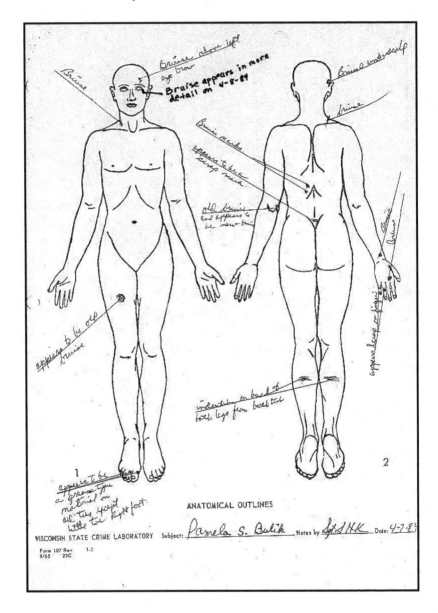

ANATOMICAL OUTLINES

WISCONSIN STATE CRIME LABORATORY Subject: *Pamela S. Bulik* Notes by *Sgt S H K* Date: 4-7-8

Form 107 Rev 1-2
9/65 25C

Above the buttocks, Skarphol said there were abrasions that ran parallel to Pam's spine. The defense attorney handed him a photo of the wooden garage steps and asked: If Pam had been pulled up those stairs, could that have caused the scrape mark?

Finne's objection, saying that the question had to be answered to a reasonable degree of medical certainty, came too late—Appel had already implanted that picture in the jurors' minds.

Skarphol noted that Pam's left eye showed bruising that extended up the forehead. Both pathologists agreed, this injury had been caused by blunt trauma—either her head had struck something or had been struck by something. The object did not have a sharp edge. It would've been something either flat or somewhat rounded, and could have included the edge of someone's hand.

Appel asked Skarphol if the bruise to Pam's left eye had more likely been caused by something flat hitting the head, as opposed to a fist?

"It had an area of straight linearity to it, going up the forehead..."

"The smooth surface of a bathtub?"

As Skarphol said, "Right. Possible," Appel cracked a smile.

Blunt trauma had also caused the two bruises on the top of Pam's head and the three located in the right occipital region, just above the back hairline. All of the bruises, Skarphol confirmed, had occurred prior to death and all were between one and a half and six hours old. The presence of inflammatory infiltrates showed that healing had started. The injuries to the back of the skull had very prominent infiltrates, but there were not enough present in the left eye bruise to time that wound. That didn't mean the bruises hadn't occurred at the same time. One might not show a reaction until a later stage, say at five hours, while another bruise might start earlier, say, after two hours.

Dr. Young believed that the right occipital bruise had occurred at least four hours prior to death. It was a good, healthy bruise, and the absence of a fracture didn't mean that force hadn't been used. "Because it is under the major curve of the skull, it is not an easy area to traumatize."

"Have you seen similar...occipital injuries in your career?" Finne asked.

"Yes, I have, sir. In my experience a vast majority of cases have been a blow specifically to this area with a blunt instrument."

Finne nodded. "Have you seen that type of occipital damage when someone had fallen down?"

"No. It would be rare...if you fall, you hit the prominent areas of the skull. It's described as the zone where your hatband would sit."

During the autopsy, Dr. Skarphol said he'd also discovered a tiny hemorrhage in the right cerebral peduncle, one of the structures that attached the brain to the spinal cord. A rotational twist of the head most frequently caused this area to be injured. The two pathologists differed, however, in which trauma had produced the rotational force. Skarphol believed it had occurred from the right occipital injury while Young placed her bet on the forehead blow.

The defense attorney now had to counteract the State's premise that Pam's bruises were severe. To do this, he asked Dr. Skarphol to tell the jury what a contra-coup injury was.

The brain, Skarphol said, was supported by fluid separating it from the skull. If somebody was hit, especially in the middle of the back of the head, their brain could accelerate forward and slam against the bony tissue in the frontal area, causing a hemorrhage. This was called the contra-coup injury. The brain hemorrhage at the underlying point of first impact was called the coup injury.

"Did...Mrs. Bulik have a contra-coup or coup injury?" Appel asked, lifting his brow.

"She did not."

"And with a more severe blow, you would expect to find a coup/ contra-coup injury to the brain, would you not...?"

"I think you have it the opposite way," Skarphol said. "When I see a coup and contra-coup injury, then I think of severe trauma to the head, rather than severe trauma always producing coup and contra-coup injuries." Dr. Young added that the coup and contra-coup injuries were frequently seen with a head in motion type of trauma, for example, an automobile accident. She felt a contra-coup injury was not required to have a healthy bruise to the scalp.

Dr. Skarphol, though, did concur with the defense attorney that only two of the bruises to the head were visible during the external examination: the forehead bruise and one of the right occipital bruises. The latter was very faint and did not even break the skin. The remaining head injuries were discovered only after the skin was retracted during autopsy.

Royce Finne next handed Dr. Skarphol a Styrofoam neck and head model and asked him to use a black marker to circle each of the trauma areas he'd just discussed. The prosecutor then placed it on the evidence table as a constant reminder to the jury.

Both pathologists provided an important opinion to support the prosecution's theory. Even though there had been no contra-coup injury, they said that the head traumas to either the right occipital or to the left forehead had been sufficient to produce unconsciousness.

"Dr. Skarphol," Appel's forehead creased, "can you tell this jury that these bruises on Mrs. Bulik's head caused her to be unconscious?"

"No." He shook his head. "I can't say that without seeing her at the time they were inflicted."

The defense attorney firmly nodded.

Skarphol agreed with Appel that there'd been no bruises, abrasions, or lacerations to Pam's lips and the teeth appeared intact. There had also been no internal injuries, often evident after a fight, and nothing under Pam's fingernails. But in less than a fourth of Skarphol's cases had he found anything significant under the nails. And in this situation, Pam's hands had been in the bathwater for some unknown period of time, possibly providing a cleansing effect.

Bruises had also been discovered on Pam's right index finger, right wrist, and the backside of her left elbow. In Dr. Young's work, these kind of injuries often occurred if a victim assumed a defensive posture. Usually one or both hands were placed in front of the body, in an attempt to ward off blows, and to protect the abdomen, chest, face, and head. In her experience, the backsides of the arms and hands were most frequently traumatized. She pointed to the photos of Pam's bruises provided by Finne. "In this kind of fashion."

The defense attorney's next goal was to show that Dr. Young's belief, that Pam had protected herself during an assault, was only one theory. In separate questions he asked both doctors to assume that Pam had been in a coma while inside the van. If Bob had grabbed and lifted his 146-pound wife, could those specific hand and arm bruises have occurred?

Both doctors confirmed that the force exerted by grabbing could cause the bruises on the left elbow and on the right hand, but not the index finger. It showed very prominent swelling implying greater force than grabbing. If Pam had been in a coma-like condition in the van, they agreed that she would have lost her muscle and skeletal control. So, during her rescue, her arms and head would have moved about freely as gravity dictated. Based on this assumption, the bruise to the index finger and the ones to the back and top of her head could have occurred from banging on the steps, the doorway, the garage floor, the van door or, both pathologists had eyed Appel, if Pam had instead been hit by something.

The prosecutor lastly tackled questions about the carbon monoxide's affect on Bob. Appel's cross-examination was minimal. His own expert pathologist was scheduled later on the docket to address this key part of Bob's defense.

Finne asked Dr. Skarphol, if a person entered a carbon monoxide-laden atmosphere, were there certain things a physician would need to know to determine how that individual would be affected?

"We'd need to know what the concentration was and the duration of the exposure." Skarphol added that the latter was the most important factor. After a long period of time, the body's carbon-monoxide buildup would be much higher than the air concentration. In Bob's case, neither the concentration level nor the duration was known.

"Dr. Young, do cigarettes produce carbon monoxide?" Finne asked.

"Yes, sir."

"Do you smoke?"

"Yes, sir."

"What level of carbon monoxide would a smoker typically maintain in their system?"

"With cigarette smokers, it's usually somewhere between 5 and 6 percent. With cigar and pipe smokers, it may go up to 10 percent. Maybe even up to 15 percent."

"Those people ordinarily get along on a daily basis?"

Young smiled at Finne. "They appear to."

The prosecutor ended with a vital question posed to each doctor separately: "Are you aware in your experience or studies, of anything to indicate to you, that loss of memory from carbon-monoxide poisoning occurs without unconsciousness having occurred?"

Both pathologists said that they were not aware of any reports on the incidence of amnesia without unconsciousness.

~

Onlookers were antsy. Before Pam's orthopedic surgeon was finally sworn in, the defense had lost a motion to keep him from doing so. Appel had argued that Dr. Rolff Lulloff's testimony would be subjective and thus waste the jury's time. The prosecution team was pleased with the judge's ruling, since this witness's testimony was being elicited to hopefully show that Bob's reason for drawing Pam's bathwater was a ruse.

In addition to being a physician, Lulloff said he'd been a runner for fifteen years and had competed in both the Boston and

New York Marathon. He'd treated Pam for leg and back problems from July 1980 until July 1983 and had prescribed their home whirlpool for her therapy. During the last eight months of Pam's life, no subsequent appointments had been scheduled.

Finne asked Lulloff, as a physician and an experienced marathon runner, to explain how soaking in warm or hot water, just prior to running, would affect a person's body.

"When someone warms up, what they effectively do is increase the temperature of the muscles." This could be done through exercise, Lulloff said, or passively by, for instance, soaking in warm water. But, overheating a muscle would burn up stored fuel and there was a limited amount available for a race.

Appel asked whether "soaking in lukewarm water, perhaps body temperature water, for a short period of time, might not be bad?"

"Depends on the temperature of the water and proximity to the time that you're going to exercise." This was not a black-and-white situation, Dr. Lulloff said. He believed the ideal temperature for optimum muscle performance to be in the range of 98 to 100 degrees Fahrenheit. "If you get above a hundred degrees, the metabolism of the muscle increases to the point that you're burning fuel, but it's not serving any purpose. You're wasting fuel. At less than ninety-eight degrees the muscle is not efficient—it doesn't utilize fuel well enough to be effective."

It was quite common, Lulloff said, for a runner to soak in warm or hot water after a race. But prior to, say, running a half marathon, he personally would not. Nor would he advise anyone else to. Even though he'd never specifically talked to either Bulik about soaking or not soaking prior to running, he thought nearly every serious runner would know better.

◇◇◇◇◇◇◇◇◇◇◇◇◇◇◇◇◇◇◇◇

Before leaving for tonight's Fun Run, Beezie and I'd received calls from the district attorney's office. The testimony was taking longer than expected. Neither of us would be needed in court tomorrow.

Following the run, while we gathered in the hosts' living room with food and drinks, Beezie provided a trial update from Marcy's notes. Since Dr. Lulloff was a familiar face at local runs, all were interested in his testimony. We wondered what the odds were that Bob had drawn the optimal 98 to 100 degrees of bathwater for Pam. Jim and I bathed Collin in our antique claw foot tub, which had two spigots. Because I'd worried he might turn the hot water knob and burn himself, I'd checked out a temperature that was safe for a baby. We now kept our water heater set at 120 degrees Fahrenheit.

There were three guys who'd taught at Edison Junior High School with Bob, including Rod Leadley. Yesterday, a *Press-Gazette* reporter had interviewed a number of the school's eighty-person faculty. Tonight's article mentioned how some of the 1,400 students at Edison had looked up Bob's picture in the school's 1983 yearbook. They knew he was on trial for murdering his wife, but couldn't remember who he was.

Rod agreed that Bob was pretty remote at school, virtually never making small talk with his fellow teachers. One of them said, "I got two, maybe three hellos from him in the last five years." Another said, "He wasn't a loner in a weird sense, but he just went about his business and left everybody alone." Another Edison teacher was quoted as saying, "The only thing outside of teaching I ever heard Bob Bulik mention was running. But when he was approached to possibly help out with the track program he had no interest in it. If he had been involved in any extra-curricular activity at all, this would have had more impact."

As a special education teacher, Bob saw the same few students daily and rarely had contact outside that small circle. Friends thought his teaching job fit his introverted demeanor. It was interesting that Pam had performed a similar job, although she'd also helped coach the Freedom High School volleyball team. After the August assault, I knew she'd been disappointed to give up that responsibility and personal enjoyment.

Within the greater Green Bay community, the ongoing gossip was about Bob's trial. Because the principals were professional people, everyone was engrossed. Many had known the Buliks or Linda through some school connection. The trial embodied the shadowy side of respectability, igniting an undeniable fascination. It was Green Bay's own soap opera, temporarily ousting *Knots Landing*.

Everybody wanted to see whether Bob Bulik was guilty or not.

∞∞∞∞∞∞∞∞∞∞∞∞∞∞

On day three of the trial, the events surrounding Bob's activities on Friday April 6, would be the focus for the next six witnesses. These included Sergeant James Taylor, two Marine Corps reservists, and three Glenview Naval Airbase personnel. Both prosecutors would take turns handling the direct examination. Their goal was to show that Bob's original plan, to attend his reserve weekend in Denver, was to have been a skillfully architected alibi, orchestrated to divert attention from Bob's possible involvement in Pam's death. Appel in turn would extract testimony from the same witnesses to validate Bob's statement claims.

Sergeant Taylor was recalled to first delve into the investigative work he and Assistant DA Lasee had completed in Illinois on June 20. The detective then confirmed he'd received some new information following that trip. The Illinois State Police had been able to furnish a taped transmission verifying that a trooper had assisted Bob near Waukegan Road on April 6 at 3:20 p.m. by driving him to the Richard Smith Standard Station.

The defense attorney eyed Taylor. "When you [first] learned from the Illinois Highway Patrol that there was no such record of any officer assisting Mr. Bulik, then you and other police officers suspected that his story was not true, isn't that correct?"

"I thought it might not be true," Taylor admitted, "but I also know how police departments operate. It could have been misplaced."

While in Illinois, Taylor said he and Lasee had stopped at that same Standard station. The detective confirmed for Finne that they still had no record that any work had been performed on the Buliks' Monza.

Reservist Daniel O'Connell, an important witness for the prosecution, testified that he lived in Manitowoc, Wisconsin, a community thirty miles south of Green Bay. Shortly after hearing of Bob's arrest, he'd contacted the Green Bay Police Department to share some pertinent information. Earlier in the year, he'd met Bob at a social gathering and had discovered that he drilled out of Denver. On the evening of Wednesday, April 4, O'Connell said he'd called Bob at his home to ask how to go about finding a military hop to the West coast.

"Did you ask the defendant about the time the flight left Glenview for Denver on Friday afternoon, April sixth?" Finne asked, crossing his arms.

"Yes, I did. Approximately 2:30."

"2:30 p.m.?" The prosecutor repeated, for the jury's benefit.

O'Connell concurred. "I had asked Major Bulik if he would be interested in car-pooling to Glenview that afternoon." Bob had told him that he'd work a half day at school and leave Green Bay right around eleven o'clock. "He normally got down to Glenview just before the aircraft departed." On that call, O'Connell said that Bob had also provided him driving directions to the base.

Naval investigative agent Richard Edmonds said he'd driven from Glenview that morning in three and a half hours, at a speed of 70 to 75 miles per hour. The prosecutor handed him a scrap of paper that had been discovered inside a brown paper bag recovered from the Buliks' bedroom wastebasket. Edmonds said the scrap included southbound driving directions from Green Bay to Glenview Naval Air Station. Today he'd taken a faster route than the one specified, and bypassed the slower speed limits and stoplights in the town of Glenview.

On April 4, Bob had also provided reservist O'Connell a Glenview Naval Air Station telephone number to call. It provided a taped recording of proposed military flight times and was available three days prior to the flight, in this case, from four o'clock Tuesday April 3 until Saturday, April 7. The information recorded for Friday, April 6 listed the 2:30 p.m. flight.

James Gregory, the Glenview traffic controller said, "It was the only one available to Denver that day." But, depending on the mission of the command, he agreed with the defense attorney that there could have been a second flight.

"Is there such a thing as a regularly scheduled flight time?" the prosecutor asked.

"No, sir, there isn't."

Lasee nodded.

It was not a requirement at Glenview, Gregory said, but flight personnel asked reservists to get there about two hours prior to flight departure time since pilots could take off an hour ahead if they chose. If Bob had missed his flight, the Base Operations could have tried to find him another way out. O'Hare Airport had an air national guard unit and an air reserve unit. They usually had a few flights going out to the West Coast daily. Like Glenview's flights, they would've been provided to Bob at no charge.

On April 6, reservist O'Connell confirmed that the flight had actually left the base at 2:28, two minutes before the 2:30 time Bob had provided.

Bill Appel conferred with his client briefly before addressing O'Connell. "I understand that when you arrived in Denver, there was a phone call for Mr. Bulik that you heard being paged, correct?"

"That's correct."

"...You wouldn't know who was calling, or trying to call Mr. Bulik, or check up on him, would you?"

"I have no idea."

The prosecutor had Agent Edmonds now review an exhibit. "When you searched these records at Glenview," Lasee said, "did you search for all the preceding flight manifests that they had available...where Mr. Bulik's name appeared on a passenger list?"

"Right." Between January to April of 1984, Edmonds said Bob's name had been listed on only the February 3 manifest. Bill Appel retrieved that same exhibit, angrily jabbing at it. He wanted the record to show that today was the first time he'd seen this document, which proved that Bob had taken a flight with a 4:00 p.m. planned departure and a 4:30 actual takeoff.

Returning his attention to the naval investigative agent, Appel had Edmonds then confirm he was also a marine reservist. On the weekend before Pam's death, Edmonds said his unit had traveled with Bob to Denver and then picked up the rest of Bob's unit before flying on to Yuma, Arizona. This was a Marine Corps flight. When Edmonds had checked flight records for the police back in June, he'd only looked at Base Operations.

"Agent Edmonds," Appel said, "if Mr. Bulik had missed his drill with his unit in Denver, could he have made up the drill with your unit in Glenview?"

He nodded. Because Bob's unit drilled the first weekend of each month, and Edmonds's drilled the second, he said that on several occasions, Bob had done just that.

Michael Clark, who manned the BOQ, said that about one hundred officers had checked in on Friday, April 6. The rooms were configured with two beds per room, and two rooms shared a connecting bathroom. Bob had been assigned room 118 and had paid the $4 in advance for the room. This was policy if an officer planned to leave the next morning before 6:00 a.m. Around 8:30 p.m., room 118 had also been assigned to Captain Haralson. Two other officers had shared room 120. If Bob had alerted the front desk that he was checking out of the BOQ, on the evening of April 6, Clark said the space would've been reassigned to another officer.

The final witness was Captain David Haralson. Finne asked, with a confident demeanor, "When you got to your room was there any sign of anything that had been disturbed or used?"

"There was a used towel in the room."

The prosecutor looked startled. "In the bathroom?"

"It was hanging on the wall in our room."

Evidently, Finne had been caught off-guard by Haralson's altered recollection. The prosecutor looked perturbed as he watched Appel stand, a big smile on his face. "Mr. Haralson, I never talked to you, have I?"

He concurred.

"As far as the neighbors in room 120, when you use your common bathroom, you have the opportunity to lock them out, don't you?"

"Right."

Appel's grin was still in place as he took his seat next to Bob.

≈

Both sides had won some points in the morning's round. The afternoon would begin with a theme that the prosecution wanted to drill into the jurors' heads: That in the days prior to Pam's death, she'd been planning for her future and working hard to improve her physical health—certainly not acts of a person contemplating suicide.

Dick Lytie's name was called. Dressed in a suit he wore only to weddings and funerals, he plodded up the aisle. In his slow drawl, Dick explained that he owned the Jogger's Joynt running store and handed Finne a copy of Pam's April 7 Spring Classic entry form. "If you registered before April first you saved a dollar on the shirt. Pam came in somewhere around that date. Being a good friend and all, even if she'd come in late I would've given her the cheaper rate."

Dick said that Pam's running had been really improving. "She ran her best, what we call PR—personal record—in January at the YMCA Jack Frost Run. It was like, I'm guessing, a minute or two faster than she'd ever run that distance before." As a buildup to the Green Bay Marathon, he said Pam's plan had been to run his Spring Classic. "It's one of the tougher half marathon courses

in the state. Runners have to be in pretty good shape to participate. Pam was ready to do it."

The last witness for the day would offer some key prosecution
testimony. Thomas Bennett, one of the Buliks' neighbors, had
been an eyewitness to certain events that occurred on the morning of Pam's death.

That Saturday, Bennett said he'd taken his car out to be washed.
After returning home he'd looked at his vehicle's clock. It was
exactly 9:00 a.m. At that point he'd started to rake his front
yard. Around 9:30, Bennett had noticed the Buliks' van leaving
the neighborhood. It had driven past his house, to the end of the
street, and turned left.

Later, Bennett said he'd taken a break from raking and leaned
on his car. He'd checked its clock again and noted the time of
10:30. About 10:45 or 10:50, he'd seen the van return. Then fifteen to twenty minutes later, Bennett confirmed that an ambulance had driven down the Buliks' driveway.

"Were you able to see who was driving, who was inside the
van?" Royce Finne asked.

"No, I had my back to the van as it passed both times. And it has
those dark tinted windows, so it's very difficult to see inside."

The prosecutor's face was intent. "Between the time when the
van returned at 10:45 or 10:50, and when the ambulance came
approximately 20 minutes later, did the van leave the area?"

"No, it did not."

Bill Appel moseyed up to Bennett. "That particular Saturday morning...what you remember seeing is the van leaving at
approximately 9:30, headed toward Preble High School...And the
other thing that you noted was sometime shortly before 11:06,
the van left again?"

"No." Bennett shook his head emphatically. "The van returned."

Appel frowned. "And the third thing you noted was that you
saw the ambulance coming some 15 minutes later..."

"Approximately."

"...If anything else had occurred, with respect to the Bulik family, you would have seen it?"

"In regards to the movement of the van, yes."

"How many vehicles does the Bulik family have?"

"Two that I'm aware of."

"What is the other one?" Appel quizzed.

"A small blue Chevy. I'm not sure of the make. A Monza, I believe."

"Thank you, Mr. Bennett." Appel smiled and joined Bob.

◇◇◇◇◇◇◇◇◇◇◇◇◇◇◇◇◇◇◇

Jim and I'd watched the highlights of Bob's trial on the 10:00 news before retiring for the night. Again the DA's office had called. I'd have another reprieve, this time until Monday.

My bedside clock read 11:10 as the ringing of our phone startled Jim and me awake. At this late hour, a red flag always went up.

He reached for the phone, listened, and then with a sharp intake of air, uttered, "Oh God, no!"

I grabbed his arm. "What's wrong, Jim?"

He shook me away. "Are you at Bellin Hospital or St. Vincent?"

Barely breathing, I waited.

"I'll be right over," he said and hung up.

I stared at his stunned face in the moonlight. "Jim, what is it?"

"It's Melissa Kapalin..."

Fear coursed through me. "Is she hurt?"

"No Lynda," he reached for my hand. "She's dead."

≈

In the kitchen, I waited for Jim's return, hugging my shivering body. How could Melissa be dead at the innocent age of twelve? How would the Kapalins ever survive?

Melissa had been their child who'd frequently snuck out of bed and quietly climbed into her daddy's lap, knowing he'd let her stay. She'd been the one that had ridden shotgun with her mom on family trips, sharing secrets in the dark while the rest of the family slept. Melissa had always treated her younger sister, Jessica, as a peer, including her in sleepovers and fun times with friends. Melissa had been the uncomplaining sister who had cleared the table so Molly and Matt could take off. And, when Melissa would get into trouble, she'd been the child that would say, "I didn't try!" and immediately everyone would forgive her, seeing the unabashed sincerity in her blue eyes.

Melissa, however, had also been the one that had said, "Why

1984 Wausau Triathlon.
Left: two sisters – Jessica and Melissa – watching out for Collin.
Right: Matt Kapalin holding Collin. Jessica Kapalin in center
with her head turned and Melissa at her sister's right.

do things always happen to me?" On a recent vacation, she'd been badly stung by a jellyfish, and on a ski trip weekend accompanying another family, their vehicle had spun out of control, rolled over, and landed in a ditch. Everyone had fortunately been unharmed.

But now, the inexplicable had occurred.

I heard the door lock click. Disheveled from running the couple of blocks to the hospital and back, Jim's eyes met mine. I could tell he'd been crying. I pulled him to me, encircling his body with my arms.

"It was terrible," he said, talking into my hair. "The whole family was gathered in this stark white room in unbelievable pain."

"How did it happen?" I had to ask, my voice muffled against his shoulder.

"This week Melissa made the senior varsity swim team that Matt's also on." Jim pulled away. "Tonight was her first practice with the older kids. Apparently a teammate offered to drive both Kapalins home. Nobody knows why, but the car swerved into the opposite lane and smashed into a light pole, right where Melissa was sitting."

I cringed. "Matt was in the car, too?"

He nodded. "Thankfully, he has only some superficial cuts from the shattered windshield. Moments after the crash, I guess, he tried to talk to Melissa, but she didn't respond."

I closed my eyes. "Where did it happen?"

"Just a few blocks from their house."

It was too much to fathom.

"Matt sprinted home and returned with Kathy and Daryl. By then, the police, rescue squad, and Jaws of Life were already on the scene. I understand that while they extracted Melissa, Kathy stayed by her side, talking to her, encouraging her to hang on, telling her that she could do it," his voice caught, "that she was strong."

"Oh, Jim..." I bit my lower lip and looked at the floor.

"I know..." He slid his arm around me. "In the rescue squad, I understand that Melissa had no vital signs. When the coroner confirmed that she'd died on impact and didn't suffer, it comforted the Kapalins."

I clung to Jim thinking about the horrific finality of this young life, yet below the surface there was also that familiar twinge of guilt. I couldn't help it. I just felt so grateful that our Collin was safe.

Back in bed, Jim and I spooned together, his hands gently cradling my belly. It was hard to comprehend. Now, in addition to

Pam, Melissa was dead. All night, our emotions continued to resurface for our dear friends, who'd lost their "Little Red."

10

Motives for Murder

Amidst a flurry of gossip, spectators funneled into the court-room for day four of the trial. Word was out that "the girl-friend" would take the stand today. But before she did, the State would set out to prove that an additional motive existed, prompting Bob to murder Pam.

Donna Harrison, loan processor for IDL Mortgage, explained to the jury that the Buliks' home was currently appraised at $120,000. In October of 1983, Bob had applied for a refinanced $106,000 VA loan. It was now locked in at nine and a half percent for fif-teen years, with a monthly payment of $1,305. In the last five months of Pam's life, the Buliks had been late on their mortgage. At least one check had bounced, and on the day of Pam's death, payments had been outstanding for March 1 and April 1. Harri-son, however, concurred with Bill Appel that the Buliks did not have mortgage life insurance. This was where Harrison's com-pany would've guaranteed payment of the mortgage in the event that either spouse died.

In quick succession, the next witnesses were brought forward to explain the insurance Bob could collect upon Pam's death. Daniel Ruder, the agent for the group life insurance at the Green Bay Board of Education, testified that Bob's insurance also cov-ered Pam for an additional $5000 with no restrictions. This pol-icy had been kept in the Buliks' home folder, as had the next one, discussed by Richard Beverstein, the Buliks' independent insurance agent. In January of 1983, he'd initiated a call to Bob to update their policies. They'd met and agreed on a $25,000 life insurance policy for Pam. Beverstein told the jury that this was not an excessive amount for a woman her age with dependent children. The paperwork had been signed in April of '83. It contained no accidental death or double-indemnity clause, but if Pam's death were deemed a suicide, and occurred within the first two years of policy signing, the payout would only be $125, the amount invested.

The last policy was from Freedom High School and had not been located at the Buliks' residence. To determine its value, Marjorie Randerson, the district bookkeeper, first testified that Pam's annual salary was $19,412. Next, Fred Evert, a field representative handling the school's group insurance, explained that Pam's policy was equivalent to her salary rounded up to the nearest thousand dollars. If her death were deemed accidental, the beneficiary would receive an additional one-time salary rounded up.

Two scenarios played out regarding the insurance payout. If Pam's death were ruled a suicide or homicide, Bob would receive no more than $25,000. But—if it were ruled accidental—Bob would get $70,000.

≈

A buzz of excitement began to resonate with the anticipation of Linda VandenLangenberg's testimony. In addition to the spectators already cramming the courtroom, legal secretaries, courthouse workers, and off-duty officers were taking personal time for a voyeuristic peek into the private lives of two points of the Bulik love triangle.

Judge Greenwood first granted a motion by Linda's attorney, John Evans, barring the media from taking her picture. "Photographs of this woman would be calculated to make her the subject of derision, ridicule, and public scorn. She's not on trial."

Pleased with the ruling, Evans joined his client in the rotunda outside.

As Lasee stood to call Linda, Evans rushed back in, addressing the judge. "The TV cameras are trying to photograph my client in the hall." Evans pointed in that direction. "They have a large light and they've got her pinned up against the wall." He made a motion to have the guilty parties found in contempt and said, if the bailiff would open the door, "the court could see it going on."

"Well, you can open the door," the judge said, rising from the bench. He then strode down the center aisle, the court reporter at his heels. In the rotunda, Greenwood approached Linda. She was standing in a corner, her thick mane of dark curly hair hanging loose to her shoulders. "Have you been photographed, Miss VandenLangenberg?"

"Yes I have," her voice bristled with rage. "I turned my back. The one right here," she thrust a manicured finger at a Channel 5 photographer. "He has been taking my picture."

"I've made the record," Greenwood said, gesturing toward his court reporter. "However, none of these things were done in my presence, so, under Wisconsin law, I am not empowered to exercise criminal contempt sanctions." That said, the judge returned to his courtroom, settled in his chair, and turned toward the prosecution section of the shared table. "Call the next witness."

Assistant DA Larry Lasee's boyish face projected an air of innocence as he stood. With his tie tucked inside his tailored suit, he was ready to take center stage. His powerful voice announced, "State calls Linda VandenLangenberg."

Whispers erupted as the crowd gazed toward the double doors at the back of the room. There was an aura of mystery about Linda. In an unhurried fashion she entered, gracefully heading down the center aisle in high leather boots and a professional suit, buttoned over a polka-dotted turtleneck.

After being sworn in, Linda targeted her dark eyes at Lasee, not giving the spectators the pleasure of seeing her steal a glance at Bob. Her testimony would obviously be an embarrassment. Colleagues, or parents of her students might be sitting in the courtroom, judging her.

Until this point, Lasee had come across as a hardworking guy, a little on the quiet side—not a grand-stander. But, he certainly could be passionate when he believed the witness was a contributing factor in the death of an innocent victim. Those present would be shocked and surprised as he tackled Linda's testimony.

Since Linda had agreed to take the stand, she was technically not a hostile witness, although the prosecutors expected her to be antagonistic. Unlike their previous witnesses, they'd had no opportunity to meet with Linda. Other than her testimony at the John Doe and the recent motion hearing, Linda had been unreachable. Today, the State finally had its chance. Their goal was not to demean her, but to elicit testimony to prove that a substantial relationship existed between Linda and Bob that had, in turn, motivated his actions on April 6 and 7. The prosecutors knew they had an obligation to be as aboveboard as possible and had decided to be soft on Linda, even though the spectators and jurors might love to hear the lurid details of the affair. Explicit questions could sometimes backfire, making the State look bad.

With his square body, Lasee looked like a high school wrestler ready for combat. He began by asking Linda, "Where do you reside ma'am?"

"I decline to answer that question on the advice of counsel." Her expected response sent the attorneys and judge into rounds of legal jargon. Greenwood finally announced, based on the district attorney's motion, he was granting her immunity to any immorality crimes.

"Thank you," Linda said politely, nodding at the judge. She then eloquently explained that her official residence was her duplex, but since Bob's release from jail in May, she'd been staying at the Bulik home with her two sons. Her sixteen-year-old was actually a foster child who'd lived with her for ten years, while the six-year-old was her natural son. "I maintained my duplex so that my children and Bob's children are very aware that this is not just a living arrangement. We are there to help and support them in this emotional turmoil and very difficult time."

Edison Junior High Special Education Department in 1980-81 with Linda standing next to Bob.

Lasee gave her a dubious look and then asked, "How did you meet Mr. Bulik?"

"We taught together at the same school ... Edison Junior High..."

"When did that contact turn to a personal nature?"

In the hushed courtroom Linda stared directly at Lasee. "I guess it's difficult to say. You don't name a day that you begin to feel differently about someone rather than just as an acquaintance."

"I'm not asking for the day. I'm asking for some time reference. How many years or months ago?" He crossed his arms, tapping his foot.

"Can you rephrase the question?"

"Well, how long have you been having an affair with him?" Lasee blurted out.

"Having an affair? I guess if that's how you want to term it. We've had an intimate relationship for about two years." Linda confirmed it had begun soon after the Red Cross CPR training that she'd attended with Bob in October 1982.

As Linda testified, Bob's face was showing no emotion.

"Did you know the deceased, Pamela Bulik?"

"I knew of her. I met her ... maybe a half a dozen times." From things Bob had related, Linda said she'd believed his relationship with Pam had been an unhappy one. Though Bob hadn't mentioned that anything was wrong with his marriage until the affair had started. At that time, Linda's marriage to Kevin VandenLangenberg had also been struggling. She'd met with Dr. Wellens twice for her own marriage difficulties before referring him to Bob. In obtaining her November '83 divorce, Linda said, "I think just about everything in my life was a factor. Bob was a factor. Bob was in my life."

Lasee fixed his eyes on Linda. "Pamela found out about the affair…do you recall when that was?"

"In October of '83."

"Do you recall that it was on Pamela's birthday?" Lasee's lips tightened.

Linda seemed startled. "I didn't know that."

"Do you remember how Pamela found out?"

Her voice subdued, Linda said, "I believe she found an envelope with my name on it." Bob had told her this.

"Do you recall where you discussed it?" Lasee peered at her.

"In Texas," she whispered.

"You've got to talk louder." Greenwood admonished Linda.

She repeated the answer, just slightly louder, a flush brightening her cheeks.

The judge frowned, turning to the court reporter. "In Texas she says. In Texas."

Linda shifted in her chair and then explained that while Bob was on his Texas military leave, she'd joined him for the week "to rest and regroup." It was her understanding that Pam had found out about the affair just before Bob had left. During that week, Linda had learned that Pam had attempted to contact her, so Linda had called Pam from Texas, concealing the fact that she'd actually been with Bob.

Lasee showed her a State exhibit provided by the Green Bay public schools. It was a copy of Linda's and Bob's attendance records from November of 1982 until Pam's death. It showed that while Linda had been in Texas, she'd called in sick for three days. The other two days had been provided for teachers to attend the Wisconsin Teacher's Convention. In addition, Lasee highlighted eight other coinciding days where she and Bob had both been absent due to sickness.

The prosecutor next moved into the weeks of January and early February 1984 when the Buliks had been separated. Linda agreed that during that time period, she and Bob had started to discuss the possibility of a future together.

"It wasn't Bob who filed for divorce, was it?" Lasee challenged her.

"He was still in the process."

"Can you answer my question?"

"No he had not!"

"Had you discussed what would happen, for instance, in terms of property division between Pam and Bob, in the event the divorce occurred?"

Linda's assumption was that Pam would've gotten the home. In response to Lasee's question about the Bulik children, Linda said, of course Bob had wanted custody, but since they generally remained with the mother, they'd both felt that would probably have happened in this case.

Lasee's eyes found the jurors'. While first working as an assistant DA in Milwaukee, he'd been trained to believe that they would do the right thing, but over the years he'd discovered that wasn't always so. Now Lasee treated them differently. He realized that each juror had a unique personality. He needed to be conscious of what they might be thinking and get a sense of what they believed. He needed to play to them and follow their faces as he questioned each witness.

Now satisfied with their response, Lasee handed Linda a document taken from the cardboard box inside the Buliks' closet.

She identified it as a rough draft of the will she'd authored in December 1983. Subsequently, she said she'd signed it.

Lasee had Linda read the specific paragraph that documented her desire for Bob to become her child's guardian, if her ex-husband had been unwilling, unable, or incapable. As she did, Lasee's jaw muscles tensed, his eyes again darted toward the jury, checking their reaction.

Pleased, he retrieved the exhibit from Linda, and then asked, "On Valentine's Day, Bob told you that it was over between you and he ... Was that a traumatic event for you?"

"Yes it was."

"He went back to his wife, is that right?"

"He moved back in his home." Linda corrected him.

"The fact is, it wasn't over between you and Bob, was it?"

"We remained friends."

"You saw each other on a fairly frequent basis didn't you?"

"Not at first."

Lasee scowled. "As a matter of fact, in the week before Pamela Bulik died, you saw Bob every day, isn't that correct?" He crossed his arms and waited.

"I'm not sure if I saw him every day. Possibly... It's difficult to remember."

At the John Doe hearing, the prosecutor reminded Linda that she'd testified that she'd seen Bob every day from April 1 to 7. As Lasee picked up the transcript, she interjected, "I guess I would believe you."

"Thank you. Do you know where Bob was April first?"

Linda looked at a calendar provided by the judge. On that Sunday, she said Bob had been out of town in Yuma, Arizona, for reserves. On Monday, April 2, Linda admitted that she'd picked him up at the airport after his delayed flight returned from Denver. Earlier that morning, Pam had left for an educators' conference in Milwaukee.

"Now, the day before Pamela died, do you recall if you saw Robert Bulik?"

Linda's eyes didn't waver. "Briefly, yes." During her lunch hour from school, at approximately 11:45, Bob had stopped at her duplex for about three minutes and then left for reserves. The next time she'd heard from him was on Saturday, April 7, sometime after 7:00 p.m. Bob had phoned her and said that Pam was dead.

During the John Doe hearing, Linda had testified to specifics of that conversation. Lasee again picked up the transcript and this time read the questions Royce Finne had asked with Linda's responses:

Q: Did he tell you anything about what he did with Pam after taking her out of the van?

A: I think he said he carried her in.

Q: Did he tell you where he carried her to?

A: No.

Q: What is the very next thing he told you that happened?

A: ...I didn't ask him, and he didn't tell me...He carried her in and I just assumed he laid her in bed or put her on the floor. I thought, I guess, she walked, or something, at some point.

Q: He told you that she walked at some point?

A: I don't know if he said that. I just feel like he said that she was all right or something...He didn't say to me specifically that she spoke to him or anything. I just got the feeling that he felt she was all right.

Lasee ran his eyes down the transcript and found another spot. "You testified that the kids normally went to bed about nine o'clock, is that right?"

"That is what I believed, yes."

Lasee continued to jab away, using the John Doe transcript as proof. "You testified that Bob said Pam was in the tub when he got up. Do you recall that?"

"I don't recall that."

To refresh her memory Lasee read from the transcript again.

Q: Did he tell you where Pam was when he woke up Saturday morning?

A: In the tub.

"I said it. I don't recall that he said that."

"You testified that Bob told you that he took the kids to neighbors, specifically to the Maddens...And you testified, Bob told you nothing about attempting any first aid or CPR...?"

"I don't recall."

Lasee read back:

Q: After he told you about this business of finding Pamela in the tub did he tell you anything about attempting to administer any sort of first aid to her?

A: No.

"Does that help refresh your recollection?"

"He didn't tell me."

"Now, since April seventh, would it be a fair characterization to say you've assumed the role of wife and mother in the Bulik family?"

"No, I wouldn't say that."

"Well, you've expressed concern about the children … and obviously you have some concern for Bob … and I assume that your relationship with him continues to be a sexual relationship?"

"Yes," Linda said, an edge in her voice.

At this significant juncture, Greenwood suspended her testimony until after the noon hour.

◇◇◇◇◇◇◇◇◇◇◇◇◇◇◇◇◇◇◇◇

Christmas decorations were strung from streetlights in downtown Green Bay, but our Fun Run group wouldn't be enjoying our annual festivities this weekend. The party had been cancelled due to Melissa's death. Friends would instead be attending her wake tonight and funeral tomorrow morning.

Since rumors had spread yesterday that Linda might testify, Bruce MacNeil had requested a personal day off to attend today's trial. Because of this most recent tragedy, I'd also taken the morning off from work. After Beezie and I'd stopped at the Kapalins, we joined Bruce and his sister for lunch at the 1001 Club on Main Street. A smoky atmosphere greeted us along with a jukebox belting out Christmas tunes.

Adhering to Green Bay's Friday tradition, we all ordered fish plates. First we discussed the Kapalins' horrendous loss. Then Bruce and Marcy talked about the trial. Most disturbing was that soon after Valentine's Day, Linda and Bob had resumed their affair in earnest. I now realized that when Jim had seen them holding hands, it had just been one more instance among Bob's never-ending deceits. Once again I felt pangs of remorse. Would it have made a difference if I'd told Pam?

While reading Marcy's detailed notes, Beezie relived Pam's discovery of the affair. We now knew the truth. Linda had actually accompanied Bob to Texas. It certainly appeared as if our tax dollars had paid for Bob and Linda's sexual enjoyment.

∞∞∞∞∞∞∞∞∞∞∞∞∞∞

In the hushed courtroom, Linda VandenLangenberg was once again composed. Her dark curls framed the confident jut of her chin as Larry Lasee resumed his direct examination. "Have you and Mr. Bulik formulated future plans at this point? Do you plan on marrying?"

"We haven't formed any plans beyond this week and this time."

Lasee located some State exhibits, again seized from the cardboard box located inside the Buliks' home. He showed Linda a small book, asking her to read the title and to explain when she'd given it to Bob.

Linda reddened. "It's a Charlie Brown book called *You're My Best Friend Because* ... I have no recollection when I gave that to him."

Lasee leaned against the witness stand and paged through the book. "There are various spots at which you have handwritten entries ... for instance there's a page that has printed on it: 'and the same classy taste in entertainment.' Then it has a cartoon with Snoopy and I think that's Schroeder, is that right?" Lasee tipped his head sideways as the spectators laughed.

"I guess." Linda shifted uncomfortably in the witness chair.

"And you've written some things on that page. Would you care to read that to the jury?"

"Is this necessary? ...It's very embarrassing ... It was written as something just personal and funny."

"Would you care to read it to the jury, please?" Lasee persisted.

"Well, I will, but I don't want to!"

"Read it loud," Greenwood ordered. "I can't hear you talk."

Linda took the book from the prosecutor and read:

We've shared escargot and rubbery popcorn, a room at the Burbank Holiday Inn and a BOQ room, dinner at Anthony's, and beer at Wertel's Tap, and it was all wonderful because we were together.

In response to Lasee's probing, Linda said she and Bob had shared the rooms in June of 1983 while she'd been on vacation in California and Bob had been there on military assignment. Anthony's was a San Diego restaurant and Wertel's Tap was in Green Bay.

"Would you care to read your comments on that particular page?" Lasee pointed, listening with the jurors as Linda reluctantly read:

When I'm under the weather you help me feel a little more cheerful. Flowers, a newly installed icemaker, and a visit from the plumbing inspector. What more could a girl want to brighten her spirits on a dismal weekend?

Lasee eyed her. "Can you tell me what the plumbing inspector refers to?"

Linda's crimson flush was spreading. "It was a little joke about the ice maker."

"I'm not going to ask you to read this particular page unless you care to read that," Lasee prodded. In this book, some of Linda's handwritten comments had described the erotic lifestyle she and Bob had enjoyed.

"You know I don't care to read any of this!"

Lasee didn't push it and set the book down, returning with a card. He then asked Linda to read the words inside.

Her confident tone returned as she did:

The ultimate paint of creative visualization—to make every moment of our lives a moment of wondrous creation, in which we are just naturally choosing the best, the most beautiful, the most fulfilling lives we can imagine.

The prosecutor checked the jury's reaction. He next handed Linda some small strips of paper, which she explained were hand-made coupons she'd created for Bob on Valentine's Day. She'd left them in his apartment before she knew he'd reconciled with Pam. Each one had given Bob a specific favor: a massage, a run together, a batch of popcorn, chocolate chip cookies, a night of not mentioning their problems, and a whipped-cream sundae for dessert, on her.

The judge's stern eyes stilled the spectators' whispers.

In the same vein, Lasee handed Linda another card, which she confirmed having given to Bob after Pam's death and just prior to his family's trip to the Bahamas. Linda attested that she had not accompanied them. Per Lasee's request she read:

> I am thinking about you every moment that you are away, missing you and hoping that you can find some solace for the pain, some peace of mind in this world gone crazy. I wish that I could promise this will all be better by the time you get back. I can promise that I will always, always be your friend and that you will have the best of all my love always. Linda.

The prosecutor asked her to go through the same routine with yet another card that she'd given to Bob in the weeks before his arrest.

> You're doing what four people would have a hard time doing well and you're doing it all beautifully, as only you can—with sensitivity, style, and more than a little craziness. You have become mother, father, coach, mechanic, gardener, tutor, chauffeur, world-class athlete in training, travel agent, dependable son, best friend, lover, and fantastic Saturday night date. I could go on, but I'm running out of time and space. You are one terrific example of energy and self-discipline. Being in your life energizes me and inspires me and I love you more every day.

Both the jurors and spectators had been listening with rapt attention, their eyes constantly jerking between Linda and Bob. It was obvious that an intense relationship had developed between the two. Bob, however, was being very cautious and still not displaying any emotional response.

Lasee moved on, now asking Linda about the days immediately following Pam's death. On Monday, April 9, Linda admitted that she and Bob had driven down to Appleton to purchase a suit for him to wear to Pam's funeral. On Tuesday, they'd returned to pick it up.

"Did you see Bob on the day of the funeral?"

"I don't recall. I don't believe so."

"...Do you own an automobile, ma'am?"

"Yes, I do." Linda looked perplexed at the question. She said it was an '83 Pontiac LE 6000.

Lasee's eyes zeroed in on her. "Do you recall if you came to the home after the funeral?"

"If I came to the home?" She hesitated. "No, I didn't *go* to his home."

He frowned, but didn't dig deeper.

Lasee now moved to closure, addressing Bob's level of physical fitness.

Linda confirmed that while the Buliks had been separated, she'd bought a YMCA membership for Bob. It had been cancelled after the Buliks reunited and then reinstated following Pam's death. This past summer, Linda and Bob had camped together about eight to ten times. The trips had included four or five triathlons in which he'd also participated.

"Would you describe Mr. Bulik as being in good physical shape, good condition?"

"Oh, yes!" As long as Linda had known Bob, she said he'd been in good shape. It was very important to him.

Lasee's eyes tracked the jurors' final reaction as he sat down.

Now it was Bill Appel's turn to direct the dialog. "Linda, you told the jury, you have two sons." In naming Bob as her second guardian choice for her natural son, Appel asked whether she'd given appropriate thought as to how Bob would care for the boy's physical and emotional needs?

"Of course," Linda said, and then explained that her decision had been based on the way Bob interacted with his own children. She'd admired the way he expressed his warm feelings and concern toward Abby and Alex.

"You indicated... when Mr. Bulik was released from jail, you thought about whether or not to see him, or be with him."

She nodded. "At that time I consulted with various people and thought about it very seriously, because, I guess, I knew this day would come..."

"Can you tell the jury, from your experience of having lived in the Bulik home, if that bathroom area on the first floor is used by all members of the family?"

"Oh yes, it is. It's an area that everyone uses for showering and as a large dressing area."

Appel paused before tackling his final questions. He asked Linda, in addition to the half dozen times that she'd mentioned having met with Pam, whether Pam had ever contacted Linda from January through March 1984.

Her brow creased. "It's a difficult question to answer." During those months, Linda said she'd received phone calls in which Pam had identified herself, but Linda had also begun receiving anonymous calls. "The phone would ring and no one would talk, but the connection was not broken, so you could hear someone was there... I suspected that it was probably Pam calling to see if I was home... I came to realize the phone calls came whenever Bob was out of town."

Assistant DA Lasee now scrutinized Linda. "I'm not certain, but I assume from your testimony that you're suggesting that these anonymous phone calls were made to you by Pamela?"

"I believe so... I started making a note of them in January."

The prosecutor hesitated. "For what period of time did they continue?"

"Actually, they continued until April sixth." On the day before Pam's death, Linda said she'd received her last call. It came into her workplace at Anne Sullivan School.

Lasee seemed surprised by this information and filed it away for future use. "It appears from your testimony that you and your family have fit in pretty well at the Bulik household. It's pretty much home for you, is that correct?"

Linda's dark eyes pierced the prosecutor. "We have fit in well, yes."

11

Censored Therapists

The courthouse clock tower chimed eight on day five of the Bulik trial. It was to be a special Saturday morning session focused on the Buliks' three therapists. At this hour, downtown traffic would normally be light, but it was the Christmas season and merchants on the small side streets as well as the mall had opened early with enticing sales.

Inside Circuit Court I, the Christmas spirit was on hold. Yesterday, the judge had announced, "Members of the jury, I understand that you've requested some exercise and fresh air. I'll allow you to take walks if a bailiff accompanies you, but you can't go Christmas shopping … It's just too risky. We don't want to chance a mistrial." Disappointment had been obvious on the jurors' strained faces.

Since Tuesday, tension had marked Bob's face, too. His jaws had clenched frequently as his eyes and ears had followed each witness's testimony. Stress had also sent Pam's father to the hospital with chest pains. After listening to Linda's testimony he'd complained of dizziness and shortness of breath. Last night he'd been taken by ambulance to St. Vincent Hospital. Luckily, it had just been a scare. He'd been released and planned to return for the rest of the trial on Monday.

Tension was also evident on Judge Greenwood's face. Before summoning the jury, he requested that the lawyers approach. "Yesterday, I made some judgmental rulings with respect to photographing Linda VandenLangenberg. My wife received a call that said the judge was sharing her with Bulik and hung up. I'm not making a complaint, but for the record, I want the courts to know the climate of this trial."

Waiting in the wings to take the stand was first Dr. Gerald Wellens, the Buliks' joint counselor, who'd been chief psychologist at Brown County Mental Health Center and clinical director at the Green Bay Correctional Institution. For the past eight years he'd been offering his psychological services in private practice. Second was Pam's individual therapist, Dr. Michael O'Neill, who'd been specializing in psychiatry for approximately eleven years. And third was Jean Weidner, Bob's psychiatric counselor, who had a master's degree in psychiatric social work from the University of Wisconsin Milwaukee.

But before the therapists could testify, Greenwood had requested a preliminary review in chambers. He had then ruled on what the jury could and could not hear. Now a subset of the Buliks' thoughts, previously shared under the confidentiality of patient/client privilege, would be revealed to the public today.

Dr. Wellens was appalled at what had just taken place in Judge Greenwood's chambers. He felt that the Bulik case was being tried outside the courtroom and believed that his upcoming testimony would be ineffective given all that he couldn't say about his two former patients, one of whom he'd cared for dearly, while the other still made the hair on his arms stand up.

In addition to barring testimony about the reason for Bob's original referral, that being the August incident, Greenwood had ruled that the doctor's concern about Pam's physical well-being, and the potential for domestic violence in the Buliks' marriage could not be discussed. The judge had said, "I have a great deal of difficulty finding whether the potential for domestic violence is within the purview of expert testimony ... Isn't there a potential for family violence in every marriage or many marriages?"

From the witness chair, Dr. Wellens first discussed Bob's individual therapy, and then the Buliks' joint treatment. Wellens's face registered disgust when he explained how Bob had broken his agreement to have no contact with Linda the first time. "On November twenty-eighth, I think it was a Monday … both of them came in for their appointment. It was discussed that his wife, Pam, had gotten a key to his office at the school, and made a copy of his key, and then went in and found letters from Linda. Bob also admitted that, apparently, he told Pam that he was not feeling well, so that Pam and the kids went to church, and then he went over to Linda's house and had sex with her." Wellens shot a nasty look at Bob. "Pam was pretty upset with that."

The spectators tittered.

Then, in January of 1984, Wellens said Bob had again breached their contract. Even though the Buliks' counseling was subsequently terminated, the doctor had continued to have sporadic contact with Pam. "If there was a crisis, she called … I would imagine, altogether, probably twenty, maybe thirty times. It seemed like quite a bit."

"What was Bob's attitude towards divorce?" Lasee asked.

"He was opposed to getting a divorce. He thought it would upset his two children. I asked him what he thought would be the best solution in fantasy?" Wellens picked up his notes to find the direct quote. "He said, 'If Pam would move out and go to Florida where I could have the kids and the house, that would be acceptable.'"

Lasee paused, letting Wellens's last words sink in, as an undertone again rumbled throughout the courtroom.

The doctor said he'd pressed Pam pretty consistently to separate from Bob, but admitted to Appel that she'd been very uncomfortable with the idea.

Dr. Michael O'Neill explained why he'd also encouraged Pam to pursue a divorce. As the course of her therapy had progressed, it had become clear to him—and eventually to her—that the Buliks' marriage had been deeply troubled for years. O'Neill had felt that their issues could not be resolved. Pam had been distressed by Bob's lack of communication and their difficulty with conflict resolution. Some financial problems had also been present. Bob had told O'Neill that early in the marriage there'd been a pattern of overindulgence toward Pam on his part. "He tended to resent that, and she also saw it as something that should change." Because Pam's turmoil had been severe, the doctor said he'd been concerned about her emotional well-being. But like Dr. Wellens, O'Neill could not mention his fears about Pam's physical well-being in open court.

The defense attorney approached Dr. O'Neill with a smile. The two knew each other personally. Bill Appel stated that Bob hadn't been the only one at fault for the Buliks' marriage problems. "It was a two-way street, was it not?"

O'Neill nodded. "Some of the marriage difficulties that I described as longer term certainly were on both parties." Pam's poor self-image, he agreed, had stemmed from her childhood. She'd felt that she'd been unattractive. Because it had been ingrained, it took longer to treat. Pam's return to work in January of 1984 had been important to her—a milestone in her progress toward achieving greater independence. Pam had admitted, though, that she would have preferred not to work outside the home. On two occasions, she'd mentioned that teaching was difficult for her. The last time had been in March of '84.

Pam 5th Grade and 11th Grade

The therapists each talked about the Buliks' two-week separation period.

Jean Weidner said that this had been a very difficult time for Bob.

On February 1, Dr. Wellens testified that Pam had called him. "Bob told her that Mrs. Weidner said the only way they could reconcile would be to go back and live together. I said, 'Pam, you know what I think. I'm opposed to that, but you'll have to do what you think is right.'" Wellens said he'd certainly been surprised by Jean Weidner's advice. A two-week separation, versus what he thought would have required several months, had shocked him. He'd wanted to confirm this with Weidner, but professional ethics had prohibited him.

Today, Jean Weidner firmly told the jury that she had not advised the Buliks to reconcile on Valentine's Day. On February 9, she'd received a call from Pam. At that time, only Bob had been Weidner's client. Because of patient/doctor confidentiality, she'd told Pam that she could not answer her questions concerning Bob. Pam had seemed upset on the phone and told Weidner that she couldn't make it emotionally without Bob. "I advised her to talk to Dr. Wellens or Dr. O'Neill."

Dr. O'Neill said Pam had called him. He'd been pleased when she'd separated from Bob, but during those two weeks, Pam had required outpatient treatment. Her emotions had "reigned supreme," outweighing her logical reasons that had prompted the separation.

Also on February 9, Jean Weidner said she'd met with Bob and noted that he couldn't stand Pam's pain. Earlier in judge's chambers, Weidner had also related that during that session Bob had fantasized about Pam skidding off an icy road and being killed. Greenwood had determined his comment simply reinforced the existence of a love triangle and had ruled that it could not be discussed in open court.

Like the other therapists, Dr. O'Neill stated that he had not advised the Buliks to reconcile, and had been upset when they did.

Once again, because of Pam's need to be with Bob, she'd heard only his promises to recommit to their marriage.

After the Valentine's Day reconciliation, Weidner said she'd conducted the Buliks' first joint session. Pam had verbalized her problems while Bob had been more withdrawn, more restrained. "I worked on communication with him." Bob had felt that Pam was very dependent on him, Weidner testified, and to a degree she'd believed this was true, but not to a dangerous level.

"As a matter of fact," Lasee said, "Pamela was employed outside of the home ... She had a large circle of friends ... She was a runner and actively training for upcoming events ... And she was looking forward to things in the future?"

Weidner nodded along, saying yes at each pause.

"Any main evidence of her dependence came from the defendant, is that correct?"

"Plus Pam's telephone call to me." While the Buliks had been separated, Weidner reiterated, "Pam expressed an emotional dependence."

Lasee curbed a frown and quickly moved on, asking Weidner to discuss the Buliks' March 12 therapy session.

In that meeting, she said that the couple had entered into a verbal contract. "Bob was to tell Pam if his friend Linda called. And if she did, Bob was to tell her not to contact him anymore." At that point, Weidner felt that Pam had been the one concerned about this problem. She'd raised the issue. The contract had also assumed that Bob would not initiate contact with Linda.

At the Buliks last meeting, on March 23, the issue hadn't come up. If Pam had been concerned, Weidner felt sure she would've mentioned it.

Lasee now asked Weidner about the morning of Pam's death.

Bob had contacted her, Weidner said, around ten minutes of eleven, very upset. "He told me that he had drawn Pamela's bath water and left the house and when he came back, he found her in the bathtub and she was cold ... I asked him if he had done anything about it ... I assumed Pamela was alive and I was questioning him as to whether or not he had tried to resuscitate her ... He said no." Though, Weidner admitted to Appel that her question had been very general. In her mind she'd been thinking CPR, but she'd never said those specific words.

She then had asked Bob if he'd called the rescue squad and again he'd said no. "I told him, several times, to call 911, and that people there could help him take care of Pamela. And I told him I was hanging up, and then he said, 'What about the children?' And I said, 'What about the children?' And he said they were going to leave shortly. And I told him, whoever was picking up the children to call them and tell them to pick them up immediately. And he said he was driving them. And I said, 'Well send the children to your neighbor right away and call 911.' And I told him I was hanging up."

"Did you at any time instruct Mr. Bulik to take the kids to the mall?" Lasee asked.

"No."

"Did you attempt to reconnect with Mr. Bulik?"

"I called back, oh, probably about five minutes after the hour, and his line was busy. And I waited a few minutes, and I called back again, and his line was busy. So I assumed that he was getting help."

The defense attorney now wanted to drive home a critical point. He asked Weidner, on the morning of Pam's death, whether Bob's concern for his children, and what had been best for them, had been quite in character for him?

She agreed that it had.

During Dr. O'Neill's testimony, Appel had also asked him if he too agreed that Bob had been, and continued to be, devoted to his children and family.

"Pamela always told me that her husband was a good father ... His devotion to the family, obviously, is a different issue."

◇◇◇◇◇◇◇◇◇◇◇◇◇◇◇◇◇◇◇◇◇◇

While the trial was in session, a larger crowd had gathered for Melissa's funeral at Resurrection Church. Last evening, at Schauer and Schumacher Funeral Home, a huge number of mourners had lined up for two hours for the wake of this precious young child.

Jim and I were now en route to the Kapalins' home. Shortly after the funeral, Dick Lytie had organized the group to run a five-miler in memory of Melissa. Our well-intentioned friend felt the physical exertion might lighten the Kapalins' heavy hearts.

As everyone arrived, the usual Fun Run joviality was replaced by a subdued sense of respect. Eventually, we headed outside through the Kapalins' foyer. On the wall I noticed Kathy's framed Irish Blessing. I'd often passed it, but had never taken the time to read it. Today I did.

May the road rise up to meet you.
May the wind be always at your back.
May the sun shine warm upon your face.
And rains fall soft upon your fields.
And until we meet again,
May God hold you in the palm of His hand.

Blinking back tears, I stepped outside and grabbed Jim's hand. I tilted my head toward the heavens and felt the winter sun warm my face and the road stretching out before us. Somehow I knew Melissa was up there with Pam's comforting arm around her, both nestled in the palm of God's hand.

∞∞∞∞∞∞∞∞∞∞∞∞∞∞∞∞∞

Key to both the prosecution and defense was Pam's state of mind at the time of her death. Back in the courtroom, the Buliks' therapists were being asked for their expert opinions on two subjects: Pam's reaction to anxiety and stress, and her potential for suicide.

Appel had Dr. O'Neill identify a letter he'd sent to Pam's insurance company. Dated March 30, 1984, it explained why her treatment would continue for another three to six months. At that time, O'Neill stated that her diagnosis had been acute stress response syndrome with depressive features. "And you write that symptoms have included sleep disruption, concentration impairment, feelings of despondency, hopelessness, anxiety, sense of futility, fear of the future, pervasive apprehension, inability to tolerate stress." Appel looked up from the letter. "You characterize Mrs. Bulik in that fashion?"

"During the course of therapy, yes." But, O'Neill explained that his letter had included Pam's symptoms from the beginning of her treatment. It didn't mean they had all been current symptoms or hadn't changed.

Appel appeared unconvinced, but moved on, ready to tackle a major aspect of Bob's defense that had been discussed hours earlier...

In Judge Greenwood's closed chambers, surrounded by the scent of leather bindings from law books, Bill Appel asked Dr. O'Neill, "As Pam's treating psychiatrist, were you aware that she did have, at times, what appeared to be states or conditions of psychological withdrawal?"

"I was aware of one episode," O'Neill said, and stated that Pam had first reported it to Dr. Bressler in January, but its actual cause had never been determined. "She was acting somewhat strangely and seemed not to have a good recollection and memory recall for that episode." Pam had entertained the thought, O'Neill said, that Bob might have been giving her some drug, a white powdery substance, like one might get from a drug capsule. O'Neill had alerted Jean Weidner, as well as Dr. Reinhard, the psychiatrist in their practice who'd originally prescribed Bob's sleeping pills, to be aware that Bob might be attempting to harm his wife.

The defense attorney quickly countered, "There is not clarity, Judge, on that crushed up medication." Appel understood that Pam had found a pill bottle damaged, containing medication, also damaged, along with a prescription. "This is all hearsay statements," he said, and turned back to Dr. O'Neill. "The type of reaction that you saw, or know of in January, could that be caused by stress?"

"Yes, but there could be other possible causes."

Appel turned back to Greenwood. "My intention, Judge, is to only ask Dr. O'Neill if he's aware that an episode like that occurred."

"Yeah, but that's a one-way street," Greenwood said, wagging his finger at the defense attorney. "You're asking for your apple pie and you want to eat it too."

The judge ruled that if Appel introduced Pam's memory loss incident, the State could ask about other clinical causes.

Now, in the courtroom, Appel took that plunge and asked Dr. O'Neill, what he thought could have caused Pam's reported December/January memory loss?

This amnesia episode, O'Neill said, could have resulted from a recent or chronic head injury, drug toxicity that affected the brain, or a dissociative fugue state. The last option was a psychiatric condition where a person has an altered state of consciousness. The individual would not be aware of their actual behavior for a certain period of time and then would come out of that state without clear recollection. "It's considered to be an anxiety type of disorder," O'Neill added, but also agreed that a dissociative fugue state could result from stress.

"Emotional stress over finances, work, marriage problems?" Appel said, lifting his brow.

"Let's just say emotional stress, or severe anxiety, is one of the known causes of a dissociative state."

Appel shared a significant look with the jury before taking his seat.

Lasee stood, ready to edge into the door that the defense attorney had opened. "Dr. O'Neill, Mr. Appel has referred to an incident that, apparently, Pamela described in January of 1984. It may have happened sometime during the holiday season. How did Pamela relate the incident?"

"Am I free to state how I became aware of it?" Dr. O'Neill's eyes slid toward the defense side of the table, priming the jury for something important.

"Sure." Lasee smiled confidently.

Given his blessing, O'Neill said, "On January fourth, or shortly thereafter ... I received a letter from Dr. Bressler, who had treated Pamela."

Lasee retrieved this State exhibit and asked Dr. O'Neill to read the initial portion.

Judge Greenwood interjected, "Could I look at it for a moment?"

Lasee placed the letter into his outstretched hand.

As Greenwood read, the courtroom waited in anticipation. Eventually, the judge handed the letter to Dr. O'Neill and told him to proceed.

Clearing his voice, the doctor began:

> Pam was seen today with a rather bizarre history of memory loss ... The details of this are very difficult, obviously, because of her impairment. But as she describes it, after an evening of drinks, following skiing, she has no recall for a period of approximately 36 hours.

Lasee retrieved the letter and asked, "Doctor, how did you have occasion to be referred to Pamela?"

Appel went on the alert.

"She was initially referred to me by Dr. Bressler."

"Was this as a result of a head injury?"

"Yes, it was ... Dr. Bressler had asked me to see Pamela after she had suffered a serious life-threatening injury, subsequent to, which she showed many symptoms of emotional distress, which would not be surprising." That was why, O'Neill said, he'd diagnosed Pam with acute stress response syndrome.

This was a significant development, and the jury appeared to want more insight.

"Doctor, from your knowledge of Pamela's condition, was there a physical residual from her skull fracture that would have accounted for that early January or late December incident?"

"No," O'Neill said, and explained that Dr. Bressler had given Pam a clean bill of health.

"Was Pamela taking any prescribed medication during the course of treatment?"

"I prescribed Dalmane, which is a sleeping medication. Very often, in acute stress syndrome, they have sleeping disturbances, often nightmares."

"The letter indicates that after an evening of drinks, following skiing, she had no recall for a period of approximately 36 hours. In your opinion, Doctor, could the combination of alcohol and drugs account for that loss of memory?"

As O'Neill answered, "Yes," Appel tensed further, however Lasee could delve no deeper.

The prosecutor lastly had Dr. O'Neill reiterate the meaning of a dissociative fugue state. This time, O'Neill added that in this altered state, triggered by anxiety and stress, suicide was not considered a high risk.

Lasee stole a look at the jury before asking another key question. "Do you have an opinion, Doctor, as to whether or not this particular state, as described by Pamela, is likely to be stress related, anxiety related?"

O'Neill pursed his lips while shaking his head. "In my opinion, it's not my first choice." Even though Pam had been suffering from substantial anxiety, O'Neill felt she'd not been prone to dissociative states. A certain set of personality characteristics went along with the condition. The most common was that the individual was not in touch with their feelings, which therefore found expression outside the individual's actual consciousness. "Pamela was very much in touch with her feelings and exploring them very openly."

The prosecutor nodded his approval. During the last round of questions, he'd made his best attempt at trying to link Bob to Pam's reported memory loss, and, with any luck, creating some speculation about her head injury. Still, the jurors seemed confused.

The dilemma was that under the judge's restrictive rulings, there was no way to clear up these two mysteries.

Before recrossing Dr. O'Neill, Appel curtly said, "I have a motion..."

Once in chambers, the defense attorney vehemently argued for a mistrial. He accused Lasee of introducing the skull fracture and drugging to intentionally create the presumption that Bob had been responsible for a previous crime.

Lasee seemed taken aback. The court had ruled, he said, that if Appel raised the December/January incident, the State could ask those questions. "As a matter of fact, the State asked Dr. O'Neill not to read the next line of the letter, which would indicate Pamela felt she was being drugged. We intentionally avoided that issue."

Listening to the exchange, Assistant DA Finne frowned, recognizing the State's error. "What happened out there," he said, "probably gave the jury a false impression on this issue." Finne felt they would now believe that Dr. O'Neill had given Pam the medication. "It deflects suspicion away from Mr. Bulik."

"The motion is denied," Judge Greenwood announced. "I find no grounds for a mistrial."

Back in the courtroom, the defense attorney quickly regrouped and picked up Dr. O'Neill's therapy notes, pointing out a section. "There's also an entry from December sixth, 1983 of Mrs. Bulik experiencing some numbness in her arms." Appel asked Dr. O'Neill to explain this to the jury.

On that date, he said that Dr. Bressler had seen Pam for that problem. After completing tests, he'd found Pam to be physically well and felt the numbness had been related to her anxiety and stress. And, O'Neill said, "I agreed."

Appel nodded, his face smug, his eyes zeroing in on the jury as if to say, I was right, Pam did suffer from physical symptoms related to stress.

Next to be broached was Pam's potential for suicide. Lasee's objective was to provide the jury with convincing evidence that at the time of Pam's death, she had not been in any frame of mind to take her own life.

From the stand, all three therapists echoed what they'd told Lasee and Taylor in their office interviews: None of them believed that Pam had been suicidal.

Now, Bill Appel's job was to put some doubt in the jurors' minds about Pam's therapists' convictions.

The defense attorney told Dr. Wellens that he'd like to review Pam's MMPI (Minnesota Multiphasic Personality Inventory) with him. She'd completed it on November 3, 1983. The purpose of the MMPI had been to capture Pam's emotional and psychological profile at that specific point in time. Appel asked Wellens to look at his copy. "In the area of paranoia it indicates that she is overly sensitive and suspicious, does it not?"

Wellens ran his finger down the page. "Yes, this profile clearly would reflect that she'd found out her husband was having an affair the week before."

"In terms of depression it indicates significant depression" Appel eyed the doctor, "two standard deviations from the norm…?"

"It's over what's considered normal limits." Wellens fidgeted, perturbed. "What you're doing is reading the computer narrative, which really, I would caution you not to do."

"Doctor, I'm allowed to do what the court will allow me to do."

Lasee eventually came to Wellens's aid, and asked him, which category had received Pam's highest score.

"Anger. She was really angry. That's a healthy response to hearing that her husband was having an affair." Because Pam had verbalized her problems and feelings, Wellens considered that another healthy sign, making her less likely to commit suicide. His eyes sought out the jurors. "Rather than keeping her feelings bottled up, Pam could talk to me or Dr. O'Neill or some of her friends."

At intervals, Dr. O'Neill told Lasee he'd discussed with Pam whether she'd ever considered suicide, particularly at moments where she'd seemed more distressed. "I did not discuss it regularly with her because I saw no need." When things had been very bad, he said Pam, at times, had a feeling of hopelessness that things might not work out. But he'd never felt she'd required a no-suicide contract, hospitalization, or medication for serious depression. "A person can have depressed feelings when your life seems to be falling apart." That didn't mean there was a serious depression, O'Neill explained. They were two different things. If Pam had not been treated properly for acute stress syndrome, according to research, this could've led to serious depression. "In fact, the treatment is an attempt to prevent that. And I think the record shows that it was successful."

Previously, on three or four occasions, O'Neill said Pam had called him when she'd been particularly distressed or upset. If she'd had issues between her last appointment on March 15 and her death, he expected that she would've done the same.

Lasee asked Dr. O'Neill a critical question: "Is it your belief that Pam was prepared for a life without Bob, if necessary?"

"That would have been very, very difficult for Pamela, but in my opinion, she was prepared to do it, if necessary."

Lasee nodded his approval and sat down.

Bill Appel picked up Pam's green journal that had been seized from the Buliks' home. He turned to the last entry, titled "I Am Afraid" that was dated March 31, 1984. Then handing the exhibit to Dr. O'Neill, Appel asked him to read it to himself.

The spectators had perked up. They had speculated about this entry ever since those words had been splashed on the front page of the local newspapers back in early June. Most assumed that Pam had been fearful of her husband, but if the defense attorney was introducing this evidence, maybe that wasn't so.

Chewing on his lower lip, Appel studied the doctor until he looked up. "Does that change your opinion as to whether or not she may have been entertaining some personal destructive thoughts?"

"No it does not."

Obviously, it was not the answer Appel expected. "I would like to read part of that out loud, then, if I may, your Honor."

"We're going to object," Finne announced. "Throughout the course of this trial we have attempted to offer, in evidence, the statements of the deceased in this case—"

"May I clarify my answer?" Dr. O'Neill interjected. "I did not state, or intend to state, that Pamela Bulik never had any suicidal thoughts... The distinction I was trying to make is that I never considered her a suicidal risk. I never felt that she had an impulse to commit suicide or a plan to commit suicide."

Appel's eyebrows arched. "Then you recognize that this document has suicidal thoughts?"

"No, in that document, I don't."

The attorney seemed peeved. "I'd like to ask the doctor about some of the language..."

Greenwood cut him off. "I'm going to check the law on this." Before court resumed on Monday, the judge wanted to meet with the lawyers in chambers to resolve the admissibility of this evidence.

≈

Back on Monday, December 3, Judge Greenwood had presided at the Washington County Courthouse in West Bend, Wisconsin, a community of around 22,000 residents, located about a hundred miles south of Green Bay. The judge had warned the potential jurors: "This is going to be a serious imposition on your time. You'll be sequestered in Brown County and to be honest, the trial will probably take all week and possibly into Monday of next week."

Six hours later, the new panel had clamored onboard a bus, en route to Green Bay. Most had felt the impending first-degree murder trial sounded like an exciting adventure.

But by Sunday, December 9, monitored around the clock, the jurors had now spent five intense days listening to the excruciatingly detailed testimony. In addition, on a second floor wing of the Downtowner Hotel, reserved exclusively for their use, televisions had been removed from rooms and newspapers had been off-limits. Instead of an adventure, the trial had become a lockdown. Tomorrow was the promised Monday, and the prosecution hadn't even rested their case. Everyone knew the trial's duration would be a far cry from the time commitment they'd signed up for.

Today, at least, they could get their minds off the proceedings. The judge and attorneys had sanctioned an afternoon spousal visit. In the community room, decked out for Christmas, a brunch had been laid out that included fresh fruit—a welcomed spread after days of eating the rich German food from the Stein Supper Club, conveniently located near the courthouse. Two jurors had asked to use the YMCA, but their request had been denied. Although, this morning, under the bailiff's watchful eyes, a number of jurors had at least taken a brisk walk to attend nearby churches. Others had done their laundry in the housekeeping section of the hotel's basement. Many had not packed sufficient clothing for the lengthy trial.

At noon, their guests began to arrive. The group clustered around the single television in the common room anticipating the start of the Packer-Bear game. The bailiffs patrolled, decked out in Packer gear. Alcoholic beverages were provided, livening up the atmosphere. With the stress of the trial off their minds, a camaraderie feeling surrounded the group. The game was exciting as the Packers secured another win.

But, by 5 p.m. the floor had been cleared of guests. The jurors had taken advantage of their one day of freedom. A few felt a bit guilty recognizing their purpose for being in Green Bay until Friday's sightings were mentioned. First, through the windows of the jurors' room, they'd noticed Bob Bulik and Linda VandenLangenberg emerge from Bob's car. Later in the day, the bailiffs had announced that the jurors were due back in court. In the hallway, reserved for court personnel, Bob had stood, chuckling with his attorney. The jury members all agreed that if the defendant could have a life outside the courtroom, so could they.

The week ahead would be rough. The jurors realized that Bob Bulik's future was resting in their collective hands. It was an extremely sobering thought.

∞∞∞∞∞∞∞∞∞∞∞∞∞∞

The hubbub in the courthouse heightened for the second week of the trial. Inside the rotunda I located Beezie and Sylvia. We were to remain in the hall until a bailiff would individually call us to enter. Since all of our husbands worked for the Green Bay schools, we'd asked them not to take a personal day to attend. Their presence would only have made us more nervous.

It had been a draining weekend, but at least today I was carrying a bit less guilt. After the newspapers provided highlights of Jean Weidner's testimony, I realized that even though I hadn't shared Jim's information with Pam, she'd probably had an inkling that Linda was back in the picture.

Beezie pointed out Dr. Michael O'Neill. I'd heard lots of good things about him from Pam, but had never met him. His eyes appeared kind and with his dark curly hair, he was a handsome man. The bailiff opened the courtroom doors and motioned him in.

∞∞∞∞∞∞∞∞∞∞∞∞∞∞

As Judge Greenwood announced that Pam's journal and other writings were admissible, an excited undercurrent spread. Both the spectators' and jurors' curiosity had been piqued after Saturday's testimony.

Bill Appel stood to resume his cross-examination of Dr. O'Neill, again opening Pam's journal to the "I Am Afraid" entry, dated March 31. "Mrs. Bulik attempts to express some of her thoughts... She starts out saying: 'I want to cry, scream, laugh, run, and dance. Why am I so confused?' And she talks about her emotional needs and feelings...I guess what strikes me, as a layperson, is the ending—'Lord, help me be better and stronger and good. I want to live.'—underscoring live one, two, three, four, five times." Apple asked O'Neill if this didn't strike him as a kind of overstatement?

"Well, it struck me as an emphatic…affirmative statement partly in response to the kinds of concerns she was expressing."

Now, the defense attorney looked confused. "If she makes this statement, 'I want to live,' and underscores live four or five times, wouldn't that lead you to suspect that she was thinking the opposite?"

The doctor shook his head. "I don't feel that way."

Appel frowned. "Did you have a chance to talk with the district attorney's office over the weekend about this particular diary entry…?"

"Yes, I did." The doctor also confirmed that he'd had the opportunity to review Pam's entire journal.

Locking eyes with the prosecutors, Appel scowled. As he set the journal down, it was now the spectators' and jurors' turn to be confused. They still had no definitive answer on why Pam had written, "I Am Afraid." If Appel wasn't going to provide it, hopefully the prosecution would later.

The defense attorney next retrieved Pam's fifty-two-week James Fixx running log. It was something that the police had overlooked and now was marked as a defense exhibit. During the week of January 15, under mental attitude, Appel said Pam had written: bad, depressed. Then for the remainder of January and throughout February Pam's feelings had seemed to oscillate. One week she'd been depressed, the next week improved, and the next day low and tired. In early March, Pam had felt lousy, empty, and hurting. On March 11, she'd been feeling anxious and confused. Finally, on March 31, the weekend before her death, Pam had written:

> Ran partly with Lynda and Barb. In an emotional down. Bob gone to Yuma. Said he'd call last night and didn't. Was disappointed.

I miss him so right now. I really had to kick myself to get going today. Slept little last night.

Appel looked up from Pam's running log and asked Dr. O'Neill if those entries confirmed his clinical impression that Pam had been emotionally confused, often depressed, and mentally stressed over her marriage problems.

"I would say, more or less, they would." But, he said, he hadn't heard anything that had surprised him or run counter to what he'd already testified about.

Appel was going nowhere with this witness and for the moment, sat down.

With Pam's journal in hand, Assistant DA Lasee approached Dr. O'Neill and asked him to give the jury his overall opinion about its contents.

"I didn't see anything ... to indicate that Pam had not been open or honest with me, which would have been a concern." The diary entries, O'Neill said, were called a personal inventory. Pam had been looking at her life: her future and her past. They had different titles. The doctor turned the pages as he read: Appreciation, Success List, Self-Esteem List, Self-Appreciation, The Reason I Can't Have What I Want, Why I Don't Like Myself. Then Pam had listed her Ten Most Important Goals. The final entry was titled "I Am Afraid" and had been the one that Bill Appel had referred to, in which Pam had ended with the words "I want to live."

"I think," O'Neill said, "that the final line has to be taken in the context of this entry."

Lasee nodded and asked the doctor to read Pam's entire March 31 entry and provide his professional interpretation.

Dr. O'Neill began:

> I want to cry, scream, laugh, run, and dance. Why am I so confused? Why can I not move on my desires to fulfill my emotional needs without guilt and fear or repression? What makes me smile one minute and hate the next? What is this leading to? Have I lost control, or the burning desire to make it right? Or am I

concerned about making it right for Bob and neglecting my real inner needs?

...I felt today, I could have severed the last physical interference in my ability to move positively forward, but didn't mobilize or act out of fear. Fear of how Bob would have reacted. Now I am angry at me for not following through on my needs to cut...that last string and at Bob for being gone right now when I truly need him to help cope with loneliness, sick children, job pressures, feelings of emotional exhaustion, feelings of non-importance. He could remember trivial other things, but didn't see it important to remember to call when he said he would...

Am I not that important, or has he become so detached that I mold in with the woodwork, plaster, paint, doll house, etc. I quit. I don't like feeling so confused and miserable. I no longer will allow the flow of energy to proceed in the direction of the past two years or last six months.

I believe in me, in Bob, and in us. I need him to remind me of that last, lest I continue to worry. I will tell him I need to hear romantic and loving assurances as long as they are genuine and true.

The doctor paused to interpret the portion he'd just completed. "Pam's going through some very difficult considerations. She expresses in here her concerns...not recognizing her own needs. That she is thinking of Bob only. She's recognizing that this is no longer a good thing for her...She's talking about the dependency that she feels, but she's also talking about her struggle towards being able to live without him, if that's necessary. That's what she's doing in this entry."

O'Neill found the spot where he'd left off and said in the later part Pam stated:

I love you Bob, but will be happy with you only as long as I know you are happy and satisfied with me.

"She's conditioning it. In other words, she's stating, I'm not going to just stay there if it's going to be a harmful relationship to me."

And then O'Neill said that Pam had ended the entry with:

> Lord help me be better and stronger and good. I want to *live*.

"She's finally coming to the conclusion ... that despite the fact it may be without Bob, she's going to live and she's going to make a life for herself."

Lasee nodded his approval and rejoined Finne.

Even though the jurors and spectators had finally heard Pam's entire entry, some ambiguity remained. Unfortunately, the only one that could have cleared this up was Pam.

Before O'Neill was dismissed, Appel's goal was to plant some final seeds of reasonable doubt in the jurors' minds concerning Pam's emotional state. He retrieved her journal, turned to a specific page, and read:

> Because the prospect of aloneness and proceeding down life's path, as a single unit, frightens and paralyzes me into non-action and non-movement.

He showed it to Dr. O'Neill. "She writes that?"

"Yes."

Appel chose another entry and read:

> Because I'm still a little girl, insecure and frightened at the prospect of living alone without the love, care, understanding, and acceptance of me by Bob.

Again Dr. O'Neill acknowledged that Pam had written that and also the last entry Appel now finished with:

> Because I've become angry and bitter at what life has dealt me, and I feel I deserve escape.

12

Friends with Conviction

"Lynda Drews," the bailiff's baritone voice resounded inside the rotunda.

My heart pummeled my ribs as Beezie and Sylvia offered encouraging words. Discretely, I adjusted my pantyhose, which had slipped below my pregnant belly, took a deep breath, and stood. I remembered feeling this same way eons ago…

Back in 1964, my mother, siblings, and I had arrived near midnight at our Stormy Lake cottage. Gravel crunched under the tires of our station wagon as my mother maneuvered the long rutted driveway, secluded in our five wooded acres. Sounds of a persistent owl and noisy crickets greeted us. A sliver of moon disappeared behind the clouds, and the wind rustled, permeating the air with the scent of conifers. My mother left the headlights on as we three kids unloaded the luggage. All of twelve years old, I led the way, gingerly stepping through weeds that should've been virgin, but clearly had been trampled. "It looks like someone's been here," I said, unsettled.

We all jumped when we heard a snap behind us. At this point my little brother was close to tears, and my younger sister put a stranglehold on my arm.

My mother assured us—it was just an animal.

That didn't help.

When I reached the back porch I stepped up nearly slipping.

Shattered glass covered the porch stoop, and the screen door hung ajar. I knew we had no phone.

Now, the same panic I'd experienced entering our cabin enveloped me as I stepped into Judge Greenwood's courtroom. Back then, fortunately the intruder had already made his exit and no one had attacked us. With any luck today, I'd have the same result handling Bill Appel's questions.

Situated in the witness chair, I smoothed my paisley blue maternity dress. I sensed Bob's critical eyes and avoided his stare, only to rest my eyes on the Styrofoam head model, reminding me of Pam's terrible ordeal. After explaining that I'd known the Buliks for nine years, Larry Lasee asked if I'd considered myself a close friend to Pam.

"I was a really good friend. We ran together for all those years."

"Do you recall the last occasion on which you saw Pamela Bulik?"

I nodded. "April first, the Sunday before her death, we ran about five miles together from her house, toward the bay, and back."

"How was Pamela that day?"

"She was real happy," I said remembering our conversation. "We discussed the upcoming Jogger's Joynt half marathon and the Green Bay Marathon in May. Pam was

At four months pregnant, I testified at Bob Bulik's trial.

running extremely well—the best in her whole life—almost better than I was. And she'd never been able to beat me in a race."

"Were there any other runs that Pamela was interested in?"

"On May fifth was the Bonne Bell Race on Milwaukee's lakefront. When I went there to register I discovered that she'd preregistered and already sent in her entry fee. Because we were in the same age group I ran under her name...I ran the race for Pam." I'd managed to hold my emotions in check, but now blinked hard.

Lasee kindly waited a moment and then asked if I'd also seen Pam the Saturday before her death. I took a calming breath and said she'd run from her house to mine, where Barb Delong and I'd joined her to complete approximately fourteen miles that day. A fourth friend, Maureen Shaughnessy, had ridden along on her bike.

"Do you remember what you were talking about?" Lasee asked.

"Maureen had recently split up with a guy she'd been seeing for twelve years." I hesitated. "He'd been cheating on her. Pam said she understood what Maureen was going through and gave her some *Self* magazines with good articles on coping and helping you feel good about yourself."

I could still picture that day. We'd stopped for water at Pam's house and she'd gone through some boxes of magazines to find the specific ones she'd mentioned. Then, as Maureen had strapped them to her bike, promising to return them, Pam had shaken her head with a courageous smile and said, "I don't need them anymore."

From the witness stand, I now added that Maureen and Pam had also made plans to attend a self-help seminar at UWGB over the summer. "There was one earlier, but Pam was going to be in the Bahamas so she couldn't go."

I'd been keeping tabs on the jury. The fourteen sets of eyes were focused on me. Thankfully no one was dozing. At IBM, I frequently presented to clients and would watch their facial expressions and body language, but this was not my usual bunch. All I could do was to truthfully relate the past, while trying to reveal a bit of what had made Pam endearing to me.

"Now you've indicated that Pamela was running pretty well at this particular time, is that right?"

"It was just unbelievable." Like in the prosecutor's office, I answered questions about Pam's running, her weight loss, and her lack of recent leg problems. After I stated that I'd never known

Pam to soak her legs before a run, Lasee asked, "Did she ever soak her legs after she ran?"

"She and Bob would invite people to use their hot tub after a run. Then she would soak her legs."

Lasee glanced at the jurors, apparently pleased. He then asked,

Bulik hot tub after 1983 New Year's Run

"Do you remember ... the morning Pamela died?"

As I nodded, my baby kicked wanting to be part of the action. Gently resting my hand on the spot, I said, "I expected Pam to be at the Jogger's Joynt race ... I even had what's called a Red Plate that says YOU'RE SPECIAL. I was giving it to her that day."

"Now, did this run go near the Bulik home?"

"It went on the street below their home. Because Pam hadn't been at the start, I expected to see her waiting on the corner with her kids to cheer us on." I tipped my head toward the jury. "She was very supportive. But when she wasn't there it went through my mind that there was something really wrong."

I knew Larry was going to ask me "the damaging question," beating Bill Appel to the punch. "Now, you remember making the statement to the police to the effect that you hoped Pamela didn't kill herself?"

As I said, "That's right," I watched furtive whispers being exchanged within the spectator section.

"Do you remember why you made that statement?"

"Bob was out of town. You know, Pam was like any of us," I said, my eyes locating a woman on the jury that was about the same age as me. "She was more depressed and disappointed on weekends when he wasn't around. Pam had to take all the responsibility for their home and the kids. Also, most of our social activities as couples happened on weekends, like going out for fish. If Bob were home she would go, otherwise she often stayed home. She may have felt left out sometimes." I looked down at my hands for a moment. "That weekend Bob was gone again. I guess I thought she might have done something, but I don't really know why... It was just sort of a feeling." I was trying to explain, but didn't know how.

"If you'd known that Bob was at home, would you have thought that?" Lasee rested his hand on the witness box, surveying me.

"No," I shook my head firmly.

"Do you know if Pam was seeing professional counselors?"

"Yes, she was, but on March thirtieth I went out to lunch with Pam. She told me that she and Bob were not going to be seeing a counselor anymore because Bob felt it wasn't necessary."

Appel abruptly interjected, "Mrs. Drews really should not be allowed to say what Mr. Bulik supposedly said."

I blushed, realizing my mistake.

"Well, if you have an objection, just make it." Greenwood waited.

Even though Appel looked peeved, he kept his mouth shut.

"I have nothing further." Lasee gave me a broad smile and sat down.

The easy part was over. My stomach churned as I watched Bill

Appel rise. He positioned himself in close proximity to Bob, placing him in my line of sight. I flushed further at Bob's penetrating gaze.

Appel began pleasantly enough saying, since I'd been a very good friend of Pam's, "I would imagine it's difficult for you to appear today and testify?"

"Yeah," I said, tentatively, not sure where he was going.

"Your very first thought, when you saw Mrs. Bulik was not at the corner to cheer you on…was I hope she didn't commit suicide?"

"That's right." I shifted my body in the uncomfortable witness chair.

"You must have known then, Mrs. Bulik was depressed?"

My eyes met Appel's. "She was extremely depressed back in January, or around Christmastime, and improved a ton since that point. But the real bad times still come back to my mind."

He paused, trying a different tact. "Mrs. Drews, you've indicated that you ran with Mrs. Bulik the weekend before her death…Her running diary to your left reports running with Lynda. It's L-Y-N-D-A. That would be you, wouldn't it?"

"Right."

"Did you run with Mrs. Bulik many times throughout that spring, February and March?"

"Right."

"And during those runs you talked with her? …She shared her problems with you?"

"Yes."

"And again your first thought, when you did not see her that morning, is you hoped she didn't commit suicide?"

Nodding, I brushed my bangs away from my eyes. "I don't know why, but that's what I thought."

"In fact, you told the police that you changed your mind…and have now concluded she did not commit suicide because you now know, at the time of her death, she was not wearing any clothes."

Appel's brow wrinkled with skepticism.

"When that statement was taken, the only thing I thought caused her death was drowning in the water. I knew nothing about carbon monoxide in the van."

"I appreciate—"

"I didn't know any of the other things." I frowned at him. "You've got to wonder how somebody can drown in a bathtub. When I learned Pam wasn't wearing any clothes, then I said she didn't commit suicide because she would never have wanted to be seen naked."

Appel jumped back in, taking charge. "When I learned you were going to be a witness for the government...I called you up and asked to talk to you...But you did not want to talk to me, did you? You told me that you and your friends were all against Bob."

I nodded. "We all think he did it."

The spectators again murmured.

"And with that thought in your mind, you come to court today, to testify?" Appel's tone was harsh.

"That's right." Color rose from under my dress's red collar as I glanced at Larry Lasee. Surprisingly, he gave me a thumbs-up sign, boosting my confidence.

"Now, Mr. Lasee had you testify that Pam was not having any trouble with her legs or thighs or anything prior to her death?"

"She didn't complain one time on Saturday and Sunday about it."

"How about anytime during...March of 1984?"

"Since Pam lost her weight—nearly thirty pounds—I don't remember her mentioning anything about her legs bothering her." I hesitated. "She was tired, physically tired, because she was running many, many more miles."

"Your statement, to this jury, is that Mrs. Bulik was not having trouble with her legs or sore thighs and things like that in...February and March of 1984?"

"She used to with her calves around her varicose vein area."

"If I told you, in that running diary next to you, there were twenty to twenty-two entries from February seventh to March twenty-fifth of '84 about sore tired thighs, would you find that surprising?" Appel's eyes sparked beneath thick eyebrows.

"She might've had tired thighs just because she was running more miles." Again, my eyes met his. "But they weren't bad enough that she complained about them to me. Prior years, when she had leg problems, it was the number one priority."

I could see Bill Appel was not giving up. He reiterated his words about Pam's running entries.

"Objection," Lasee finally broke in, coming to my rescue. "It's argumentative."

"It's argumentative," Greenwood agreed. "Sustained."

Appel looked extremely unhappy with me. "When you ran with Mrs. Bulik on March thirty-first and April first, she was in good spirits … feeling happy, no problems with depression?"

On Saturday I knew Pam had mentioned being disappointed when Bob hadn't call her from Yuma, but I also knew that she'd quickly snapped out of her depression. What's more, she'd spent most of the run counseling Maureen, so I responded, "If anything, I said she was trying to help somebody else with her problems on Saturday. Then, after running on Sunday, Pam and I sat at her table eating some cranberry bread that Bob had made." My voice was adamant, "We were having a really nice day."

I often reflected back to the last time I saw Pam. In addition to the bread, we'd gone through multiple cups of coffee, and on a caffeine-high, laughed and chattered away. I'd remained seated when she'd stood up, energized, and had begun preparing food that she then had planned to freeze for their Bahamas' vacation. As I'd left that day, I'd told Pam how proud I was of her. She'd hugged me tight and whispered in my ear, "Lynda, I've never had a sister, but if I did, I'd choose you."

Now, returning from my thoughts, I was flooded with relief as a tightlipped Bill Appel sat down.

Larry Lasee asked me one last question. "Did Pam ever mention anything to you, suggesting that she was considering killing herself?"

I shook my head hard. "She never said she would kill herself."

Greenwood excused me and called for a ten-minute recess. I rushed down the aisle, out of the courtroom, and past my friends. In a bathroom stall I broke into tears. Were hormones making me so sensitive? Just as I'd feared, I felt Bill Appel had attacked me.

The door to the bathroom creaked open. "Lynda, are you in there?" Beezie's hesitant voice asked. "Are you all right?"

"I'm okay." I blew my nose on toilet paper and then left the stall to wash my hands. "I know crying is silly, but I felt Bill Appel was accusing me of lying."

"Lynda, I'm sure you did great up there! Don't take it so personally. He was just doing his job."

I shook my head. "I can't believe I just said, we all think Bob did it!"

Her eyes widened. "He actually asked you that?"

I nodded.

"Well Lynda, we nearly all do."

≈

For a week I'd heard about the trial secondhand. Now that would change. I found a spot next to Marcy and settled in, ready to listen to the testimony of Beezie, Sylvia, and Pam's former school colleagues. Each friend would provide some personal insight into the last days of Pam's life.

From the stand, Beezie told Finne that after Bob's affair had been discovered, she and Pam had talked nearly every day. Their last conversation, however, had been on Sunday, April 1, six days before Pam's death.

Like me, Finne had to ask Beezie a harmful question before the defense. "Mrs. MacNeil, during that period of time, did Pam express to you thoughts that things might be easier for Bob and the kids if she were dead?"

"In October, Pam did tell me that," Beezie admitted. "It was like the day after she discovered the affair."

While the spectators around me nudged their neighbors, I checked the jurors' reaction. A few of them had frowns on their faces. Back in November, Beezie had shared Pam's distressing comment with me. At that time, we'd both discussed how Bob's affair was awful, but things could've been far worse for her—Pam's kids or she could've had some incurable disease. In addition, Pam would never have wanted "that woman" living in her house and raising her children...It was crazy, but that's exactly what had happened. Even though I'd felt relieved when Beezie had said, "Pam's never uttered those words again," I knew that her comment had continued to gnaw at me, especially when Pam was particularly down.

Now on the stand, Beezie was saying that the period from October through December had been the lowest in Pam's life, but by January and February, when she'd returned to work, Pam's outlook had continually improved. During March, Beezie said that Pam had often talked about being a single parent. "I think she was finally able to decide that she could do this on her own, although it would have been difficult... Pam was stronger than I'd ever seen her. I think she'd finally made up her mind that if Bob was going to decide to be with Linda, Pam could accept that."

Finne nodded his approval and moved on. "Do you recall being at the Bulik home in August of 1983 when Lynda Drews came to the house?"

"Yes." Beezie looked frustrated at having to zip her mouth. Instead of being able to explain that she'd been there to assist Pam after her life threatening assault, Beezie had to leave the jurors in the dark. "That day," she said, "I was alone in the family room doing some stitchery. The television was not on...or the radio. The only thing I could hear was the clock ticking. Lynda drives a diesel Oldsmobile, and she knocked on the back patio door, scaring me half to death...I didn't hear her car."

"Didn't hear the car come in the driveway?" Finne asked checking the jury's reaction.

"No."

"Weren't able to hear it when it was in the cul-de-sac or coming down the driveway?"

"No."

The prosecutor raised his eyebrows and sat down.

Bill Appel referred to Beezie's police statement. "You told Detective Parins...that Pam would go into depression when something surfaced about Bob and Linda?"

"She would become very upset about it," Beezie said, her sharp eyes focused on Appel, "but she could always talk about it. She was more in a rage rather than depression. You and I are defining depression differently."

Appel pointed at her comment. "Did you tell Detective Parins depression?"

She reviewed it. Her mouth tightened into a stubborn line. "Evidently, I did."

Appel next addressed Beezie's last conversation with Pam, on Sunday, April 1 at 10:00 p.m. "She was upset and crying?" he asked.

"Yes she was. Her daughter was sick, and Pam was leaving for a conference in Milwaukee the next morning. Bob wasn't going to be home because he was stranded in Denver."

"But those two factors—the husband being stranded...and her daughter being sick—drove her to the point of tears?" Appel seemed dubious.

"Well, she was upset because she didn't have anyone to leave her children with when she had to leave town at six in the morning." Beezie crossed her arms. "I think I would be upset, too."

"...And you know that after her husband came home, he took the children down to Milwaukee to see her...because Mrs. Bulik was upset?"

Full of skepticism, Beezie said, "Bob—told me that he did."

Moments later, as Linda Maves, a former colleague of Pam's settled into the witness stand, Beezie squeezed in beside me.

On April 2 and 3, Linda said, she and Pam had attended the Milwaukee educators' conference together, and met for lunch on that Tuesday. "Pam thought there was some hope...she felt the marital problems would be resolved." Pam hadn't mentioned that

Bob and the kids had driven down the evening of April 2, even though Linda said she'd asked her where the children were. Pam had just explained that they were home with Bob.

Debra Fantini said she'd last talked with Pam at school on Thursday, April 5. Because Debra had been a runner for ten years, their conversations had often revolved around the sport. "Pam had lost at least twenty-six pounds, and was in great shape ... She had just run ten miles Wednesday night at an eight minute pace, and I was congratulating her ... I asked her if she was sore ... She said no, just a little tired."

When Debra explained that she'd only known Pam to soak her legs in the Buliks' hot tub after a run, I felt better. Someone else had substantiated my testimony. I then watched Appel step forward to put Debra on the spot, like he had me.

"Your testimony is that Mrs. Bulik never complained about pains in her legs, or having trouble with her legs, while running?" Appel waited.

"I said she did not complain that Thursday."

"Had you heard her complain before?"

"No, not that I recall."

He frowned, picking up Pam's running log. "Would it surprise you to find out ... that from February seventh of 1984 until March twenty-fifth of 1984, she had some twenty to twenty-two entries ... complaining about sore thighs and sore legs?"

"No." Her eyes were steady. "Not with the mileage she was running."

Nancy Gloudeman, a reading and language teacher at Freedom High School said she'd last talked to Pam on Friday, April 6. Since Pam had completed her special education certification the previous summer, she'd told Nancy that this summer, she was looking forward to spending more time with Abby and Alex.

"Was it your impression that Pamela was devoted to the children?" Finne asked.

"Very much so."

Sylvia Madden said, around suppertime on Friday, April 6, she'd seen Pam at the Port Plaza Mall on the second floor of the Boston Store. She'd been in a hurry shopping and looking for Abby, who had just wandered off. "Pam looked like she had just come from school and was dressed up. She looked very good, very alert."

Finne asked Sylvia whether her son had been scheduled to baby-sit for the Bulik children the weekend of Pam's death?

"Yes...Saturday night. Pam was planning on going to a faculty party in Freedom, Wisconsin."

In response to the prosecutor's question about Pam's attitude, during the last few weeks of her life, Sylvia said, "In March, I thought Pam's outlook was very positive. She was becoming more confident, and was realizing that she could handle a lot of the family situations she didn't think she'd be able to do. She was looking to the future."

"What about her physical condition?"

"Excellent!" In addition to Pam's running regimen, Sylvia said that on the evening of Tuesday, April 3, they'd both purchased a three-month membership at the New Horizons Health Club. "Pam was going to go there to work out, oh, at least three, four times a week."

With bright eyes, Royce Finne sat down as Bill Appel stood. "Mrs. Madden, you were given access to Mr. Bulik's home by him, were you not?"

Sylvia concurred and explained that, in addition to having secured a key from Bob at the time of his arrest, she'd helped Beezie pack up Pam's things. Sylvia agreed that Bob had provided the two women full access to his home while his family had been in the Bahamas.

Sylvia also confirmed that after Bob had made bail, her daughter had played at the Bulik home and accompanied the family on a white-water rafting excursion. Then, this school year, she'd shared car pool responsibilities with Bob during their daughters' basketball team tryouts, but added, "Our children arranged that."

"From knowing Mr. Bulik," Appel gestured Bob's way, "you would agree he's totally devoted to his children?"

"I assume so."

Sylvia next identified the May 25 church bulletin she'd removed from the Buliks' refrigerator and subsequently turned over to the police. On the back she said there was a paragraph that had been written by Bob, just prior to his arrest. Sylvia explained that it was text to be inserted into Bob's will. In the event of his death, he was awarding custody of Abby and Alex to Linda VandenLangenberg.

Appel asked, "Do you remember telling Bob Bulik's father, John Bulik, that one of the reasons you brought up ... the church letter bulletin, with Bob's writing on the back, is because you were concerned about his depression and committing suicide? He was depressed and emotionally affected by his wife's death, wasn't he?"

"I can't say that for sure." Sylvia's eyes met Appel's. "My concern was that he was going to commit suicide."

On the morning that Pam died, Sylvia agreed that she'd seen Bob in his van at about 9:30, heading west, in the general direction of Preble High School.

"And he waved at you, didn't he?" Appel tilted his head with brow raised.

"Yes, he did." Sylvia also confirmed that she hadn't seen anyone else in the van.

As each friend had testified, the prosecution team had posed the same question: "Did Pam ever give you any impression that she was contemplating suicide?" Other than Pam's October comment to Beezie, each friend adamantly stated that Pam had never mentioned any such thing.

Ending on this high note, the prosecution rested its case against Bob.

13

Fugue and Family

"The State's case is completed in chief," Judge Greenwood announced. "If you have any motions, I'll entertain them now."

In the spectator section, Beezie and I were again situated beside Marcy for the rest of the trial. Sylvia had returned to her classroom after we'd eaten lunch at the Stein Supper Club, where the jurors had also dined, segregated inside a private room. They had yet to return to the courtroom as Bill Appel now stood.

"Thank you, your Honor." The motion, he said he'd like to make was to move the court to dismiss Bob's charge of first-degree murder. "We have to have some clear proof ... that Mr. Bulik intentionally committed an act intending to cause the death of his wife and I don't see it here."

Royce Finne retorted, "It's apparent to me that Mr. Appel has been hearing a different case than the one the jury has, but for the record we resist the motion."

We three held our collective breath until the judge's voice boomed, "Motion is denied."

It was show time for the defense.

With the jury now seated, Dr. Ralph Baker took the stand. In addition to being the medical director for Green Lake County Mental Health Clinic, he was the psychiatric consultant to both Winnebago County Mental Health Clinic and Lutheran Social Services. The doctor said his credentials had given him the opportunity to testify in hundreds of criminal cases. He'd reviewed Pam's autopsy report, the notes of her therapists, and the police statements in preparation for today.

I assumed Appel's intended goal for this expert witness would be to cast doubt on the validity of the State's earlier witnesses' beliefs.

First, Dr. Baker shared his observations about Pam's emotional state. He'd noted numerous references concerning her depression, starting with Pam's "absolute state of despair" when she'd discovered Bob's affair in October, her own comments in her journal and running logs, and Dr. O'Neill's belief, noted in late March, that Pam still required months of treatment to deal with her acute stress syndrome. Baker then pointed out the police statement of a neighbor of the Buliks, Mary Teixeira, who had talked to Pam as recently as the Friday evening before her death. At that time, Pam had expressed to Mary that she'd been feeling "depressed and down."

I caught Beezie's eyes. Pam's comment upset me especially when I added it to another regret. At our April fourth Fun Run, Pam hadn't shown up. When the hostess, Barb Eversole, had called her home, Pam had told her, "Things are not good." I'd meant to follow-up, but instead had decided to wait until we could talk in depth while running the Joggers Joynt half marathon, but of course, by then, it was too late.

Baker was now saying that the results from Pam's MMPI, completed in November 1983, had revealed that Pam had a tendency to be impulsive. And a person, who was impulsive, Baker said, was a person who did things on the spur of the moment, without necessarily planning things out for long periods of time. The MMPI also indicated that Pam had hysterical tendencies. That went along with impulsiveness. If a person was hysterical, they might do something on the basis of their emotions.

Dr. Baker pointed out that Pam had suffered from low self-esteem. He highlighted her comment to Mrs. MacNeil that perhaps Bob and the children would be better off without her. "It's the kind of thinking—I'm not even good enough to have the children." Pam's impulsive/hysterical traits and her low self-esteem, Baker said, were likely to be long lasting. They'd been part of her personality, whereas her depression might have tended to wax and wane.

In Dr. Baker's professional opinion, he felt that Pam's depression had increased the risk that she might have committed suicide. Because of this, he'd been surprised that none of Pam's therapists had ever noted that Pam had suicidal tendencies or that she had not. He felt an initial suicide evaluation should be done and then periodically repeated. To do this, Baker said a therapist would need to ascertain whether their patient represented a suicidal risk by talking to them about their thoughts and their feelings. As the therapist gained rapport, and the patient's trust, the therapist could then ask the patient if they'd considered suicide, if they'd ever had a plan in their mind. "If they are suicidal, you make a contract with them to call you before ever trying to commit such an act."

Appel looked intently at Baker. "If that process were done, it would be normal practice, in your profession, to make a notation in the medical records of that?"

"Yes. If anything, you put negative and positive indications in the record that this person denied any suicidal thoughts. And I do teach that to my residents who I'm training to be psychiatrists."

Appel gave a knowing nod. He next asked the doctor to address the topic of dissociative fugue states.

In the newspapers, I'd been surprised to read that even though Dr. O'Neill had said that a dissociative fugue state, initiated by anxiety and stress, could've been one possible cause for Pam's December memory loss, it had not been his "first choice." It now appeared as if Pam had simply grabbed hold of this option to explain away her doubts concerning Bob. But O'Neill's testimony had also brought back the surprising conversation I'd had with Barb Delong. Because she'd told me that the police had shown little interest in Bob's revelation, that Pam had gone into a fugue state and drowned, I'd forgotten about it.

So had this condition been a factor in Pam's death or not? I leaned forward to hear Dr. Baker's opinion.

He was saying that one type of dissociative state was called a fugue state, in which, for example, someone might travel to another city, return, and not remember any of the travel period. Eventually, the individual would come out of that state with no memory of, say, the past twenty-four hours of his or her life. Someone talking to a person in that state might not notice much difference since the individual could still carry on a conversation. In a more severe dissociative state, Baker said, a person might appear to be in a stupor and would be uncommunicative.

Appel asked if a layperson could visually discern the difference between an individual in a severe dissociative state from an individual immobilized by, perhaps, the toxic effect of carbon monoxide?

"I think it would be hard," Baker said and elaborated. If, for example, somebody would come into an emergency room in one of those states, he didn't think the examining room physician would know the difference without conducting an examination.

Appel seemed satisfied and next asked the doctor to address the subject of carbon monoxide poisoning.

Baker said that after reading Pam's autopsy report, he'd referenced a standard manual on internal medicine to better understand the effects of carbon monoxide on the human body. "I didn't know 48 percent was that high." Also, Baker admitted, he'd been surprised to discover that a 10 to 30 percent carbon monoxide level could cause some cognitive impairment.

"In terms of cognitive impairment are we talking about ability to think rationally?" Appel asked.

Baker concurred, and added that carbon monoxide, also at the 10 to 30 percent level, could impair memory and the ability to perform calculations and higher-level kinds of tasks.

Pleased, Appel sat down.

It was Lasee's turn. "Doctor, you concede that you were surprised to find that at such a low level of [carbon monoxide] concentration, that there could be memory loss, is that correct?"

"Not permanent memory loss, but an inability to remember."

"Are you aware, Doctor, that studies have shown there is no memory loss without a coma?"

"Somewhat," he hedged.

"You have no specific expertise in the area of carbon monoxide induced poisoning, do you?"

A flush appeared above Baker's white collar. "I'm not an expert on carbon monoxide, no."

"And the knowledge, you indicated, is what you gained just in reviewing that text. When was that?"

"Last night," Baker said, turning a brighter hue.

His point made, Lasee moved on. "In terms of this dissociative state, you referred to a fugue state, is that correct?"

"That's one example, yes." Then matching Dr. O'Neill's earlier testimony, Baker said that an individual in this state would usually not be self-destructive or suicidal.

Lasee's intense gaze met the doctor's. "Just so the record is clear, it is not your opinion that Pamela Bulik committed suicide, is it?"

As Baker cautiously said, "No," the prosecutor smiled, his eyes straying to the jurors.

To assess Pam's potential for suicide, Baker agreed she'd had a number of healthy methods for coping with, what he termed, her roller-coaster depression. Pam had sought out treatment, been actively running, and verbalized her problems with family, friends, and doctors. There had also been no evidence that Pam had ever been physically self-destructive, and other than the MMPI assessment in November 1983, no evidence of any impulsive or hysterical acts.

In Pam's journal she'd listed six categories of personal goals. Lasee had Baker read the ones she'd noted for creative self-expression. These included: to develop piano skills, play in the symphony, sing in a choir, and learn to write poetry. Because Pam had documented these, and the positive steps to achieve them,

Baker confirmed that this would have lowered Pam's potential for suicide as well.

The prosecutor located another section in Pam's journal. "Mr. Appel has pointed out that Pamela apparently had problems with her self-image, with her self-concept." Lasee had Dr. Baker read Pam's "Success" and "Self-esteem" lists:

- I have developed into a warm and caring person.
- I have achieved a feeling of success in an area of professional work where I previously thought myself incapable and inept.
- I have been a faithful and loving wife to the best of my abilities and knowledge.
- I have been a loving and nurturing mother, having given love, life, and meaning to my children...
- I have achieved a level of fitness and self-worth never before thought possible...
- I like my smile and the warmth it conveys when I truly feel happy and content...
- And I like my capacity to accept, understand, and forgive.

"Does that indicate relatively healthy self-concept and self-esteem?" Lasee asked.

When Pam wrote that, Baker said, he didn't doubt that she'd been feeling good about herself, been working on her self-esteem, been making progress.

Lasee nodded. Possibly ready to tackle a vulnerable area, his forehead now creased. "Doctor, do you feel that someone who had a professional therapeutic relationship with an individual would have a more valid opinion, on the ultimate question, whether or not that person was capable of attempting suicide?"

"Well it has its advantages and disadvantages in terms of its validity."

"Let's talk about that suicide evaluation, for instance. Would it be important for whoever conducted this evaluation to have some sort of rapport with the patient?"

The doctor said this was critical. "If you don't have rapport with the person, when you are asking them if they are considering suicide, they could say no. They could lie to you."

"Does it appear that Pamela developed a fairly significant rapport with Dr. O'Neill?"

"My impression is that she had rapport with all of her doctors."

"You feel that if someone had a substantial relationship with a professional, they felt they could trust, that would diminish the potential of suicide?"

"That's probably one of the most helpful things, if they have somebody they could call rather than acting on their feelings of wanting to kill themselves."

Lasee asked Baker to turn to the journal page titled "Appreciation" and to read the third entry from the bottom.

The doctor read:

> For having found a caring professional person who cares enough to give the most of what he can to help me.

"Would this suggest to you that Pamela apparently had some type of relationship with someone?"

"I would think so. She says so."

"Unfortunately, Doctor, you never had the opportunity to speak to Pamela, did you?"

"No."

"You feel your opinion would be more valuable if you would have had that opportunity?"

Baker acknowledged that it would have been more valuable if he could have examined Pam, "certainly the day before or the week before her death."

As Lasee placed the journal on the evidence table, the set of his mouth looked satisfied.

Bill Appel retrieved the journal, opening it to a particular spot. "There's a page here entitled, 'Why I Don't Like Myself.'" Appel read:

- I have not been an understanding and more compassionate wife and given more of what Bob needed.
- Because I'm not naturally as beautiful and physically attractive as is Bob.
- Because I react from my heart and emotions and not logically and calculatingly.

Baker agreed these were statements about Pam's self-perception. "And of course her goal, and the goal of the therapists, was to try to get her to feel better overall." Baker felt that 90 percent

1982 Milwaukee Marathon Bob ran full and Pam ran half.

of Pam's journal entries were positive. A therapist tried to teach a patient to set realistic goals, and by reaching them, the individual should begin to feel good about his or her progress. But, Baker concurred with Appel, "If you set unrealistic goals and you can't achieve them, then you can cut the other way and can become depressed."

≈

It had been difficult hearing my friend's private feelings and innermost thoughts today. Until this stage, I'd been buffered. Since I'd first known Pam, it had been a given that I'd often need to provide the right words to boost her confidence and self-image. But when she'd been in college, things might have been different.

Back then, Randy Albright*, who'd coached Bob's college swim team, had been about the same age as Pam and single. Between Bob and Pam, Albright had considered her to be the outstanding one. "Pam was my swim team manager and such a special person, a fantastic young lady. It had nothing to do with her looks, though she was sleek, blond, and fair. Her personality was what had made her remarkable. She was such a neat person and was going through a tough phase then because her brother was a POW. If you put together a human ladder, I'd like to have Pam around me more than Bob." Albright had known Pam would be successful.

Another local runner, who worked in administration for a Green Bay area school, had also attended the University of Wisconsin Stevens Point with Pam. Don Zander said she'd been in the center of everything with loads of friends. Pam's positive and upbeat personality had made her fun to be around. She'd had a great smile — genuine and real. If she hadn't been so enamored of Bob, Don said there'd been a number of guys on campus who would have asked her out.

In college, Pam (center) was in Sue (Christensen) Weimer's wedding

When I'd first met Pam in 1975, like our fathers' alcoholism, low self-esteem had been a trait we'd had in common.

I'd known my husband since grade school where we'd played sardines and kick the can together.

Jim had been the cute, freckled, blond kid. From the hoods to the brains to the athletes, he'd been everybody's friend. By tenth grade he'd never dated, preferring sports to any girl. I'd had a few fleeting dates and innumerable crushes—Jim among them. With encouragement from friends I'd asked him to a Sadie Hawkins dance. He'd turned me down. The following year I'd been humiliated whenever I'd seen him or his friends, so I'd been astounded when he'd asked me to Junior Prom. Jim had been the star basketball forward and top runner in our high school. Now, unbelievably, he'd picked me.

Attending the same college, it had been a whirlwind of excitement dating UW-La Crosse's top cross country and track star. Jim's aura had included me. My identity had become entwined with his. During our first years of marriage in Green Bay, I'd still enjoyed basking in Jim's limelight, being known as the wife of the local running celebrity. Then, as I gradually gained a sense of my own self-worth, through my job and running, instead of believing that Jim's persona defined me, my own uniqueness emerged.

Throughout Pam's life, she'd had a special quality that her friends had always perceived. Inexplicably, she had not. Today, while Dr. Baker testified, it really hit me how devastating it was that in the last few months of Pam's life, she'd finally been recognizing her own unique potential. But the quandary was, that even as Pam had been succeeding in her eyes and quite possibly Bob's, the other woman had refused to give up *his* relentless pursuit.

◇◇◇◇◇◇◇◇◇◇◇◇◇◇◇◇◇◇◇◇◇

Both Kapalins were present for day seven of the Bulik trial. Their shoulders looked weighted down by their unbearable loss. Only four days had passed since Melissa's death. It seemed so wrong that Daryl had to appear, but his testimony was required. Kathy had insisted on being there to provide him moral support.

Bill Appel started out slowly, empathetically, asking Daryl where he worked.

"The House of Ryan, a Dodge dealership in Green Bay. I'm the parts manager there."

"Do you know my client, Robert Bulik?"

Bob gave Daryl a tentative nod, who, without reciprocating, said, "Yes, I do."

Since Melissa's death, Daryl's neutrality had changed. At the crash site, he'd watched the rescue squad's determined effort to save his daughter even though she had already been dead. He now believed, if Bob had called 911 when he'd first found Pam in the van, she could still be alive. Where Melissa didn't have a chance to live, Pam certainly did, but Bob's inaction simply took it away.

"Mr. Kapalin," Appel said, "I've asked you to come to relate to the jury an incident you saw sometime last year…"

On December 19, Daryl said he'd come out of the backdoor of the parts room, near the service department where the Buliks' van had been in for repair. Pam had been getting out of the passenger side of their blue car and walking around the vehicle to get in the other side. "I said hello to her first, and she said hello back. Pam then got in her car and drove away."

It had been around 5:00 p.m. —quitting time. Daryl hadn't seen Bob, but figured he must've been the one picking up the van. After Daryl had retrieved his keys and coat, he'd climbed into his car to head for home. "And as I was driving along, I noticed a car up ahead hit the snow bank of the roadway, back into the road, and then proceed to a stop sign, oh, maybe 300 yards from that point. I don't know if it was Pam's car or not. I wasn't positive at that time. I noticed cars were moving away from that vehicle to protect themselves. Whoever it was, got to the stop sign, made a right turn, and again hit the median strip. I did suspect it could be Pam. I turned and tried to go around the block to see if she was all right, but I never saw her after that." Daryl confirmed that the car had been going in the general direction of the Buliks' home.

"Did you talk with Mrs. Bulik about that incident at some time after that?" Appel asked.

"Yes, I did … She did not recall that evening, as far as driving or anything, and I guess I was concerned after I heard that."

"When you first saw her at the House of Ryan and said hello, did you feel there was anything unusual about that?"

"I did feel she was distant at that time. But knowing that the Buliks were having marital issues, I thought Pam was just having a bad moment and wasn't herself."

Assistant DA Finne now asked, "Mr. Kapalin, you're not positive that car was being driven by Pam Bulik, are you?"

"I'm positive Pam was driving a car, but it was dark outside and there was heavy traffic, so I'm not positive she was the one that hit the snow bank."

"All of us, from time to time, have things on our mind, or problems get in our way, and we get preoccupied, maybe appear distant to other people, is that right?" Finne asked.

"Yes we do." Daryl's weary eyes briefly sought out Kathy's.

"Now, you saw Pamela Bulik again in March of 1984...What was she doing?"

"I noticed a runner coming at me on the sidewalk, and just the movement of the runner, and the attitude was one of being very happy and serene, running along and having a very good time by herself."

"And that was Pam?"

"Yes, it was."

≈

Everyone had speculated whether the Bulik children would be taking the stand on their father's behalf. Other than Bob, they'd been the only individuals in the home that could possibly shed more light into their mother's confusing death. So when each child's name was actually called, there was a rustle and stir in the courtroom. The spectators and jurors, alike, craned their necks to catch the first glimpse of Pam's children before each would take their turn on the witness stand.

Abby was outfitted in a bright red sweater and a matching plaid skirt. When asked by Bill Appel for the date she'd turned ten, she hesitated, thinking hard, before blurting it out. At her slip in memory, a smile momentarily crossed her lips aimed at her dad. Those who had known her mother could see Abby's striking resemblance.

At twelve, Alex could be picked out of any crowd as Pam's child, too. He said he was a B average student, while Abby stated that she'd earned four A's and one B on her last report card. Recently, she'd tried out for the basketball team and made it.

"Good for you!" Appel smiled.

"Everybody made it," Abby said, modestly.

In addition to playing basketball, football, and golf, Alex said he liked to run. Pride of accomplishment briefly crossed his face when he announced that he'd recently completed a triathlon with his dad.

Appel then gently proceeded with each child, asking them about the weekend their mother had died.

On Friday, April 6, Alex testified that he'd eaten lasagna prepared by his mom before leaving for an evening of roller-skating at St. Mary's. A friend's mother had driven him home at around 9:45 p.m. About ten o'clock his mother and sister had walked in from shopping. They'd both bought swimsuits for their upcoming Bahamas trip. At this point, Alex said he'd still believed that his dad was in Colorado with the marines.

"Did your dad do anything for your mom before he left?" Appel asked.

"Yes, he bought her flowers," Alex quietly said, his voice displaying good control. "I saw them sitting on the counter."

"...Did you see your dad later that night?"

"Yes, I did." After Abby had gone to bed, Alex said he'd been using the computer in the family room. Around 10:30, both he and his mom had been surprised when his dad had entered the house through the door leading in from the garage. Since it had been late, his dad had told him to go to bed. Alex confirmed, for the prosecutor, that his mother had seemed fine and happy when he'd gone upstairs.

Appel asked Alex, "Where is your bedroom located?"

"It's on top of the stairs, right above the family room..."

"After you went to bed that night, Alex, did you hear any noise, or your mom and dad arguing or fighting or anything?"

"No, I didn't." Usually, he said, he could hear noises—like the TV—from his room, since his door was louvered, not solid.

Abby stated, while in bed, she hadn't heard any noises from downstairs either.

Both children were next asked to step through their recollections of the morning of Saturday, April 7.

Neither could remember whether there had been any windows open when they'd awakened, but both said they'd felt sick and dizzy. "I had a headache," Alex said, "and my stomach wasn't feeling good." In the past he'd had migraines, but that morning his headache had felt different. "When I have a migraine it usually hurts and I usually go to bed. And that morning it wasn't hurting. It was just kind of dizzy, more like." At the April 18 John Doe hearing, however, Alex had testified that his headache had felt like a migraine.

In court today, Alex said that after getting up he'd watched TV in the family room and tried a bite of a doughnut, but "it didn't feel so good." Then his sister had entered the room. At the John Doe, Alex had said that it had been about 7:45 a.m.

To get to the first floor, Abby explained that she'd had to slide down the stairs sitting on her bottom. "My dad ... told me to take an aspirin." She'd gotten one from her mom and dad's bathroom and returned to bed. Her dad had then brought up a bowl of cereal for her. Later, she'd eaten a second one downstairs.

"Do you remember, Abby, if you saw your mom at all Saturday morning?" Appel asked.

"Yes...When I was going into the bathroom, their door was slightly open and I saw her laying on her side in the bed." Her mom had appeared to be asleep, Abby said, and she'd been wearing something blue and red—possibly her running suit.

That morning, Alex related that he hadn't seen his mom, and

he couldn't remember if his dad had been up before him or afterward.

"Do you remember if your dad was doing anything that morning?" Appel asked.

"He was going to pick up the car at Preble."

"How do you know that?"

"He told me."

Alex had testified, at the John Doe, that his mother had rarely used the big bathtub, however, he'd heard water running into it, before his dad had left for Preble at about 7:30 a.m.

"Do you ever use that big bathroom area?" Appel asked.

"I used to," Alex said, "when I was littler."

While in bed, Abby said she'd also heard the water running. In the past, she'd used the big bathtub with her mom.

At the earlier hearing, Alex had testified that his dad had been away from the house for about five to fifteen minutes. After he'd returned with the vehicles, Alex's friend, Scott, had come over to see if Alex could go to the mall. "So I asked my dad and he said it was okay. And we arranged a time, and my dad brought us down there." Abby said that her dad had also agreed that she could invite her best friend, Allena, who lived on their cul-de-sac.

Before they'd left, Alex had taken his dog for a walk. Afterward, he said he'd felt better.

A key question concerned the actual time Bob had driven his children to the mall. At the John Doe, Alex said they'd left about nine o'clock. Today, he agreed that was right, and that he'd made plans to meet Scott by the big clock at about 9:30.

Finne asked Alex, "When you went down to the mall that morning, you took your van, right?"

He concurred.

"And the van has two captain chairs in front … and two bench seats behind … You sat on one of the bench seats, and your sister and her friend sat in the other?"

"Yes."

"So nobody was sitting in the seat next to your dad?"

As Alex said, "No," Finne glanced toward the jury and sat down.

Appel's final question for Alex was an important one for Bob's defense. The attorney asked if the master bathroom, off the foyer, had been used "just for your mom and dad, or do you kids use it, too?"

"We all use it."

≈

As Abby and Alex had testified, I'd been thinking of Pam. She would've been so proud of her children today.

14

Friendly Fire

Electricity crackled through the room when Robert Bulik's name was called. The spectators' usually restrained voices elevated to a roar knowing that the focus would now shift directly to the defendant himself.

I'd figured all along that Bob wouldn't pass up this chance to talk to the jury. After all, he'd tried during Appel's opening statement. Bob had the competitor's belief that he could deal with any challenge from his opponents. Per Johnson had told me how detailed and organized Bob had been while competing in triathlons, how he'd think through every contingency, even figuring out the best way to tie a shoelace to speed up his transitions between the swim, bike, and run. Today would simply be another test of Bob's skills.

In a gray suit, white shirt, and red tie, Bob looked handsome, though his deep-set, dark eyes seemed to have receded even further under his brow. If he was nervous, he didn't show it. He took the stand, his head held high and shoulders straight.

Appel's first goal was to have Bob personalize himself to the jury. As I listened, my memories about Pam couldn't help but intermingle. Other than her journals, the testimony of her therapists, and the brief testimony of her friends, how would the jury feel a connection to Pam? It seemed such a travesty to focus so much attention on the man who may have murdered her, yet not reveal the history surrounding the victim's life.

Bob spoke to the jury in his familiar calm voice—one I'd not heard for nearly eight months. As he reviewed his background, his demeanor was formal, evidence of his military training. Bob explained where he'd been born, and detailed his schooling, and extracurricular activities at the University of Wisconsin Stevens Point, including the swim and tennis teams, having been president of the Lettermen's Club, and recording secretary for his service fraternity. He also said that he'd met Pam in college.

Bonnie Metzger told me that while Bill had been a POW, she'd returned to school at UW-Stevens Point. Three days a week she and Pam had swum laps together. That was where Bonnie assumed Pam had first set eyes on Bob. "I could certainly see why she fell for him: athletic, very bright, a good looking kid—tall, dark and handsome."

UW-Stevens Point: portion of Letterman's Club – Bob in back row

UW-Stevens Point 1969— Pam on Cheerleading Squad

Fellow UW-Stevens Point graduates, Herb and Judy Waymire, told me that Bob and Pam had been one of the "big couples on campus." In addition to Pam's role as the manager of the men's swim team, she'd been a cheerleader, on the yearbook staff, and a member of both the Pem Club and Women's Recreation Association.

Bob was now telling the jury that he'd graduated from college in January of 1970 with a bachelor's degree in biology and a minor in physical education. Pam had graduated in June with a degree in physical education. They'd been married on August 15 of that same year.

According to Sue (Christensen) Weimer, it had been a candlelight service. She and Bonnie had been bridesmaids. "Oh my gosh!" Sue said. "The dresses were kind of amazing—empire waisted with red, white, and blue plaid skirts—and we're talking big plaid! Pam wore a turban with a veil. It was ugly, but interesting. Never guessed she would've picked it."

Bob next told the jury that after a short stint as a substitute teacher in Kenosha, he'd accepted a job at Southern Wisconsin Colony, a state-run institution for mentally challenged individuals. There he'd focused on preschool children. "One project that I worked on was reconstruction of a walker... My supervisor submitted that project to the state and I won a governor's award..." At that point, Bob said he'd committed to a three-year enlistment in the Marine Corps. While on active duty in California, he'd earned a master's degree at the US International University in San Diego.

"Those early years of their marriage, when he was in the marines, there were a lot of good things about Bob, positive things," Bonnie Metzger said. "And when Alex and Abby were born, he was right there." Bonnie thought he'd been a good person then, and a good husband. "More than anything else, he was a really good father."

After his discharge from the marines, Bob said he'd accepted a teaching position at the Green Bay Correctional Institution.

That's when I'd first met Bob, who, ironically, had been teaching physical education to criminals. I knew he'd never cared for that job. One of my husband's former East High students had worked at the correctional institution. Two of his co-workers had been there with Bob. They said he was intelligent and had often given suggestions for improvements, but he'd had a poor working relationship with others. Bob had expected favors and cooperation, but hadn't reciprocated. I knew Bob's goal had been to get into the Green Bay Schools. In 1979 he'd finally achieved it.

Bob looked intently at the jury as he next explained that upon his family's arrival in Green Bay, he'd also joined the local Marine Corps Reserve unit. He'd progressed to the rank of major before joining the Denver reserve unit, in which he'd earned about $7,800 last year. He'd also been chosen to participate in a school for amphibious warfare last summer, but had been unable to attend because of bail restrictions. This would've provided an additional $6,000 in income. "I'm under no further contractual obligation to the Marine Corps," he said with a proud jut to his chin. "I could quit at any time, essentially, but I choose to remain with them."

Bob next related the history behind his home mortgage. The Buliks had initially bought a ranch home in Green Bay. Four years later, they'd sold it and used the equity to buy their lot on Traders Court. To pay for the outside of their custom-built home they'd taken out a construction loan. When the family had moved in, little of the interior had been finished. To complete it they'd taken out second and third mortgages.

I knew that Bob and Pam had subcontracted some jobs, but they'd primarily worked side-by-side and completed much of the work themselves. Pam's friends had marveled at her skill with power tools. Most didn't even know their names, let alone their uses.

Bob told the jurors that their three mortgages had eventually been combined into the current fifteen-year VA mortgage with IDL. Both he and Pam had been working at the time and couldn't see any problem making the monthly payment. "We also decided that as the kids grew up, this would be a good way to provide some security for their college education."

As Appel moved into Bob's affair with Linda VandenLangenberg, I leaned forward, focusing on Bob's testimony, intent on not missing a single detail.

Bob told the jury that they'd already heard about his and Pam's long-standing marital problems. He believed Pam's discovery of his affair had brought everything out in the open. Initially they'd started counseling with Dr. Wellens, but Bob said, "I guess...the way he had us approach the problem was not real comfortable for either of us. We didn't make a whole bunch of progress until we went to see Jean Weidner. And after perhaps three or four sessions...I felt we were making some progress, some good progress."

"Bob," Appel's voice was intent, "during this time period, did you ever notice your wife, Pam, having certain types of emotional states or withdrawals?"

My ears perked up as Bob said there had been a number of times. The first, he explained, had occurred in middle or late November after his affair with Linda had come out. He and Pam had been sitting in their outside hot tub. "She just spaced out. She was not there with me." Bob had helped her out, and she'd willingly followed his lead. "As we walked into the house she came back to reality." He assumed the cold air had helped. "I encouraged her to tell Dr. O'Neill about it and she did."

Bob said he'd noticed some other brief lapses, when, for example, the kids would be sitting at the counter and would say, "Hey there," in front of Pam's face. She'd snap out of it, Bob said, but it had become apparent she'd not been attuned to what had been going on. Another time he'd found her down in the basement. "She was just kind of sitting and staring at what, I don't know." Again, he'd helped her to bed where she'd slept deeply for twelve hours.

I nudged Beezie and whispered, "I bet I know the reason Pam

was in the basement." I quickly wrote a note to catch Larry Lasee at the break.

Bob was now saying that friends had also seen Pam in that condition. "We were at a party one time...I wasn't in the room. She appeared to space out...dissociate is a better term...Pam didn't appear to be herself. I took her home. She was all right on the ride home."

My eyes connected with Beezie's. This was news to us. Pam had never remembered anything about that night.

Bob also mentioned how other people in the running group had told him about Daryl Kapalin's concern for Pam, how she hadn't remembered driving home from the Dodge dealership that day. "Pam told me, Dr. O'Neill indicated to her, that they were called fugue states."

"Did Pam, during this time period of December, January, February, March, have trouble sleeping?"

"Yes, often." From time to time, Bob said she'd taken medication prescribed by Dr. O'Neill to help her sleep.

Now Appel moved on and began to address the Buliks' separation.

Bob said that Pam had filed divorce papers at the end of January. Even though he'd moved out of the house, she'd asked him to watch Abby and Alex after school since Pam couldn't get home from Freedom until 4:30. "I had the opportunity to have contact with the children on a daily basis for those two weeks...They were visibly distraught." Bob looked down, showing his first signs of emotion. "It tore me up to see the kids in that kind of a situation...I didn't feel that I could just walk out on thirteen years of marriage." He'd felt that he couldn't leave his family in the chaos and pain he'd caused.

Dr. Wellens earlier approach to the proverbial triangle, Bob said, had been for him to say goodbye to either Pam or Linda. "I decided to attempt saying goodbye to Linda." By February 13, he'd moved back home. At that time, Jean Weidner had suggested that he and Pam start making small verbal contracts. Then, as the positive completion of those would occur, they'd gradually start rebuilding some of the trust and deep feelings they'd lost.

Appel handed Bob a three-ring binder and asked him to read something he'd written to Pam on January 29, right after she'd served him divorce papers.

"I'll try..." Bob said, clearing his throat.

My hurt can't be solely identified as separation distress. There were needs that were fulfilled by someone else, but change does occur. Look at yourself now. You can do all those things you never dreamed of before. You are strong. It's too bad I discovered the new you when I did. All my other inept suggestions at how you need to develop your own worth and your own pride, not that which was created by me, by having me around, didn't work. But you've lost the weight, improved your self-image, related better with the kids.

And change for me can occur, also. I need to be free of hurt... It would take as much work for you as it would for me. You have one job: to forgive me, then attempt to forget the pain of the last two years, and the last five months in particular. I have two jobs: to forgive you for the pain that I have felt led to an affair, then to give up and forget that affair. It won't be easy for either of us.

I suggested last night, and this morning, that I need you to be open to me, and try with me contract time. And I would take your word for it. Faith and love for one year. I, in turn, would honestly say good-bye to that other relationship. It will hurt me, also, for a long time, but I'm willing to bet, we'll both have that sparkle back before the end of that year.

As Bob's voice faded away, I saw Appel give him a kind look while retrieving the binder. I frowned. Now knowing that Pam had heard those same words from Bob during her emotion-filled weeks of separation, I could see why she had, again, wanted to believe in him.

Appel had selected a card, which Bob now identified as the one that Pam had written to him when he'd been heading out to Yuma,

Arizona, the weekend before her death. "She generally gave me cards whenever I left for a drill weekend. I usually carry a flight bag and an open leather briefcase with me. And she will sometimes put a card in either one of them."

Rather than having Bob read it, Appel slipped on his glasses and began:

Everything is fine, will be fine, as long as I keep looking forward and believe we are together in spirit and love. I wish emotionally I was stronger and I am trying to be. At times I feel so overwhelmed by the upward and uphill climb, to a level of peace and harmony and trust and faith in our joint commitment to our relationship. I guess I've longed to hear deep and meaningful ways in which I fulfill your needs or at least am meeting them in substantial ways. I crave loving and intimate embraces of your desire for me as a lover, wife, and companion. Right now, as I struggle to find inner peace and a sense of self-worth, it's extremely important for me to hear from you whether I am meeting your needs as a companion, and if so, how?

If you truly do see aspects in our relationship that are unique and special to you, I guess I just haven't been actively listening well enough or you haven't been saying them loud enough or they haven't been said at all. More than anything, it's the kind of affirmations I don't hear said by you that makes me anxious and uptight and overly react, for fear or worry that your decision to remain in our relationship is completely out of obligation, and not out of a desire to commit to it, and believe that it is fulfilling and meaningful to you.

Those times of deep lows emotionally occur less frequently now, but they're still there and I'm working hard at dealing with it constructively. I feel as though I have been under a good deal more stress, as a result of self-induced (somewhat) pressures, as well as dissatisfied by your pressures, and that makes my ability to cope and deal with my emotional cries for help difficult. And at times, I feel so guilty for letting you see that weak and inadequate side of me—fearing I'm making life so uncomfortable here, with me, for you. If you truly are happy about our relationship building, I don't want to erode it by my inability to cope right now. I fear that the most. I hope you'll be honest with yourself and me..."

Appel looked up. "And then the rest is missing." There was a notation, he said, saying page two. He asked Bob about it.

He shrugged. "I wouldn't have any idea where that went to." I caught Beezie's eyes. This had been written the weekend before Pam's death. It seemed too convenient that the last page was missing. Like others, I could only speculate what Pam's final words might have been. Now, as Appel brought up Beezie's last conversation with Pam, I grabbed my friend's hand.

"We've heard Mrs. MacNeil testify that on Sunday evening your wife was crying, distressed, and upset. Did you call her the following morning?"

"I called her both Sunday night and Monday morning."

Appel exhibited Bob's phone bill showing those calls on April 1 and 2.

Until the squadron could bring out a spare part to fix the aircraft on Monday morning, Bob told the jury he'd been stranded in Denver. When he'd arrived home, he and the kids had driven down that same night to visit Pam at her conference in Milwaukee. They'd had pizza in her hotel room, swum in the hotel pool, and then returned to Green Bay.

Beezie gave me a wry look knowing that even if this "thoughtful gesture" had occurred, it had been on the same day that Linda had picked Bob up at the airport. And, more than likely, their encounter had progressed beyond that point.

Appel next wanted to focus on the weekend of Pam's death.

Bob confirmed it had been a regularly scheduled Marine Corps Reserve weekend to fly from Glenview, Illinois, into Denver. Before leaving on the morning of Friday, April 6, he said he'd left Pam a card in addition to buying her flowers.

Appel handed it to him, to read.

Have a good weekend, Love. Last night and this morning were great. I'll be thinking of you this weekend. Have a good time at your faculty party. You deserve this fun time. I'll call to see how everyone is doing on Sunday when I land in Chicago.

Love you,

Bob.

As he looked up, my forehead creased, wondering why he hadn't mentioned the Jogger's Joynt half marathon, especially when he'd been so concerned that Pam should soak her legs.

Appel now asked Bob, "What time did you leave Green Bay to go to Glenview...?"

"Approximately 11:40."

"In the past, Bob, have you used one particular type of flight or service to fly from Glenview out to Denver?"

Bob said he would usually call ahead to see when a navy squadron was picking up pilots in Glenview. Prior to April 6, he'd taken flights from that base many times. "They have two planes that leave. The plane I take goes to ... Sioux City, Des Moines, and then onto Denver. They have a second plane that leaves earlier in the day." The first flight would leave around 2:30, Bob said, while the second would take-off earlier than four o'clock and as late as six o'clock some nights. "I've always taken the later flight."

"When you went to Glenview... did anything happen on the way that caused your delay?"

"My blue car developed some kind of engine problem." Depending on traffic, Bob said he'd been about fifteen minutes from Glenview on I-94 near the Waukegan Road exit. He'd raised the hood and waited perhaps fifteen to twenty minutes until an off-duty Illinois State Patrol Officer had stopped and given him a ride to a gas station. Once there, Bob had explained to a mechanic that his car wouldn't start. Bob had then ridden back to his vehicle in a wrecker that towed his car to the station. "I belong to the Amoco Card Club... you get free towing, so I just used my card."

Appel showed Bob his April 6 receipts. One was for the tow, and the other was for the labor on his vehicle.

Bob agreed they were his. After the car had been repaired, he said he'd gotten back on the road around four o'clock and had driven directly to the Glenview Bachelor Officers Quarters. Once there, he'd used the phone to find out whether the flight might have been delayed, but it had already left. The last time he'd flown to Denver had been in February. Earlier testimony had confirmed that it had been delayed until 4:30.

Because I flew a great deal for IBM, I'd run into similar situations where I'd cut my time too close in Chicago or New York, not figuring on rush hour traffic or another motorist's accident, and had missed my flight. If Bob had assumed there'd been a 4:00 or 4:30 flight, I could buy into some of his reasoning.

Bob now told the jury that his squadron had been preparing for a readiness evaluation, so he'd still wanted to make every effort to get to Denver. He'd called United and Frontier Horizon Airlines, but there had been no Friday evening flights. Bob then reviewed a defense exhibit and said, "These are the notes that I took as I called the airlines." On the card, Bob had written the direct telephone numbers and a notation for the Frontier Horizons flight leaving at 7:20 a.m. on Saturday morning for a flat fee of $100. He said he'd reserved a seat on that flight.

Since he'd still been planning to drill in Denver, Bob testified that he'd checked into the BOQ. "It was a long drive to Chicago so I went out for a run … a six-mile loop." During the run, he said he'd made his decision to drive back to Green Bay for several reasons: his marriage problems, Pam's state of mind during the previous weekend, and because flying out of O'Hare Saturday morning would have been a hassle. He knew he could come back in March and make up the drill with the Glenview unit.

I'd already heard Bob read the card that Pam had inserted into his flight bag the weekend before. I wondered if she'd possibly inserted one on April 6 that Bob had discovered while putting on his running gear. Were Pam's words in that letter the primary reason he'd decided to return home? Again, I could only speculate.

Bob was telling the jury that after his run, he'd showered before driving back to Green Bay.

"Did you use the toweling provided at the BOQ?"

"Yes, I did," Bob said, and confirmed that the towel David Haralson had found must have been his.

Bill Appel checked his watch and agreed with Judge Greenwood that this was a good time to recess for lunch.

≈

I anxiously caught Larry Lasee before he left the courtroom. Was Bob's comment about finding Pam in the basement important? I told him that on the last Saturday we'd run together, Pam had mentioned something similar. She'd referenced a therapy article from one of the magazines she'd given to Maureen. There was a chance I could find it.

He told me to go ahead. They might be able to use it during Bob's cross-examination.

I called Maureen at work. She'd pitched the magazines, but remembered the article. Instead of lunch, I walked the four blocks to the Brown County Library. On the magazine racks were the three most recent issues of *Self*. The woman at the information desk located some back issues at the Ashwaubenon Branch location.

Within the hour, I drove across the river, found the article, and returned to the courthouse. Then, after intercepting Larry in the hall, I returned to my seat just before Bob's testimony resumed.

≈

In attendance today was Bill Appel's wife. As the defense attorney leaned over the rail and talked with her, Bob stood alone by the defense section of the shared table. I wondered if the jury had been noticing his lack of supporters. Other than family, no one had been there to gather around Bob to provide him encouragement.

As Bob returned to the stand, he started out by explaining his drive home from Illinois on the night of April 6. He told the jurors he'd left Glenview around 6:30 p.m., stopped briefly at a McDonald's, and arrived in Green Bay about 10:20.

"Why did you go to the Preble parking lot?" Appel asked.

"Pam didn't know I was back in town and I wanted to surprise her ... Our circle and drive are very dark and Pam, or the kids, or anyone would certainly see me coming into the circle and of course, down the driveway." Since he'd planned to leave his flight bag inside his car, Bob said he'd decided to park in the lighted Preble parking lot before walking home.

"What gave you the idea to surprise your wife?"

"One of the things Jean Weidner had talked with both of us about is that our relationship is not spontaneous enough ... It just occurred to me, she was probably right, and that's what I was trying to do."

Pam had complained to me that, other than flowers, which had actually become a standard commodity, probably due to Bob's infidelity guilt, her husband had not been as spontaneous as mine. Was Bob's reasoning possibly legitimate? Appel's nod indicated that his client's explanation made total sense to him. The two appeared to be a well-rehearsed team as Appel pressed on, asking Bob to tell the jury what had happened when he'd entered his home.

Bob said he'd walked in through the garage entrance at about 10:30 p.m. "Pam was in the kitchen ... and Alex was awake ... playing at the computer." Because it had been past his son's bedtime, Bob had sent him up to bed. "Pam admitted she was first surprised that I did come home, but slowly her surprise turned to a suspicious type nature, questioning me about how come I missed the flight? And was I really in Glenview? ...Perhaps, did I spend some time with Linda that afternoon or that evening..."

"Did she seem to accept your explanation?"

"No ... One of the problems that, I guess, Dr. O'Neill alluded to earlier was that we don't argue, discuss and talk to each other very well ... And essentially, she didn't want to hear any more. And I was too tired to even attempt to go into any kind of a discussion with her."

As they got ready for bed, Bob said Pam had asked him for a sleeping pill. He'd given her the last one he had and tossed the prescription bottle. "I'm not sure she took it. I never saw her take it … I went to bed and Pam finished up in the bathroom and came to bed." Because Bob had been exhausted from the long trip, he said, "I fell asleep, probably, instantly."

I leaned back, contemplating what I'd just heard. Marcy had said that some of Pam's sleeping pills, prescribed by Dr. O'Neill, had been found in the Buliks' bathroom vanity. Why hadn't Bob given Pam her own medication instead?

I turned my attention back to Bob who said that sometime in the early morning, before it was light, he'd become aware that Pam had not been in bed. Because he'd heard an engine running, he'd first checked for vehicles in the driveway and then had realized that the noise had been coming from their garage. "I turned on the garage light and saw Pam sitting in the passenger seat of the van." For a second, he said he'd just stood there trying to get his thoughts together. "You know—what is this? And I walked toward the van."

Beezie nudged me, whispering, "Bob said he turned on the garage lights. Do you think Pam would've actually entered a dark garage to get in the van?"

I raised my eyebrows, considering her question as Appel asked Bob, "What do you remember doing next?"

"Opened the door to the van, saw that Pam was what appeared to me to be asleep." He paused and looked intently at the jury. "About that time, it occurred to me, she may be in that sleep that she goes in after she spaces out." To turn the ignition off, Bob said he'd reached across Pam. Since it had been his intention to carry her back into the house, he remembered stepping up into the van and pulling her toward him.

"Do you remember trying to talk to her?" Appel prompted.

"I can't recall exactly what I said." Bob's forehead creased. "She was obviously deeply asleep in my perception of what was going on."

Bob next addressed his recollection about getting Pam out of the van. "In the statement to the police, I said, I thought I must have carried her because I don't remember." And Bob said he still didn't recall. "I remember some disjointed thoughts as I was going back up the stairs and thinking geez, I got to get this damn door in back of me open ... From that recollection Pam was in front of me and the door was in back of me."

I could picture those six steep garage steps leading into their house. Pam weighed only about ten pounds less than Bob. It certainly would've been difficult for him to get her into the house.

The next thing Bob said he remembered was that Pam had been lying in bed on her back. Her pants had been wet, for whatever reason, and he thought he'd undressed her and put her to bed. "I then recall going to bed myself."

Bob's next recollection was waking up in the morning. It had been light out, but he had no idea about the time. "I had a headache myself. I just assumed I was still tired from the trip to Chicago."

Bob turned to the jury. "Looking back on the situation now, I remember, as I went to get dressed, bumping into the wall in that passageway from the bedroom into the dressing area ... Like people miss a step. I just banged into the wall."

At that point, Bob said he remembered going upstairs to see Abby. She'd been complaining about feeling sick to her stomach, being dizzy, and seeing double. "I thought she was overstating the problem, as kids do." After Abby had taken a couple aspirin, Bob said she'd gone back to bed and he'd brought her a bowl of cereal to eat upstairs.

Next he remembered doing some laundry, folding clothes on the counter, and thinking that he still had to pick up the car at Preble. "I recall Pam having to run the half marathon, and we had talked about her sore legs and sore thighs for most of the spring ... She was going to try soaking her legs prior to the run."

Appel handed Pam's running log to Bob and asked him to read two entries.

For March 24, Bob read: "Five and a half miles alone into the wind. Tired and sore thighs." For March 25, he read: "Ran with Lynda. Felt strong till the last two miles. Sore thighs." Bob looked over at the jury. "This is Lynda Drews." Then his eyes found mine.

I blushed, but kept my gaze steady, until Bob looked down and began thumbing through more pages. He said there were many other entries for sore and tired thighs. "Pam had complained about it for a couple of months, and I related that when I ran my first marathon, or first two marathons, that I also got sore knees or sore thighs." He'd told Pam that it had helped him to warm up his legs with warm water, not hot. So that morning, Bob said he'd started the bathtub running for Pam to soak her legs. Since it took awhile for their floor-level tub to fill—even to the eight inches reported—Bob said he'd left the room to see how the kids had been doing.

Eventually, he'd thought that Pam should be getting up for the run, so he'd returned to their bedroom. "To remind her that I did have the water in the tub...I rolled her over, shook her, and she rolled on her back. And I said, 'Okay, time to get up...Let's get this day going.' She appeared groggy. Her eyes were open. She appeared to be waking up or in the process of waking up. I recall just pulling her legs out of the bed and pulling her arms to stand her up."

Bob's eyes took on a lost expression, as he said that he didn't recall how he'd gotten Pam into the tub area. "My impression is that she was still groggy, still having a hard time breaking out of her sleep. I thought that I would, you know, just be cute and say, okay, I'm going to dunk you in the water." Because Pam had been groggy, he said he'd sat her down next to the tub and told her to "Get in when you're ready." Again he addressed the jury, "I didn't want her to have an accident."

Bob believed that this had been when he'd decided to retrieve his car from Preble. The Monza had 100,000 miles on it and since he hadn't been 100 percent sure it would start, he'd wanted to drive the van over. To do this he'd tried to find the keys. When he flew out to Denver he usually wore a flight suit. Instead of carrying his whole key ring, he would take only the keys necessary to drive the car. "I went through Pam's purse trying to find her keys." Appel showed the jury a police photo of Pam's purse lying open on the kitchen counter. Bob continued and said that after he couldn't find the keys, it had occurred to him that they'd been in the van. "I didn't take them out that night."

Police photo that verified Bob's story of folding laundry, feeding his children, and going through Pam's purse to find the van keys.

Bill Appel now reviewed the testimony of Mrs. Madden and Mr. Bennett who had both said that, at about 9:30, they'd seen Bob drive by in his van, while he'd also waved at Mrs. Madden. The attorney asked Bob, "Do you remember what time you went to get the car from Preble?"

He shook his head. "I don't have any perception of time that morning at all." But, whenever it was, Bob said he'd parked the van in the Preble lot, climbed into the Monza, and it started. After driving the car home, he'd walked back the half mile to Preble to bring the van home. "I felt much better by the time I had returned the second time." Both his headache and upset stomach had disappeared.

"When you left the home and took the van, where were your kids?" Appel asked.

"They were up and about the house."

The attorney nodded, his eyes finding the jurors.

Bob then said that he couldn't recall if it had been before he'd left to get the car or afterward, but one of Alex's friends had come over to see if Alex could go to the mall. He hadn't been dressed, so Bob had agreed to drop his son off later and also told Abby that she could ask a friend. Since Alex had still not been feeling well, Bob had sent him out to walk the dog. "Because getting outside seemed to help me feel better. It also occurred to me, as I did that, that perhaps there was carbon monoxide in the house. At that time, I opened the windows—some of them in the family room and some upstairs."

Appel stopped him. "It was at that point in time, that you recalled the carbon monoxide from the night before?"

His voice sincere, Bob said, "First time it ever occurred to me."

About then, Bob said he'd thought it had been getting closer to the time for Pam to leave for her run. "I didn't know if she was in the bathtub. I didn't know if she was stretching and getting ready to run. I just went to check on her, to see if she needed a ride to the run, as I took the kids downtown."

With heightened intensity, Appel said, "Tell us what you found?"

Bob took a deep breath and said, "When I went into the bathroom area, Pam was laying face down in the tub … I guess I just stood there motionless for a minute and it was like—I couldn't believe it … I was just wanting to deny what I saw … My first thought was, oh, she's just kidding and fooling around or something, and she wasn't."

Pam's right arm had been down by her side in the water. Bob

said he'd moved it around so he could grab her left arm and shoulder, and then had pulled her out. "I don't recall rolling her over onto her back, but about that time, I began, or attempted to give her artificial respiration." He explained how he'd knelt down by Pam's left side and tried to open the airway by tilting her head back. "I tried to press down on the jaw to open the mouth a little further. It wouldn't move. But I attempted to blow into her mouth, which was partially open."

He didn't know how long he'd tried, but when he'd realized that his efforts weren't providing any beneficial effect, Bob said, "I just sat back... I believe I was in shock. I'm sure I was. And I heard the kids." His eyes found the jurors. "It just occurred to me that they probably shouldn't see their mother like that." Bob's voice seemed unbelievably steady as he said, "To me she was obviously dead." After getting the children busy on something in the family room, he said he'd called Jean Weidner. "I couldn't think, so I called a counselor."

"Were you able to get through right away?"

"Not the first time." But, on the second try, Bob said he'd reached her. The only thing he'd focused on had been her recommendation to get the kids out of the house. He didn't even recall the rest of the conversation. "I continued to think, I guess, just to carry on with the plan for the day." He'd had Abby call her friend to tell her they'd pick her up early, and then they'd immediately left for the mall. After dropping off the kids, Bob said he'd come back as quickly as he could, called 911, and minutes later, opened the door for Officer Peterson. At that point, "I just fell apart."

Other than Peterson, Bob said he could only remember talking to Sergeant Taylor and Officer Baenen before his interview at the police station. During it, even though Lieutenant Hinz had told Bob, he should have remembered certain events better, "I continued to tell him, I just couldn't." Since Captain Langan had told Bob that they'd seen drag marks in the garage, "I guess then I replied... I must have dragged her. I got her into the house. She was in the house."

It had been the same with the questions about getting Pam into the bathtub area. "I had no recollection of it. If they had drag marks in the carpet, they must have seen them, because they saw the drag marks in the garage."

"Did they ask you questions about your relationship with Linda?"

"I don't think so, other then asking me for the name of the woman that I was having an affair with, because I had told them that."

"In fact," Appel said, "most of the things in your statement, you told them … They didn't know about your leaving the car at Preble the night before?"

"No, they didn't."

Appel continued his repetitive questions saying that if Bob hadn't told the police, they would never have known he'd gone to Glenview, missed his flight, checked into the BOQ, taken a run around the base, or showered. With each question, Bob concurred. The rhythm was gripping. Bob ended with, "I tried to be as open and honest with them as I could…"

"You have been released on bail since late June of this year … What was your feeling and attitude about this police investigation and your willingness to cooperate?"

Bob's earnest eyes connected with the jurors. "I felt from the start that I had nothing to hide … I've traveled quite a bit and I've had five months in which I probably could have run and hidden pretty well, and I didn't. I guess I trust in the legal system. I guess I trust in your objective evaluation of the facts."

Appel rested his hand on the witness box. "When you saw your wife in the van, did you think that she may have been committing suicide or did that thought enter your mind?"

"No it didn't!" Bob shook his head hard. "My first thought, my observation was … she was in another dissociative state, because that's my previous experience with her, when she was like that, in a place where she wasn't supposed to be, or acting differently than she normally might have."

"Did you at any time that night, when you saw your wife in the van or in the process of taking her to bed, think that medically she may have been in danger?"

"I swear I didn't know that!" Bob's eyes were pleading with the jury to believe him.

"How about the next morning?"

"Not the next morning either."

Appel's pause was long and dramatic before he asked his final question. "If you had thought that, would you have called for medical attention?"

Bob's voice resonated inside the still courtroom, "Yes, I would have!"

I wanted to believe Bob, but just didn't know if I could.

15

Adversarial Combat

It had been eight months since Royce Finne had questioned Bob at the John Doe hearing. This time Larry Lasee would lead the charge. The prosecution team's goal was to show the jury that Bob's convoluted reasoning surrounding Pam's death made no sense at all.

Lasee had built a reputation as being good on cross-examination. He wasn't afraid to go for the throat. In another case he'd prosecuted, one of the local papers had printed a cartoon showing Lasee as a caged wild animal. The caption read something like this: IF THE WITNESS DOESN'T ANSWER THE QUESTION, THE STATE THREATENS TO LET LASEE OUT.

For Bob's cross-examination, Lasee had created a structured outline, but while listening intently to Appel's direct, he'd inserted new questions into his plan. Cross-examination came more from the gut than from preparation. He needed to go with the flow and to hope it was effective. He believed the defendant would give them things that would support their case. Those were the things he wanted to emphasize on cross. A defendant might say something absolutely incredible. Lasee enjoyed grabbing hold of those far-fetched admissions, building on them, and then flaunting them to the jury.

During interviews, Pam's brother had said, "Bob is intelligent and cunning." The prosecution team knew this was true. Lasee couldn't underestimate Bob's inherent ability to handle the tough questions that would be thrown his way.

≈

When the attorney rose, he set off a buzz in the courtroom. The crowd, like me, anticipated emotion-packed questions aimed directly at Bob. Our wait was short as the testimony immediately heated up.

Bob's first year teaching at Preble High School

"Mr. Bulik, now you gave the jury an extensive picture of your background, didn't you?"

"I hope so," Bob said appearing ready to face his adversary. "I was as open with them as with the police when they questioned me."

"That really doesn't have anything to do with this case, does it?" Lasee's voice carried heavy disdain. "The only purpose for eliciting that information is so that the people on the jury know something about you, so they can relate to you, isn't that right, Mr. Bulik?"

"Objection," Appel interjected, appealing to Greenwood. "That's argumentative."

"Sustained."

Lasee smiled, unperturbed. He'd still managed to execute his first jab at Bob.

In response to the prosecutor's request to describe his Marine Corps Reserve duties, Bob said he performed the job of an air defense controller. This responsibility entailed monitoring jet aircraft that were potentially intercepting the enemy and was considered a significant job for national defense.

"I assume that the military would want to put persons in that particular position who could handle crisis situations, wouldn't they, Mr. Bulik?" Lasee lifted his brow.

"They train us to do the job, just as an infantryman would be trained to do his job," Bob said evenly.

The prosecutor next brought up Bob's Wisconsin Correctional Institution job. "The people you were teaching were criminals, isn't that right, Mr. Bulik?"

"That's correct."

"Wouldn't that be considered a higher-pressure job than teaching, say, high school students?" Lasee crossed his arms and waited.

"I guess I've broken up more fights in the high school than I have in the institution where there is security," Bob retorted.

Appel shot a warning look at him.

Bob's polite demeanor returned when he admitted that there had indeed been more stress at the prison, but there had also been a certain amount in teaching his emotionally disturbed students.

Lasee looked like he'd achieved the result he wanted and switched gears. "I believe you testified that you could terminate your employment with the marines at any time, but that you choose to continue in that occupation, is that correct, Mr. Bulik?"

"I feel that's important, yes."

Then in response to Lasee's request, Bob explained why he'd drilled out of Denver. The position he'd held in the Green Bay reserve unit had a maximum rank of lieutenant. After his promotion to major, he said he'd been granted a one-year waiver. During that time, he'd looked for another squadron to work for and had been accepted into his current unit in the fall of 1982.

Wasn't it a fact, Lasee's voice lashed, that Bob's Green Bay commanding officer had recommended he be terminated, "because you were not performing your duties appropriately?"

A slight flush appeared on Bob's cheeks. "I had one bad fitness report out of fourteen years, that's correct..."

"But isn't it true that one bad fitness report recommended that you be terminated?"

"From that unit, that's correct..."

"And it happened to be the occasion in which you joined the unit in Denver, is that right?"

When Bob admitted that was also true, Lasee again looked pleased.

This last line of questioning hadn't surprised me. The husband of a friend from my bridge club had drilled with Bob in Green Bay. She'd known about his bad performance, but until Pam's death, had tactfully kept it to herself.

Lasee next asked Bob about his home. "The house is somewhat unique, is it not?"

"I like to think so."

"And you had plans to add an addition on the house, didn't you?"

Bob's eyes shifted. "Possibly."

"You referred to that at the time of Pamela's funeral...?"

"I've been trying to talk my dad into moving up with us for a number of years," Bob said, skirting around the question. "I thought this might be a good time to have him come in and help out with the kids and the house."

Lasee crossed his arms. "Yes or no ... did you talk about that at the funeral of Pamela?"

"Yes, I did." A definite edge had entered Bob's voice.

"Okay, thank you."

At the funeral luncheon, I knew that Jim Davis, a home contractor in our Fun Run group, had been approached by Bob to discuss his home addition ideas. To others he'd also mentioned his plans to purchase a new souped-up van or Corvette. Friends had wondered where Bob's money would be coming from.

Lasee began to pace, fingers locked behind his back. He asked Bob about the marriage-counseling contract he'd made, promising not to see Linda VandenLangenberg. "You had no intent to follow through on that commitment, did you?"

"My intent was to help Pam, myself, and the family as much as possible."

"How much did you think you could help Pam while you continued in this relationship with Linda?"

"I didn't agree with Dr. Wellens's approach."

Lasee stopped pacing, his eyes aimed at Bob. "Could you answer my question, please?"

"I thought I could help her keep her sanity."

"And do you think you could accomplish that by telling her that you would not see Linda and yet continue to do so?"

"Much better than saying I couldn't see her any more." At that time, Bob said he'd felt that Pam couldn't live without him.

"Well, the truth of the matter is, Mr. Bulik, that on several occasions she was confronted by the fact that you weren't honoring that commitment. She lived through that, didn't she?" Lasee challenged.

"Because I was still there with her…"

"And are you telling me she wouldn't have lived through it if you weren't with her?"

Bob paused, looking down at his clasped hands. "No, I'm not telling you that."

My eyes followed Lasee's as he turned to check the jury's reaction. He seemed satisfied that they were with him.

The prosecutor now began to discuss Bob's continued deception through the first quarter of 1984. "You indicated it was a difficult decision for you to leave the house. As a matter of fact, you weren't going to leave the house, were you, Mr. Bulik?"

"I didn't want to," Bob conceded.

"You were separated a very short time," Lasee said, picking up a document. "Apparently, at the same time you came back to Pamela, you wrote this letter to Linda." After Bob identified it, as his Valentine's Day breakup letter, the prosecutor asked him to read it to the jury.

Bob's tone of voice showed strain and fatigue as he did.

My Dear Linda,

I guess it's time for me to admit and you to realize that I am, and will always be, just a phantom. You deserve more from a relationship than an absentee lover. You deserve someone whose heart can be with you 100 percent of the time. I am too emotionally tied to what I have "created" in my family to attempt to undo it, because as I feel right now, it would undo me and eventually us. As much as I tried to separate myself from that "package deal," I found that it included me also. I am comfortable there. Not the highs we've experienced, at least not in the same way. But those I'll never forget. It happens to be my way of life. I tried another with you, but to be happy there, I'm afraid I'd rain on your parade or break your stride or change myself in ways I can't be comfortable with. You are too much of a free and independent spirit, in all the best sense, to have Kevin or I hold you back. It is just two different lifestyles.

I do love you, Linda. Always know that. However, for all the wrong and right reasons, I'm leaving the apartment and moving back, in an attempt to make things work. We have shared so much, that this is extremely hard … But our memories will always be part of me. You've taught me so much about life and myself. And I feel I've touched your life also.

I must do now what I feel is right. Some day you may understand, but maybe not. As lovers, in a secret relationship, we were great. Guilt has a way of under-mining things. All of it was great. You did all the right things. It was me, not anything you did or didn't do that led to this letter.

Linda, I could hang on and probably pull us both down. I think we agreed … if we were to split up, let's do it while we're on a high—the way we spent our whole relationship.

I will be gone with the group this weekend to ski … Pam will be back in town Sunday night. Please take the things you want from the apartment this weekend. Toss what you don't want. I'll do the same, except for the good memories. Your keys will be there on the counter. Please leave mine there in return, along with a deposit slip for your bank.

Some day I'd like to smile at you, wave, go for a run, or see you
at another triathlon. But, until that day, my love, take care! You
are important, treat yourself that way.

  Bob

I was irked at Bob's last words. He'd written that he'd like to
see Linda at another triathlon. That had to have meant that she'd
been at previous ones with Bob while Pam had still been alive.

Before the August assault, he had, once again, been training for
the Menominee Tinman. Pam had been released from the hospital on Thursday, August 25. That Saturday, many running-group
friends had stopped by to show their concern, dropping off a cas-
serole, a loaf of banana bread, or a favorite book. One had been
Wayne Hubbard, whose son had frequently hung out with Alex
Bulik at the Fun Runs. As Pam had rested in the darkened bedroom, Wayne had asked her, "Where's Bob?" When she'd said he'd
been at the triathlon, Wayne's eyes had blinked with astonishment.
He'd listened to Pam defend Bob's actions. She'd been okay with
his leaving. She'd wanted him to go—he'd trained so hard.

Wayne hadn't bought it. Pam had just been discharged from
the hospital. It had also been only a few days since the assault,
and understandably, Pam had still been fearful in her home. Bob
should've been there for his wife.

As I'd listened to Bob read his letter to Linda, I realized, there'd
been a good chance that while Pam had been naively justifying
Bob's absence to friends on that Saturday in August, he'd actually been screwing both Pam and Linda—only in very different
ways.

Lasee now crossed his arms and leaned back on one foot. "The
truth of the matter is, Mr. Bulik, you did not end your relationship with Linda, did you?"

"Pam and I agreed on a contractual agreement, verbal agreement, as suggested by—"

"Answer the question, yes or no!" Lasee's voice exploded.

"I tried to for a short time." Bob looked down.

"Was it a day later ... a week later?"

"I don't recall."

"In that letter, you wrote certain terms in quotation marks such as what I 'created.' What you're referring to is your marriage, isn't that right?"

"That's correct."

"At any point, do you indicate that the reason you wanted to end it with Linda is because you love your wife?"

Bob referred to it again and looked up, his jaw tight. "I did not write that, no."

"You do refer to the fact, though, that you love Linda, about four times in that letter?" Lasee thrust a finger at it.

"I guess if it's Linda's letter I would say that to her."

Lasee shook his head as he returned it to the exhibit table and picked up another.

Bob identified it as the letter Dr. Wellens had intercepted, dated the first Tuesday of 1984.

I realized it had been the reason behind the Buliks' dismissal.

Instructed by Lasee to read it, Bob reluctantly began:

Dear Linda,

Whenever the Chinese New Year begins, in October or November sometime, they always give it a name like the Year Of The Dog or something like that. Well, without being Chinese, I'd still like to use their custom and label 1984 as The Year Of Our Rainbow.

I came to school this morning happier than anyone else I saw. For me, my life and its priorities are now something that's becoming clearer. That was one of my resolutions for the New Year, taking charge of my life, not escaping and going for a long run to meet a beautiful lady. I've been doing that for too long—not being truthful with myself. So I am working at honesty with myself first, then with you, then with everyone else. I really want our new life together to be ... very honest, or we will just recreate our old relationships again.

I'm not in the habit of saying what my needs are, not being honest with me, but I need to change that so we can be the best for each other. I don't ever, ever want to go through this again. On the other hand, if I thought I would have to, even in the back of my mind, I wouldn't be committing myself to you as I am. You have no idea how good it feels to be back at school, that is, not at home. What a pressure cooker there. Why do I put up with it? I'm still trying to figure it out, but not for long.

I always have enjoyed camping and sleeping bags. Have a beautiful day.

Love,

Bob

I sat back, numb. This letter had been written in the midst of Pam's paranoia, when she'd believed that Bob had been drugging her so he could sneak out to meet Linda, or in Bob's words, "a beautiful lady."

Lasee took the letter back and asked Bob if he'd followed through with those New Year's resolutions. Had he been truthful with himself, Linda, and others?

"I don't think that can be answered with a yes or no…"

"Were you honest with yourself? Did you tell yourself that you wanted a new life with Linda?"

"Yes."

"Were you honest with Pam after you wrote that letter?"

"I can't answer that."

"I didn't think so. Were you honest with Jean Weidner after you wrote that letter?"

"Yes."

"Well, did you hear her testify that right up to the point where Pamela died, she assumed that you weren't seeing Linda?"

"That was her assuming, that's right."

Lasee pursed his lips at Bob's audacity. "You spoke of occasions in which you saw Pam 'spaced out,' is that right?"

"That's correct."

I leaned forward, anxious to hear this testimony.

"I understand that those occasions were all prior to the first of this year... For instance, you referred to an incident in a hot tub in November, and a party in December, and some occasions in between... when Pam would sit and stare blankly."

"Could have come after the first of the year," Bob said. "I'm not sure."

"Were you concerned about Pamela when you saw her in those states?"

"Of course I was... That's why I asked her to talk to Dr. O'Neill..."

"As a concerned, loving husband, you didn't feel it was your responsibility to bring that to any professional's attention?"

"She already had."

"Did you hear Dr. O'Neill testify that he heard about this from Dr. Bressler, not from Pam."

Bob's eyes flickered. "I don't know." A frown line creased his brow. "I didn't think it was a life-threatening situation."

With a critical squint, Lasee appraised him. "There were never any occasions that Pam was in this condition where she did anything to harm herself, were there?"

"No, not at the time that I saw her..."

"Thank you." The prosecutor firmly nodded toward the jury, apparently ready to move on.

I was disappointed. Larry hadn't questioned Bob about the magazine article I'd researched. It included a number of self-help exercises to raise an individual's self-esteem. One of them suggested that the reader should find an isolated place away from any daily disruptions—a quiet spot in the basement was mentioned. Once there, the reader was to spend time listening to what their body, mind, and heart were saying. That's what Pam had told me she'd done. I felt certain that when Bob said he'd found her sitting and staring blankly in the basement, Pam had been in the midst of this meditation exercise.

Lasee now said he wanted to address the last two days of Pam's life. He referred to the card Bob had written to Pam on Friday April 6. "You talk about how good things were the night before and that morning ... Apparently, you had sexual intercourse with Pam before you left, is that right?"

"Yes."

"And then, after you did that, you went over to see Linda?"

"I dropped some papers off for her."

"Did you go over to see Linda?" Lasee's voice was harsh.

"Yes."

"Thank you ... You testified this morning that there were two flights that left Glenview on that day, is that right?"

"There were normally two flights." Bob corrected Lasee. "I'm only concerned with the second flight. I have no idea if or when the first flight would ever leave." From his experience over the year and a half he'd traveled to Denver, Bob said he'd always caught the four o'clock flight.

Lasee asked Bob if he recalled Mr. Edmonds testifying that only one flight left on April 6, at 2:28 p.m.

"That's correct. That's when the early flight normally leaves."

"Thank you." Lasee smiled smugly. "You testified that your car had trouble." He held up the repair exhibit. "Tell me what kind of work you had done for five dollars, Mr. Bulik?"

"There was a firing problem, I was told..."

"I assume it was a relatively insignificant problem?"

"It required being towed ..."

"And was repaired for five dollars?" Lasee feigned disbelief.

"I'm not a mechanic," Bob quipped.

Lasee showed him the exhibit where Bob had recorded the commercial flight times. "Where did you keep that document?"

"I testified I carried a briefcase and, I suppose, I threw this in, along with receipts from the motor club."

"And you retained that particular document? You thought that would be important to you?"

"I threw all my paper work together..."

Lasee gave Bob a skeptical look. "Mr. Appel asked you about

the fact that you took a shower at Glenview and that Mr. Haral-son found a towel … Well, you don't know that was your towel, do you?"

"I guess I didn't put my name on it when I finished using it."

Bob's quick comeback drew appreciative snickers from the spectators seated around me.

Lasee ignored them. "The fact of the matter is … you didn't even know you had a roommate that day, did you?"

"That's correct, I didn't."

"Now, you testified that you returned to Green Bay … Did you tell Pamela you were with Linda?"

"No I didn't…I had not spent the afternoon or that evening with Linda."

The prosecutor scowled at Bob. "You heard Linda testify that she got this anonymous phone call at Anne Sullivan School … Did you assume that was Pamela?"

"That's what she has been known to do in the past, yes."

"So Pam would have known that you weren't with Linda, wouldn't she?" A sly smile curved Lasee's lips.

"I think Linda said she never answered the phone or went to the phone."

Lasee quickly countered, "Well, did Linda testify to that?"

"I don't know if she did or not, but I know that from talking with her."

Lasee left it at that. He next addressed Bob's discovery of Pam inside the van. "And your testimony is that you assumed your wife was in one of these spaced-out states … You didn't attach any significance to the fact that the motor was running, the door was closed, she was seated in the van, she was unconscious?" The prosecutor glared at Bob.

"I'm sorry, that's the first thing that comes to my mind when I see her like that."

Lasee shot him an incredulous look.

Then after Bob reaffirmed that he couldn't remember what Pam had on when he'd removed her from the van and undressed her, Lasee asked, "When you got up, did you find her clothing anywhere?"

"By her closet, I believe … a green running suit, some underwear."

"Now, is that what you took off of her?"

"I don't know…I was doing a load of wash and gathering up all the dirty laundry I could find."

"What time did you go to get your car, Mr. Bulik?"

"I don't really have any recall of time frames that morning."

"What time was Pamela supposed to run in this half marathon?"

"I believe it was eleven o'clock."

"Did you think she was going to run in that race, Mr. Bulik?"

"Yes."

Lasee's voice rose to a shout. "You thought that this person that you found unconscious in a van, with the motor running, in an enclosed garage … who wouldn't communicate with you, who was groggy, who was breathing heavily, you thought that she was going to run thirteen miles, Mr. Bulik?"

"To the best of my knowledge that's what I believed." Bob's eyes beseeched the jury. "To me, those were two different events. I didn't, at the time, relate the two of them together at all … I guess when I first recalled that in the morning, it appeared as a dream-like situation to me with some of the parts missing."

Larry Lasee's brother was attending the trial today. The attorney had told me that his sibling had suggested a question during the recess, which Lasee now posed to Bob. "If you were teaching in school and you found a student of yours unconscious in a chair, uncommunicative, blank … would you call for professional help?"

Bob paused. "If I had no previous knowledge of his medical background, yes."

"Now, the reason that you didn't call for help, for your wife, was because you knew she had previous medical problems? Is that what you're saying?"

"Because she had emotional problems."

"So then she doesn't need help because she had emotional problems?"

"That was related to—"

"Answer my question!"

"I object," Appel said. "Counsel is interrupting his answer."

"I object... it's not responsive," Lasee snapped.

After Greenwood told the prosecutor to go ahead, Lasee gave Bob a withering look, implying that his answer couldn't be believed in any event, and withdrew the question. "You testified that when you found Mrs. Bulik in the tub, you were in shock, is that right?"

"It was my wife. Yes, I was in shock."

Lasee had Bob agree, however, that his shock hadn't kept him from finding his marriage counselor's phone number, or calling her, or driving to the mall with his kids, or returning home.

"When you hung up with Jean Weidner, who did you call...?"

"I didn't call anyone."

"You heard her testify, she tried to call you back and the line was busy."

"I guess you've heard me testify that my daughter called her friend immediately after I talked to Jean... so we could go to the mall and [I could] get the kids out of the house."

Lasee gave him a skeptical look and asked, "Whom did you call after you called 911, Mr. Bulik?"

"I didn't call anyone."

"Well, you heard Eunice Hanley testify, that after your call came through, that she kept the line open and you came back on... Who were you calling?"

"...I don't recall why I went to the phone or why I picked it up."

"Thank you. You testified that after you found your wife in the tub, your thought was just to carry on with the plans for the day, is that right, Mr. Bulik...?"

"That was an automatic response, I guess." Bob's eyes, now puffy with fatigue, met Lasee's.

"You didn't want to disrupt your plans just because your wife is dead in the tub, is that right, Mr. Bulik?" the prosecutor bellowed.

Bob fought to maintain his composure. "No, it's not."

"The fact of the matter is, Mr. Bulik, that after your wife's death you did just carry on with your plans, didn't you?"

"No, that's not right!"

Lasee held up an exhibit. "Well, the plans that you expressed in this letter... the first Tuesday of January, your new life together with Linda, isn't that what you carried on with, Mr. Bulik?"

"No, that's not correct." Bob's voice seemed exhausted.

Lasee shot a last hostile look at him and took his seat.

When the defense attorney stood, the spectator section around me grumbled, unhappy to forego another round of questions, but we were in for a treat. Appel looked right into Bob's unflinching eyes, as if in a private conversation, and asked, "Did you know that night that your wife had been poisoned by carbon monoxide?"

"No, I did not."

"Did you understand that, or think that, or know that Saturday morning?"

In the hushed courtroom, Bob's final words resonated, "No, I did not!"

I watched as he wearily stepped down wondering whether there was any chance Pam's death had accidentally resulted from this string of illogical circumstances? However... it was just so difficult to believe that Bob had been telling the truth today, when he'd been such a master of deceit in the past.

16

Noble Cells

O n day eight of Bob Bulik's trial, I entered Circuit Court I and surveyed the now familiar clientele. Some were friends of the Buliks, but most probably knew them only through attending the proceedings and through media accounts. A *Press-Gazette* reporter was interviewing a few attendees. They were saying that there was this intense curiosity about the real-life drama that had been unfolding throughout the trial. It was a rarity for Green Bay since the principals were all schoolteachers, touching the upper middle class. There were also so many unusual circumstances surrounding Pam's death. "It's something different," one gentleman stated. "You usually have someone shooting somebody. Here you've got kind of a sex triangle. People like a good scandal."

The trial was nearing its conclusion. A pathologist would be the final witness for the defense.

Dr. John Fodden looked like an absent-minded academic as he helped Appel describe his impressive credentials. The doctor said he'd received his medical degree from the University of Leeds in Liverpool, England. He'd then worked as a pathologist at a number of Canadian hospitals and as associate director of laboratories at Mount Sinai in Milwaukee. He was currently director of laboratories at four small Wisconsin hospitals: Manitowoc, Two Rivers, Kewaunee, and Algoma. In addition to having firsthand experience with a dozen carbon monoxide poisoning cases, Fodden said he'd conducted his own independent study in that area. As an expert witness, he'd testified in about seventy criminal cases, more often for the prosecution than the defense.

In preparation for today, Fodden had reviewed Dr. Skarphol's autopsy results. "I found my colleague's work to be very thorough, comprehensive, and markedly detailed," he said with his clipped British accent.

The State's two pathologists, in earlier testimony, had both stated that Pam's head injuries had been severe enough to knock her unconscious. This prerequisite had been necessary if Bob had, indeed, placed Pam in the van. Appel was now prepared to provide evidence that this assertion was, in fact, false. To do this, some groundwork had to be established. He first asked Dr. Fodden to explain how he, as a physician, rated the severity of bruises to the skull area.

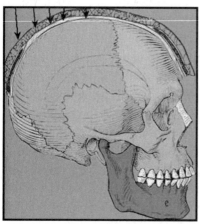

In the courtroom Dr. Fodden taught his "class" using exhibits and drawings.

"I work from the outside in," Fodden said, addressing the jury. He told his attentive "class" that the first level of severity was to the superficial area of the skin. The second level involved the entire thickness of the skin. The third level occurred in the thin, but markedly strong skullcap, known as the aponeurotic layer. "We're dealing with a severe injury, if bleeding occurred between that layer and the skull bone." The fourth severity level, Fodden said, was a fracture to the skull, and the fifth, and utmost severity level, was where a hemorrhage occurred beneath a skull fracture and on top of the membrane encasing the brain. This could be the result of a contra-coup injury after the skull had been struck from the back, front or side.

Appel asked Fodden if there'd been any indication of a "coup or contra-coup injury?"

"No," he said, shaking his head.

"Did you find any evidence of skull fracture or damage to the skull?"

"None reported."

"Did you find any evidence of damage to the aponeurotic layer?"

"None at all."

"The report of Dr. Skarphol," Appel said, referring to it, "indicates the bruising to be confined to the skin area?"

"Full thickness scalp," Fodden clarified.

Appel was now ready to ask his key question. He wanted to know whether, in Dr. Fodden's expert opinion, any of Pam's head injuries had been sufficient to cause unconsciousness.

Fodden was firm. "None of the injuries, delivered to the head, could cause loss of consciousness."

A cautious smile grazed Appel's lips. "What factors do you find significant in making that conclusion?"

"I come back to my aponeurotic layer." In Dr. Skarphol's report, Fodden said, his colleague had never mentioned wiping blood away to examine for a fracture. Also, there had been no evidence of a concussion. "In loss of consciousness, there are microscopic indications in the brain," Fodden explained. "Lots of unconscious cases recover, but in those who succumb, we usually can detect very early cell changes of brain structure..."

"In this case, there were none?"

"None."

With bright eyes, Appel nodded and moved on. "Let me ask you then, Doctor, if you would address for the jury the effect of carbon monoxide poisoning on your inspection of the bruises."

As Fodden, once again, began lecturing to his "students," the defense attorney could've played hooky. To answer Appel's question, the doctor said he first had to explain how carbon monoxide affected the body's cells. Each held a social status, where the brain cells were the most noble followed by the heart, liver, and so forth. Carbon monoxide did its damage by attacking the noblest cells first.

He then used a blackboard to draw an elaborate diagram while describing how carbon monoxide restricted oxygen, causing the red blood cells and their capillary walls to become damaged and sick. "A love tap could produce a hemorrhage, a bruise." The poisoned cells, he said, would not have had the same resistance to injury that they had when they were healthy. "I believe that is what took place in some of these bruises."

When the pathologist returned to the witness chair, Appel took charge, guiding him through each of Pam's injuries. Fodden believed that the superficial abrasion above the buttocks could have resulted from scraping against a step. The right wrist and hand wounds were also "slight, simple, and superficial." He definitely felt they were not defensive. The doctor demonstrated how women normally protected themselves by putting their elbows together, palms covering the face. In this position, the bruised areas evident on Pam's wrist and hand would've been sheltered.

The doctor believed the cerebral peduncular hemorrhage had occurred when Bob removed Pam from the van. This was based on the most factual piece of evidence, "the laboratory-proven urine." Because Pam's urinary sphincter had failed, she'd been as close to death as she could possibly have been. The only thing left to fail had been the respiratory and cardiac center of the brain. Pam's nervous system had already shut down, so her body had been like a 146-pound sack of flour, much harder to carry than a 146-pound tree trunk. Since Pam's neck had been as flaccid as a day old baby's, her head could have swung forward, backward, or sideways, causing the cerebral peduncle injury.

Fodden stated that Dr. Skarphol's autopsy drawing verified that the right occipital injury was a linear type of bruise, running from right to left, following the course of the back hairline. The pathologist believed that this had been caused by something blunt and hard, of a linear structure, and edge-like.

Steps Bob dragged Pam up that led from the garage into the house. A telephone is adjacent.

Knowing that Pam had been extracted from the van, he thought an ideal spot that could potentially have created this injury was the edge of the floor near the passenger door area. He also envisioned the edge of a step. In extracting Pam's limp body, needing both hands to remove, pull, lift, or whatever, the rescuer would have found it extremely difficult, without three hands, to control the movement of that head. Then, in terms of dragging Pam's limp body by her armpits and placing the head between the rescuer's legs, Fodden believed the head could have partially been controlled, though it still could have escaped and swung. "A door, a doorjamb, a step, dropping of the head against a door or the edge of a step, I really don't know… but I feel I have justification for my belief in the mechanism that caused those bruises."

Like Dr. Skarphol, Fodden agreed that the left forehead bruise could have resulted from Pam's head striking the surface of the bathtub. However, he believed the forehead injury's age was not the same as the other bruises. He believed those were three to five hours old, whereas the forehead bruise had occurred closer to the time of death.

The doctor had seen people with carbon monoxide levels above 50 totally recover. When Pam died, he said there had been a small amount of new urine in her bladder. This meant her recovery had begun.

Appel nodded. His next questions would focus on a key defense area—the effect the carbon monoxide had on Bob.

The doctor explained that an atmospheric concentration of 10-15 percent carbon monoxide could create early symptoms of poisoning. A very dangerous level would be 30-35 percent. In that environment, a resting person, taking 16-17 breaths per minute would survive longer than a working person taking 25-30 breaths. The first effects of carbon monoxide poisoning were sleepiness, dizziness, headache, and failed reasoning. Next was total lack of concentration and loss of muscular coordination. Walking would be staggered, in a groggy-like state. Last was the development of a coma.

"How about the memory part of the brain?" Appel asked.

"Now, that's an interesting area … Memory function of the brain is not yet, by any means, fully understood … but we do know that it is one of the first things to suffer in brain damage." Fodden hesitated, lightly tapping his fingertips on the arms of his chair. "In some cases memory can be involved."

The doctor offered one case in point. He'd had a patient who'd recovered from a 58 percent blood saturation level of carbon monoxide. The woman had driven into her garage, closed the door, and while unloading groceries into a small corridor, had mistakenly left the engine running. She'd returned to the car in search of her gloves, passed out, and been comatose when discovered. Afterward, Fodden had asked her why she'd left the car running, why she hadn't switched it off before unloading the shopping bags. She'd replied: Golly, I didn't know I did that. "She could remember what she'd bought in the shopping store. She could remember everything else," Fodden said, "but that particular critical detail, that moment of her crisis."

Intent on clarifying this important point, Appel asked, at what concentration level of carbon monoxide would an individual experience "memory impairment?"

Fodden shook his head. "That's impossible to say." Because carbon monoxide was so individualistic, he could only take a calculated guess.

"Your Honor," Finne interjected, "I object to the witness guessing."

"Sustained."

Appel tried a different approach. "You indicated that the effect of systemic poisoning is first upon the brain. Can you give us a range in terms of 0 to10, 10 to 30, 30 to 50 where you find carbon monoxide having an impact on the cognitive functions and memory impairment?"

"First failure of mental response is at the range of 15 to 25 percent saturation."

"15 percent saturation?" Appel repeated, zeroing in on the low end. "Would that include judgment…reasoning, memory?"

"You see, not necessarily memory," Fodden hesitated, "but can in individual cases…Not every sufferer from carbon monoxide toxicity manifests memory disturbance."

"I'm not talking about…permanent or long-term memory impairment, but memory impairment for an event." Appel was still after a definitive answer.

"Yes. At that level [of 15 to 25 percent saturation], too."

Finally, having received the answer he wanted, Appel asked Dr. Fodden to please assume the following: That Bob had found Pam inside the van, having lost her sphincter control, and in a condition he'd described as being asleep. That she'd weighed 146 pounds and Bob had weighed 160 pounds. That he'd physically dragged her through the garage and up the stairs into the house. That after sleeping in the upstairs bedroom, his children had reported dizziness, nausea, and headaches. "I would ask you to assume all that and ask if you can formulate an opinion…whether or not Mr. Bulik would have been affected by carbon monoxide?"

"We have a supposition to decide upon, and it's between the atmospheric concentration in the garage space at the time that Mr. Bulik entered that garage, and/or the length of time spent in that atmosphere. Now, both may apply. I don't know how we'd ever be able to decide." The doctor believed, though, that the real clue had been that the early symptoms of carbon monoxide had affected the children in their upstairs bedrooms. Because the poison had reached that area of the house, Fodden said, "I can, I'm sure, have the right to presume a high atmosphere concentration of carbon monoxide."

The doctor also presumed that Bob would've been in shock upon discovering Pam. Adrenaline would have sped up his breathing. He would've been wasting time trying to figure out how to remove her limp body. Then, trying to rescue Pam, he would have used a maximum degree of energy while rapidly breathing carbon monoxide. "One can envision a pretty high concentration of carbon monoxide over a short period of time." Fodden felt that this scenario would produce physical weakness, tiredness, and impaired brain function, causing confusion and affecting reasoning—and memory.

The State attorneys huddled during the short recess, adding final touches gleaned from Dr. Fodden's testimony. Now, Finne approached him.

"First, I am interested in this case you have described as your one and only personal experience with memory loss from carbon monoxide…Dr. Young and Dr. Skarphol both testified that they personally have not heard of, or read about, or experienced a case of carbon monoxide poisoning that resulted in memory loss without a coma or unconsciousness. That's evidently consistent with your own personal experience, is that right?" Finne tilted his head waiting for this critical answer. When Fodden responded in the affirmative, a smile crossed Finne's lips.

"Mr. Bulik testified that when he first saw his wife sitting in the van that he did not assume she was in any danger from carbon monoxide. Does that imply great anxiety, surprise, and concern over her welfare?"

Stress lines formed on Fodden's brow.

"It does not, does it?" Finne asked.

"Agree."

"Doctor, you described that, in your view, Pamela Bulik was as near to death as she could be. Seeing her in this condition, wouldn't you think that a person would conclude that she was in some physical distress?"

Again Fodden answered in the affirmative.

Pleased, the prosecutor next picked up the autopsy drawing that showed the location and description of Pam's bruises. "Doctor, how would you define blunt, in terms of a blunt instrument or a blunt surface?"

"Edge of a table, edge of a step, edge of a floor—"

Finne's forehead creased as if confused. "So your view of the term would be the existence of a well-defined ridge or edge?"

"It would, yes. We have that characteristic shown to us on one of the injuries."

Finne showed Fodden the autopsy drawing. "This one?" the prosecutor asked, pointing to the forehead bruise.

"No…the only one that Dr. Skarphol saw when he looked at the outside of the skull." He pointed to a spot on the back of the head. "There, that outline."

Finne appeared baffled. "The right occipital was a result of a sharp edge?"

"It has that characteristic. It describes it well."

"Evidently, then, you take exception with the testimony of Dr. Young and Dr. Skarphol that the right occipital was a result of contact with something that did not have a well-defined ridge or edge."

"Oh, I must—"

Finne interrupted. "I just wanted to be clear. Thank you."

The prosecutor stepped back, studying the pathologist. "Is it your view that one school of physicians would recommend taking an unconscious, comatose individual, who's poisoned from carbon monoxide, to the extent that she suffered urinary incontinence, and simply put them to bed?"

Fodden took a deep breath before answering, "No."

"I didn't think so. Thank you…And you have seen nothing, from the medical evidence, that would indicate to you, that Pamela Bulik would not have recovered if treated properly?"

Again he said, "No."

"Doctor, have you seen any medical evidence that at 48 percent carbon monoxide saturation, Pamela Bulik was conscious?"

He hesitated, before giving Finne the same response.

"If that's true, she didn't get up and stumble and fall into the tub, did she?"

"That I couldn't answer."

Finne asked Fodden, what the reaction of a groggy or clumsy body would be, "if it were to fall into eight inches of water?"

"Some uncoordinated attempt to escape from that circumstance … almost meaningless, but with some motive within that person's mind."

"That's an unconscious survival response?"

"It is indeed."

Appel's goal was to recover lost ground. "Dr. Fodden … is it necessary to have a coma condition to have memory impairment?"

"Oh, no, no." Fodden shook his head. "Neither did I imply that." He again clarified that there might be sporadic memory impairment for that fraction of time, concerning the crisis situation only.

"You were asked on cross-examination, if a 48 percent level of carbon monoxide in Mrs. Bulik would necessarily make her unconscious."

"No, it wouldn't. It is not science … At 50 percent level one may be able to walk right across this courtroom."

Appel nodded. "Do people with athletic abilities, athletic backgrounds and training, have a greater volume or concentration in their body of the red blood cells?"

"Yes, and they can draw upon them faster…"

"And would that also affect the ability to recover from a traumatic situation or a toxic situation?"

"It would in some sense …but not as much as it would affect the ability to not succumb as quickly."

Unwittingly, Appel had provided ammunition for the prosecution.

Finne was back in the driver's seat. "Doctor, what you're telling us is that an individual with a very well-developed cardiovascular system, one, for example, who regularly competes in triathlons," he gestured at Bob, "would be able to enter that atmosphere and take longer to be affected than someone like you or me, who may have trouble running across the street?"

"That's right. That's what I maintain."

The prosecutor nodded his approval and moved to closure. With intensity in his voice, Finne stated that since the following carbon monoxide factors were unknown: Number one, the individual's ultimate saturation percentage; number two, the period of time they were absorbing it; number three, the activity they were engaged in; and number four, the concentration in the atmosphere, "You can't state, with any sort of certainty, medical or otherwise … what degree, if any, this defendant was affected by carbon monoxide on April seventh, 1984, can you Doctor?" Finne asked, turning to face the jury.

"Yes, I can."

The prosecutor spun around, shocked. "You can?"

"My remarks in testimony were … what I believe to be the most outstanding fact in the entire case, the laboratory and chemically proven presence of urine—"

"I understand that," Finne said condescendingly. "I simply asked you about the defendant, not the deceased." The prosecutor again had the jury doubting the defense's expert.

"I'm sorry then," Fodden said, clearly embarrassed. "I take it back, but it was a form of reemphasis."

The doctor was in trouble. Before he was excused, Appel's job was to alter the picture Finne had just painted of the defense's renowned expert. To reestablish his credibility, the attorney asked a pointed question: "Just as carbon monoxide is a systemic poison, recovery is systemic?"

"Yes." Fodden said, his head bobbing. "Recovery is systemic and in the reverse manner to which we had it fail." He closed by explaining that the noble cells of the brain and heart, the first to be affected by carbon monoxide, would be the last to completely recover.

A handful of spectators mockingly applauded as the beleaguered pathologist stepped down from the witness stand.

Greenwood banged his gavel. "I'm deadly serious—this isn't Packer stadium, this isn't a sideshow."

The defense rested without celebration or fanfare.

No one took the stand on Bob's behalf.

17

Impassioned Closings

I nside the courthouse rotunda, the excited chatter of students greeted me after lunch. Many wore Preble High School letter jackets and said they'd received permission from their teachers to attend the closing arguments. Some of them knew Bob personally, but most simply remembered the day of Pam's death. It had been the Saturday of Preble High School's Junior Prom.

In addition to the extensive trial coverage, last Sunday's *Press-Gazette* had printed a letter from the parents of a former student of Bob's that said:

> Maybe Robert Bulik was not one who would make small talk with fellow teachers … but where a teacher really shines is in the classroom, and here he did his job, and did it well.
>
> My son … had special education throughout his years in school and we saw not much hope, that is, until Bulik's class. This man cared for his kids and took time to listen and make them feel important. When I was talking to my son about the Buliks' trial he said, "You know, Mom, maybe he was always listening to our problems and he had no one to listen to him."
>
> Maybe he was a loner, maybe he did what they say, but I can only say "Thank Goodness" he was a part of my son's life. He made a lasting impact on our lives and we want to thank him.

I wondered if this student was present in the gathering mob. It sounded like Bob had done right by this kid. Maybe he did have some silent supporters after all.

≈

The Bulik trial had reached its grand finale. With all the critical players in position, Judge Greenwood addressed the jurors: "The lawyers will sum up the case. Because the State has the burden of proof, they will argue first. Then Mr. Appel will argue only once. The State gets the last rebuttal." He next lectured the spectators. No one was to walk out in the middle of closing arguments. It was their choice, either they stayed until recess or left immediately.

Few left.

From behind the lectern, Royce Finne's face looked thinner. He'd addressed the jury at the trial's opening, and now he would offer the State's final argument. His job was to lead the jurors back to the State's perception of the truth. To show the jury that Bob's explanation for Pam's death was unreasonable and did not fit within any sensible definition of common sense.

He thrust his hands into his pockets ready to begin. "The first date I'd like to mention to you is Wednesday, April fourth." On that date, Finne said, it had been clear that Bob had known that the Friday, April 6 flight from Glenview to Denver had been scheduled for 2:30 p.m. There'd been no way that he could have anticipated Mr. O'Connor, a fellow reservist, calling the police to say, "Listen, this is what I know. Is it of any use to you?" Bob had also known that it had been a solid three to four hour drive. When he hadn't left Green Bay until shortly before noon, it would've been impossible for him to make it to Glenview on time. Finne paused, giving the jurors an ironic smile. "Doesn't it strike you as curious that this defendant would rather drive an automobile, which he had no confidence would make it … than to accept this offer of a ride from Mr. O'Connell?"

The prosecutor crossed his arms. "Now what does the defendant have to say about this? He says … I had car trouble. We know that's not true. We know when he had car trouble he was half an hour from the base and it was almost forty minutes after the plane had already left...There's no escaping the conclusion he simply never intended to get on that airplane...

"Now what does the defendant do when he arrives at the Glenview base?" The prosecutor raised his brow. Instead of inquiring about additional free military flights, he said Bob had reserved a seat on a commercial plane. He'd then checked into the Bachelor Officers Quarters, paying in advance, allowing him to leave at will. "He goes out for a run and he says, well, I'm talking to myself...and I'm thinking this is a very important drill for me to make...Well, the heck with that! What I think I'll do is go home and surprise Pam...That's from a guy who's been sexually involved with another woman for two years, has put Pamela through hell...who stopped to see his girlfriend on the way out of town...who had seen her every day that week prior to Pamela's death. The kind of a guy who says he's too sick to go to church, and when they're gone, runs over and hops in the sack with Linda." Finne drew a deep breath. "What he intended to do was to surprise Pam by sneaking into town, killing her, and sneaking back out. He's a thousand miles away in Denver when the body is found."

Leaning on the lectern, the prosecutor next asked, "What does the defendant do when he gets back to Green Bay?" Finne scowled, zoning in on the jurors. "If you were coming home from work early, to surprise your wife, do a nice thing for her, are you going to park your vehicle a half a mile away?...And what do you do when you're coming home in a car that's had trouble, and you don't have any confidence it will start again?...It's clear from that territory out there, that car could have been parked anywhere, including right in the cul-de-sac." By parking at Preble High School, Finne said, Bob had assured that no one in the neighborhood would've known he'd been there.

"What did the defendant expect to find upon his arrival back home?" The prosecutor's eyes darted to Bob' tense face and back to the jurors'. "He knew Pamela took sleeping pills when he was

**View from the Bulik's driveway apron up to their cul-de-sac.
The portion of fence knocked down was from
Pam's accident in December.**

out of town. He expected her to be asleep, zonked out." And since the children were usually in bed by nine, Finne said that Bob had expected the same of them. But things had not been as expected. Alex and Pam had both been awake. Bob couldn't just kill Pam and return to Illinois. He now had to conjure up this fantasy about suicide.

From the autopsy, Finne said, the jury knew that Pam had taken a sleeping pill "and it rendered her asleep, as they do." At that point, Pam had received blunt trauma to her head from some object without a well-defined ridge or edge. The bruises had been serious and "all sufficient to render her unconscious." In that condition, Pam had been placed in the passenger seat of the van. "The defendant," Finne glared at Bob, "then starts it and simply leaves her there. There's no way to tell how long the defendant waited...The rate at which a body absorbs carbon monoxide depends on quite a variety of factors, none of which are known. But she absorbs quite a bit. That's what we do know.

"There's also a limit to how long he can afford to wait. The longer that van is running, the longer it's spewing out fumes. It creates a number of risks for him." Finne began counting them off on his fingers. First, the carbon monoxide might poison his children. Second, a neighbor might hear the van and check it out. Third, a police car patrolling the Preble parking lot might see Bob's car, trace the owner, and show up on his doorstep. "So he waits as long as he thinks he can and hauls Pamela out." Bob might have believed she'd already been dead, Finne said, but "she's still alive, barely alive … She clearly cannot be allowed to recover. The suicide was unsuccessful." He hesitated, meeting the jurors' eyes. "Now we have an accidental death …

"That's when this defendant cooked up this story about having to soak Pamela's legs so this unconscious, comatose woman could go run thirteen miles!" The prosecutor's eyes narrowed in disgust. "When this defendant placed her against that hamper, if indeed that's what he did, she was still nearly dead, in all medical probability still unconscious, still doing things like dribbling saliva down her chin … People who are unconscious and comatose simply don't stumble into a tub full of water … There's only one way she could have gotten into that tub." He jabbed a finger at Bob. "This defendant put her there."

Under the law, motive was not an essential element, Finne said, but there clearly had been motive. "The defendant himself best stated it. His life would be ideal, if only Pam was out of the picture, maybe moved to Florida, leaving him with Linda and the house and the kids." He paused, eyes focused on the jury. "Isn't it funny how things work out? Pam's out of the picture. He's got Linda. He's got the house. He's got the kids. All one big, happy family, just like Ward, June, Wally, and the Beaver."

Finne peered at Bob. "This defendant also knew the ride on the gravy train was getting close to being over. Pam was not going to put up with this situation between him and Linda forever … When Pam died, she was confident that she could make it on her own, without the defendant, if he chose Linda instead of her." His hands clutched the lectern. "That was difficult, but she could do it."

Leveling his eyes at the jury, Finne's passionate voice moved to closure. "The divorce situation was fast approaching for this defendant. He couldn't give up Linda. He faced losing everything...and he wanted it all. The only way for him to have it all was to kill Pam...and he did." His eyes flashed at Bob. "In clear conscience and on the evidence in this case, this defendant is guilty of murder in the first-degree."

From the spectator section, whispers erupted weighing in on Finne's remarks. After hearing the fervor in his preview, they anxiously awaited Appel's closing statement and then the State's rebuttal.

The judge now motioned to the bailiff to open the courtroom doors—winter or not, the room was stuffy. Those forbidden to enter rushed in, occupying the few remaining spots.

The respectful crowd silenced when Bill Appel rose to his feet. Notes in hand, he took his place behind the lectern, debonair in his dark gray wool suit and diamond-patterned tie. In one sense his task was easier than the prosecution's. He only needed to convince one juror of Bob's innocence, or that there was reasonable doubt of his guilt.

"I told you...I never had a case weigh so heavily on me...where the presumption of innocence is more important." Appel's eyes immediately homed in on the jury. "We're human beings...we always look for the dirt and the scandalous and the unclean. We do it. I do it. This community has done it. I also sincerely believe that jurors are different."

Appel defined reasonable doubt. It didn't mean the jury *might* find Bob innocent, it didn't even mean they *should* find him innocent. It meant they absolutely *must* find him innocent.

The attorney proceeded. He said there were four factors in the case that were undisputed. First, Bob had cried after Pam's death. "When you commit murder you don't cry and sob."

Second, Bob had been completely open with this investigation.

"He did not hide his wife's running suit," Appel said, holding the exhibit up. It had been left with the laundry in plain view. Even when the police didn't believe Bob's story, he'd never requested an attorney. He'd told them about his girlfriend, about parking the car at Preble High, which, Appel said, the State placed some sinister motive on. How would the police have known without Bob having told them? By the time they'd arrived the car had already been back at the home. He'd told them about finding his wife in the van before there'd been any information about carbon monoxide. He'd taken off his shirt when they'd wanted to see his body. Bob had even been willing to tell the police things that had sounded funny. A liar wouldn't have said, "I'm going to throw you in the

**In plain view was Pam's wet sweat suit bottom
with the underwear wrapped inside.**

bathtub," Appel insisted. "Think about that!" The attorney held up cards and letters from the evidence table. "The police have these," he waved them toward the jurors, "because Mr. Bulik let friends and neighbors in the house … Does a guilty man expose himself not only to the police, the prosecutor, but also to his friends and neighbors?" He shook his head. "I don't think so."

Third, it was beyond dispute that on the morning of Pam's death Bob had left his home to retrieve his car. "Thomas Bennett said he saw everything," Appel said smugly, "but he didn't see the Buliks' blue car arrive home." Like Bennett, Sylvia Madden had testified that she'd also seen Bob drive by in his van at about 9:30 a.m. He'd been alone and waved at her. "Does a man who's just murdered his wife wave at the neighbors?" Appel's eyes widened at the question's absurdity.

Fourth, it was beyond dispute what the Glenview witnesses had told the jury. Appel said that the State had known all along that Bob had taken prior flights at 4:30. Then Mr. Haralson had been called to suggest that Bob had never been in his BOQ room, but "a dirty little towel got thrown in their face." And, Appel said, he'd been grateful that the Illinois police had been diligent in their efforts to verify Bob's car trouble.

The attorney next addressed two issues in dispute. First was Bob's claim that he'd performed mouth-to-mouth resuscitation. Appel suggested that the post-mortem pressure marks on Pam's chin occurred when Bob's hands had tried to open his wife's mouth. "And a man who intends to kill his wife doesn't try to save her." His voice was emphatic.

The second issue in dispute, Appel said, was the State's assertion that Bob's reason for drawing Pam's bath water was a hoax. Both Debra Fantini and Lynda Drews had testified that, in the couple of months before Pam's death, she'd never complained of sore legs. "Mrs. Bulik's diary is more honest!" the attorney said sharply, shaking the spiral log above his head. Then setting it down, he pointed out the testimony of Pam's orthopedic surgeon, Dr. Rolff Lulloff, "no question, a fine expert in his area," who had confirmed that warming leg muscles actively or passively, to their optimum level, was not bad.

The State, Appel said, had argued two motives: Bob's girlfriend and Pam's life insurance. The attorney gripped the lectern, his face earnest. "I've got to believe that a fair assessment ... will lead you to conclude that Mr. Bulik was sensitive to his wife, sensitive to his girlfriend, sensitive to his children. Maybe we don't approve of him having a girlfriend and a wife. And as a husband, maybe he failed." But that human frailty doesn't make Bob a murderer! Appel said, his eyes intense.

The next motive was Pam's life insurance. In the Buliks' home folder, the attorney said that two of the three policies had been located: Bob's employer family coverage policy for $5,000, and Pam's commercial policy for $25,000. The State had suggested that Pam's insurance had been a motive because of her work policy. To establish its value, they'd had to call two witnesses. Appel frowned at the jurors. "They want you to believe that Mr. Bulik knew all of that." The attorney then insisted that the Buliks had not been in severe financial straits by highlighting Bob's summer plans to earn substantial supplemental military income.

Appel was now ready to address Pam's injuries. When the rescue squad had arrived on April 7, he said Lieutenant Katers had not seen any bruises on Pam. Targeting the spectators Appel shouted, "No bruises, Green Bay!" He then refocused on the jury and said the bruises had only become apparent later, due to the carbon monoxide poisoning, causing Pam's body to be more susceptible to trauma during her rescue. There had been no defensive bruises—no clips to the mouth, no internal organ damage. Dr. Young had even admitted to the jury, that the arm and hand injuries could have occurred when Pam had been removed from the van.

The State wanted the jury to believe that a major blow knocked Pam unconscious, Appel said, so that Bob could have put her in the van. The attorney paused, letting that point penetrate. "But we've all bumped our head without being knocked out." Bruises that would cause unconsciousness should be evident below the full thickness of the skin, but none of Pam's had been. Appel used the exhibit table as a prop. If he hit his head on its surface he'd get a round bruise. If instead he hit the edge, it would produce a linear one. "That bruise to the occipital area runs along the base of the hairline ... and I suggest to you, it happened when Mr. Bulik was trying to get his wife out of the garage, up the stairs, reached behind him to get that door open ... He doesn't remember dropping her, but it happened."

Addressing the forehead bruise, Appel said that Dr. Skarphol and Dr. Fodden had both testified that it could have resulted from hitting the bathtub. And, compared to the other bruises, Dr. Fodden had also believed it had happened closer to Pam's time of death. "That bruise occurred when Mrs. Bulik slipped, fell ... bumped her head, was rendered unconscious, and drowned." There was a beat of silence as Appel paused, letting that crucial scenario sink in.

He next tackled the extensive evidence surrounding Pam's psychiatric condition. The State, Appel said, wanted the jury to believe that Pam's mental health had been good, improving. Pam's friends and therapists had said she'd definitely not been suicidal. But the attorney reminded the jury that Dr. Wellens hadn't treated her since early January, while Dr. O'Neill had felt that Pam would need at least three to six more months of treatment for her acute stress syndrome. "Dr. O'Neill did retreat from his opinion," Appel said with emphasis. "He told us, well, I'm not saying she never had any suicidal thoughts."

The attorney drew a reflective breath. "Dr. Baker said no one can tell when a person is thinking suicide. Her friends can't tell. Her doctors can't tell," Appel hesitated, "unless they ask ... There's no record that Dr. Wellens or Dr. O'Neill did that ... [Mrs. Bulik] told her friends that Bob and the children would be better off without her ... She said it, and we knew she was thinking it." And what had been the first impression of Lynda Drews, her very good running friend? Appel gave the jurors a significant look. "'I hope she didn't commit suicide.'" His lips formed a tight line. "The truth here, ladies and gentlemen, from that witness, is not what she said, but what she didn't want to say."

Appel said he wasn't saying that Pam had been suicidal, but a used tissue had been collected from the floor of the van's front passenger seat. "It tells me it was used by a distraught lady." His eyes held the jurors' as if forcing them to accept the reality of his words.

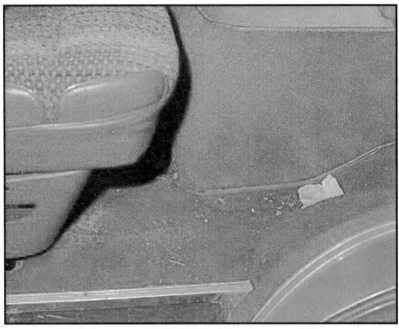

Used tissue on the floor by the van's passenger seat.

"Dissociative states." With almost painful intensity, Appel asked, "Is this a reason Mrs. Bulik was in the van? I don't know. Isn't it possible? We know she had them." He reviewed each of those prior instances. "The State wants you to believe that Mr. Bulik knew his wife was in a serious medical condition when he found her in the van. And isn't that our first thought ... why didn't he call a doctor then?" When Officer Peterson had initially checked out the van, Appel said he'd only discovered the wet spot because he'd touched it. "If you can't see it and can't smell it, how can you charge Mr. Bulik with the responsibility for knowing it is there?"

Appel pressed on, stating that Dr. Baker had testified that people simply come out of dissociative states so medical attention would not be needed. "And isn't it natural for Mr. Bulik to have a self-denial of suicide for his wife?" Appel's empathetic eyes focused on Bob. "I don't know if we have an act of suicide ... a dissociative reaction ... a combination of the two. I don't know if we have Mrs. Bulik getting in the van with some suicidal thought, maybe changing her mind, but then it's just too late, and her physical strength is gone ... All I'm telling you is ... you ought to know, her husband didn't put her there."

Next was the carbon monoxide. The attorney selected a specific photo of the Buliks' garage floor. This evidence, he said, showed that while rescuing Pam, Bob had been disorientated and physically weak from the carbon monoxide. "You can see that in the drag marks." He passed the photo around to the jury. "They're wavy ... There was enough to make the children sick. There was enough to make my client sick." The carbon monoxide had attacked Bob's brain first, and his brain had been the last to recover. That's why, Appel insisted, Bob hadn't known that Pam had been in danger on Saturday morning. He'd told the police that Pam had been groggy—an apt description of someone recovering from carbon monoxide poisoning, but also an apt description of a woman getting up after taking a sleeping pill. Because Bob couldn't remember, the police had been suspicious. "But he can't remember, and they don't know why and he doesn't know why." Appel trained his attention on the jurors. "I hope you now know why."

The attorney was ready to pose the question everyone wanted answered: "What really happened that night?" He suggested that Pam had been worrying about her marriage all week, had been upset in bed that night and couldn't sleep. She might have been stressed to the point that she'd had this physical reaction and, like her journal said, wanted to escape. She'd dressed and entered the van.

Eventually, Appel said, Bob had awakened, heard it running, and discovered his wife. The effort he'd expended to get her out of the garage, and the level of carbon monoxide in it, had so weakened and tired him that Bob had not been thinking clearly. "And it was the carbon monoxide that put him into bed when he put his wife into bed. And it was the carbon monoxide the next morning that doesn't let him remember that event very well." He paused on that critical point.

"You've had a chance to judge this man." Appel motioned toward Bob. "It's beyond dispute that he left his home the morning of his wife's death to retrieve his car." The attorney's eyes probed the jury. "If he knew the facts of her death … that man would not leave the house and create the situation of his children possibly finding their mother dead!"

Several jurors' heads were nodding. Appel's words had found their mark.

"He did not know that his wife was in danger!" The attorney pounded the lectern, willing the jury to believe. "What happened here is an accident!"

Appel explained that in addition to the charge of first-degree murder, Judge Greenwood would be giving the jury two lesser offenses to consider: second-degree murder and homicide by reckless conduct.

"Mr. Bulik did neither. He committed no crime!" Drawing bath water, taking his wife to the bathroom, even if Bob had believed that Pam had been waking up, Appel said, would not be dangerous. "Who would expect what happened would happen here?" In many cases, when the victim had been shot or stabbed, there'd be no question that a homicidal act had occurred. Often, the accused would claim that he didn't intend to kill the victim. That would be considered second-degree murder.

Appel next defined the second lesser offense, homicide by reckless conduct. It was an act creating a situation of unreasonable risk and a high probability of death, and committed with a conscious disregard for the safety of another. Drag racing down a public street and causing the death of a pedestrian would be considered homicide by reckless conduct. "Mrs. Bulik died by accident," he reiterated. "Her husband didn't know." Appel paused to make sure he had each juror's full attention and said, "Carbon monoxide is the substantial factor causing death in this case, not what Mr. Bulik did."

Appel eyed the prosecution side of the table. "Mr. Finne has a chance to give you a rebuttal argument. I do not... Sometimes, I've seen the prosecution give a short final statement, and come back up, and give a very long rebuttal argument... I hope Mr. Finne doesn't use that type of tactic. But I ask you, ladies and gentlemen... to think what would the defense have to say to this?"

Bill Appel closed with an impassioned plea for Bob. "My client only has three protections: Me, the law, and you. I'm done. I hope I've done enough. I ask you to come back and to tell him you believe him to be an innocent man."

The defense attorney had given a performance worthy of a standing ovation, but of course no one rose to the occasion. There was no doubt that Appel believed Bob was innocent. He had done an exemplary job of tying the facts together to provide a plausible story. Would the jury believe it?

⬦⬦⬦⬦⬦⬦⬦⬦⬦⬦⬦⬦⬦⬦⬦⬦⬦⬦⬦

It was now 6:20 p.m., three hours since the last break. While the jury stretched in their room, Beezie, Marcy and I joined Bruce MacNeil to stretch our own legs. Because he'd arrived just before Bill Appel's closing statement, Bruce had missed Royce Finne's. Beezie shared the highlights. She totally bought into the prosecution's theory and felt Bob should be put away forever.

As Beezie talked, I wondered whether Appel's comments had created enough reasonable doubt in the jurors' minds? I'd found certain parts persuasive, especially the premise that, if Bob had actually known Pam had been dead, he would never have allowed his children to potentially discover their mom.

I admitted to my friends that after Bill Appel had singled me out, I'd been obsessing over his comments. I didn't believe I had lied on the stand, but had I stretched the truth to portray Pam in a better light? Had her doctors? Had her other friends, who had loved her and couldn't believe, or didn't want to believe, she might have entered the van on her own?

Overhearing my words, Larry Lasee joined us. He said he and Royce were ticked off at Appel's insinuations about Pam's doctors' testimony and mine. I wasn't to worry—they'd take care of his remarks in their rebuttal.

∞∞∞∞∞∞∞∞∞∞∞∞∞∞∞

There was energy in Royce Finne's step. He positioned himself at the lectern, a smile tugging at the corners of his mouth. "In regards to Mr. Appel's final comments to you, I can only assure him and assure you that whatever method or procedure I use, he taught me during three years of tutelage, when he was district attorney and I worked for him."

In high gear, Finne kicked off his attack, focusing on Bob's state of mind on April 7. " I want you to remember that the defendant in this case never complained of any symptoms of carbon monoxide poisoning until he testified in court." The prosecutor also wanted the jury to consider Bob's mental condition that morning. He'd been able to do laundry, fold clothes, prepare breakfast for his children, attend to Abby's medical needs, drive his vehicles back and forth to Preble High School, and drive his van downtown. "He did all of those things, none, of course, show any signs of mental impairment, of lack of cognitive ability, of lack of awareness on his part." Finne took a deep breath, eyes latching onto the jurors'. "I want you to keep in mind that no witness in this case ever testified to having any experience, with any victim of carbon monoxide poisoning, having any sort of memory loss, unless they were rendered unconscious by it."

Finne referred to his notes to counter the CPR evidence that

Appel had reviewed. "The deputy coroner testified that she grabbed the chin in an effort to test for the presence of rigor mortis. That's where those pressure marks came from."

The prosecutor next selected some photos and approached the jury box. "There's an issue raised by Mr. Appel concerning the bruises. He calls them superficial and minor. I suggest to you, ladies and gentlemen, that neither Mr. Appel nor Dr. Fodden were on the receiving end of those bruises," he said, flipping through the pictures, pointing out Pam's various traumas. "There's no evidence that there was a frantic bumping, banging, dropping-type procedure going on in that garage." However, he said, revealing another photo, "the bottom of her heel clearly shows she was dragged through that grease with her heels down, as Dr. Fodden said, her head up, somehow protected."

Finne moved on to one of the central issues in the case—whether Pam had entered the van of her own accord or if Bob had, instead, put her there.

"Now, Mr. Appel talks about fugue states and dissociative reactions." Finne discussed how the defense had brought up poor Daryl Kapalin and then claimed, since Pam didn't remember that driving incident, she'd had one of these alleged fugue states. It only suggested that Pam didn't remember it, because she hadn't hit the median strip. "Pamela Bulik had a memory lapse one time ... even the defendant said it was prior to January first of 1984." The connection between that event and her death, almost four months later, Finne said, was speculative and tenuous at best.

Bob had testified, that upon finding Pam in the van with the garage full of carbon monoxide, he'd never considered she'd been in any physical distress other than these fugue states. The prosecutor glared at him. "Do you believe that?" And even if Pam had been in this state, Finne said, the therapists had agreed, she would have guarded against hurting herself.

The prosecutor next wanted to examine whether or not Pam had tried to commit suicide. He reminded the jury that on Friday, April 6, Bob had left Pam flowers and a loving card saying,

"Last night and this morning were great!" Pam might have felt depressed if she'd thought Bob had been with Linda, but if the jury believed the phone call to Anne Sullivan School, Pam had known that Linda had been in town. Even Bob said he and Pam had briefly discussed Linda that night. "In the course of this relationship between the defendant and Linda VandenLangenberg, how many times must the Buliks have had that very same brief discussion?" The prosecutor's eyes sought out each juror's. "You can appreciate, dozens and dozens of times. What's special about this time?"

Even though, Finne said, the defense needed to convince the jury that Pam had tried to kill herself, the only witness they could produce to suggest that she'd been suicidal had been Dr. Baker. "He said he could not accurately assess the suicide potential of a person without talking to that person, which he did not do, but which Dr. Wellens did and Dr. O'Neill did."

Appel had argued to the jury, Finne said, that on the night of Friday, April 6, Pam had somehow roused herself from a medicated sleep and gotten dressed. There'd been no evidence about the clothing Pam had actually worn, but there had been evidence about what had been on her feet. Two drag marks had been discovered on the garage floor, one caused by her exposed right foot and the other by her left shoe. Finne shook his head in confusion. "So she puts on one shoe to go kill herself? What sense does that make? Would you put on one shoe? Maybe no shoes or two shoes, but who puts on one shoe?" And then, getting past that, he said Pam had climbed into the passenger's side of the van, managing to squeeze around the console to start the vehicle from the driver's seat before sliding back into the passenger's seat. "Why would she do that?" His brow wrinkled.

"Mr. Appel suggests to you that Dr. O'Neill, whom he knows personally, whom he's worked with in court before, got on the witness stand and lied to you. Mr. Appel said that there's no evidence in the record to support that Dr. O'Neill ever did a personal suicide evaluation with Pamela Bulik. Dr. O'Neill clearly said he did...

"Let's talk about Lynda Drews's remark. She thought there was something drastically wrong because Pamela didn't show up for the race." At that time, Finne said that Mrs. Drews had considered suicide because she'd known the defendant had been out of town. "It is significant that she related the existence of this drastic event to his presence in the home ... If he was not in the home, there was some other cause. If he was in the home, she wasn't worried about suicide anymore ... That's significant."

The prosecutor clutched the sides of the lectern and said that the strongest evidence to prove that Pam did not kill herself had been the way she'd responded to her most serious depression in October 1983. "She had found out that a man she loved deeply had, for some time, been running around and sleeping with another woman." If Pam had wanted to kill herself, that moment, Finne said, would've been when she would've done it. "But she didn't ... or even try to ...

"Mr. Appel has made a big deal of this defendant's cooperation with the police." When Bob gave his statement, the prosecutor said he'd only told them things that would exonerate him. He hadn't said anything about his wife's condition when he'd taken her out of the van. He hadn't told them about the bruises she'd suffered. "Most importantly, he was trying, at that time, to convince the police, as he is trying to convince you, that she died accidentally ... He's trying to sell you a theory of accidental death."

Finne paused, now ready to address the crucial elements within the prosecution's theory. "Mr. Appel was very careful during his cross-examination of Dr. Young, of Dr. Skarphol, and of Dr. Fodden to have them all say that ... the right occipital bruise and the two on the top of the head occurred four to five hours prior to the time that Pamela died." Finne wanted the jury to consider that fact in relation to another. According to the pathologists, once removed from the garage, Pam would have expelled half of her accumulated carbon monoxide in a four-to-five-hour time frame.

"Pamela Bulik's carbon-monoxide level was forty-eight percent when she died. That is one half of ninety-six percent." There's been no case in medical history, Finne said, where anyone has ever lived with a 96 percent carbon-monoxide saturation. "And to the extent that's accurate, and it's clear that's the only conclusion that can be drawn from the medical evidence, the fact is, Pam was whacked on the head before she was taken out of the van not afterwards." The prosecutor paused letting that critical point sink in.

He wanted the jury to next consider the facts of Saturday, April 7. Bob had no recollection of when he'd retrieved his car, but Alex Bulik had. At the John Doe hearing, Alex had said that around 7:30 a.m. his dad had left the house and returned about five to fifteen minutes later. On the morning of Pam's death, Lieutenant Katers, of the rescue squad, had asked Bob if he had children and Bob had said yes. He'd then told Katers that he'd dropped them off at the mall around 9:30.

"The evidence in this case is undisputed that Mr. Bennett saw the van leaving the cul-de-sac at 9:30, return at 10:45, and then never leave again." Only Bob's statement, Finne said, had contradicted that fact. Even Alex Bulik had testified that they'd left for the mall at 9:00 or 9:30, not 11:05 or 11:10, as Bob would have the jury believe.

"Mr. Appel says, well, the defendant would never leave Pamela Bulik there dead for the children to find." Finne clutched the lectern and bellowed, "Well, they were out of that house!" When Bob called his counselor at eleven a.m., the children had already been at the mall. "It did not happen the way the defendant claims."

Finne was now ready to cover his bases. If the jury panel could not all agree that the defendant was guilty of first-degree murder, they should then find him guilty of second-degree murder. "Mr. Appel asks, who would know that taking someone in Pamela Bulik's condition, running tub water, and placing her next to it is a dangerous act?" Finne's face flushed with indignation. Clearly, he said, the defendant, who, just hours earlier, had dragged his wife out of a carbon monoxide-filled garage should know that putting Pamela next to a hazard that he himself had created, would be a dangerous and reckless act—one devoid of any regard for her life. "He should know, if anyone should, and so do we...

"The one thing that shines through all of the evidence is...he simply allowed Pamela to die." Finne's passionate eyes swept the jury. "This loving, grieving, caring husband...just dropped her like a sack of old laundry...and he simply goes about his life...All he had to do, to save her life, was to pick up the telephone. That's it. And dial three numbers—which he was perfectly capable of doing after she was dead."

Finne stonily regarded Bob. "The image this defendant portrayed on the witness stand was of a man in control, competent, a major in the armed forces of the United States, trained in a sensitive and complicated job to handle crisis situations. Trained to recognize signs of physical distress in other people because of his expertise in special education. Trained as a leader of soldiers. That's who this defendant says he is." This was the same person, the prosecutor said, who had told the jury, that when he'd discovered his wife near death, in a closed garage, with the van still spewing out fumes, the thought never crossed his mind that she might be in distress.

Finne stood back, his eyes burning. "Mr. Bulik wanted it all. He wanted the house, the kids, Linda—just what he's had for the last six months. The only way he could get it was to get Pam out of the way. What happened is that pressure cooker exploded in the days prior to April seventh of 1984. And that's why Pamela is dead today...

"We can't bring Pamela Bulik before you so you can get to know the victim...I'm sure you've tried to imagine the kind of person she was." With sincerity, Finne said that Pam had been a caring mother who'd loved her children very much, a wife who had loved her husband very much, despite having that love rejected. She'd been a teacher who'd loved her students and had been loved by them. "She was in many ways a very strong person. She bore this tremendous hurt of October...yet she did not lose her capacity to love and forgive." If the jurors would read Pam's journal, they'd

At Freedom High School, Pam had a definite effect on her special education students, but her own children were the center of Pam's world.

see she'd even been resolved to be nicer to Linda VandenLangenberg. Finne's eyes widened in disbelief. "Can you imagine?"

As the prosecutor moved to closure, he focused only on the fourteen people that would decide Bob's fate. Despite all of Pam's pain, he said, "She roused herself from those depths ... When she died she was on her way to that self-assurance and self-respect and, to use her words, to make a life for herself should that be necessary. At no time in her life ... had she been stronger. That progression of strength and growth and life would be continuing now, if not for the defendant," Finne's eyes found their target, "in whose plans Pamela Bulik simply did not fit."

The prosecutor glued his eyes back on the jury. "Think about the very last words that Pamela Bulik wrote ... 'I want to live.' That's what she was saying to us then and that's what she's saying to us now ... And damn it, she had a right to that life!"

∞∞∞∞∞∞∞∞∞∞∞∞∞∞∞

Royce Finne's impassioned words had touched me. He sat down to a sprinkling of appreciative applause. Most of the spectators had been with him, encouraging him with their nods. I'd continually looked at the jurors' faces, but found them hard to read.

At the start of the trial, I'd believed that Bob had planned my friend's death. This week I'd announced it in court before even hearing his defense and then had been quoted in both newspapers. Had I been wrong?

Appel said that the jurors *must* find Bob innocent if they had any reasonable doubt of his guilt. Now I'd heard all the defense testimony and Appel's closing statement. I'd been considering Bob's claim, that because he'd been overcome by carbon monoxide, Pam's death had been a tragic accident. The problem was, that unlike Finne's rebuttal, Appel hadn't given me any real proof. He could claim Dr. Fodden had provided it, but I didn't agree.

Finne had explained that reasonable doubt must be based upon reason and common sense. He'd finally tied all the facts together and provided the proof I'd been looking for. As he'd explained his theory behind the timing for Pam's bruises, and when the children had gone to the mall, and then added Bob's feeble reason for parking at Preble, the defense's story totally collapsed. Finally, I felt relieved—Royce Finne's logic had substantiated my earlier belief. I wanted the maximum punishment for Bob.

The trial had taken eight grueling days. The judge instructed the jury that after full and complete consideration of the evidence, they were to reach a unanimous decision on one of four verdicts: first-degree murder, second-degree murder, homicide by reckless conduct, or not guilty.

In the closing statements, I'd been surprised to hear that the two additional verdicts had been added and wondered whose decision that had been. Now the jury's job seemed more complex.

At 8:29 p.m. on Wednesday, December 12, the bailiff escorted the jurors to their room near Judge Greenwood's chambers. It was deliberation time.

Before leaving the courtroom, the MacNeils and I approached Pam's father, who was standing with the prosecutors. Because of his heart-attack scare, Mr. Metzger said he would not be present to hear the verdict. While he expressed his appreciation to Royce and Larry, Beezie and I added our own. They promised to call us when the verdict came in. More than likely, it would be a lengthy wait, though it never paid to second-guess a jury.

As we turned to leave, a reporter approached the prosecutors, pad in hand. "How do you feel the trial went?"

"We're happy." A smile crept onto Larry Lasee's face. "We had our day in court."

18

The Verdict

Today's *Press-Gazette* reported that more than fifty people had waited inside the courtroom until the jury returned near midnight—without a verdict. At that point the judge sent them "home" to the Downtowner Hotel for some sleep. Deliberations would resume this morning. I knew this could go on for days. I enjoyed cereal with my son and his nanny and drove to the IBM offices, listening to Christmas carols on the radio.

I asked our receptionist to hold my calls so I could wade through my stack of mail and electronic notes. When my phone rang I nearly knocked over my coffee. The district attorney's office was on the line. The verdict was in. It had taken the jury only six hours to reach their decision.

"Wow, that was fast!" My heart raced.

I met Beezie in front of the courthouse. Others that had gathered in the rotunda were discussing what a quick verdict might mean. People in the know were shocked. They'd seen swift ones before, but never in a case with so many special circumstances. The consensus was: the jury hadn't even looked at the evidence before reaching a decision.

The police had cleared the courtroom. Before entering, Beezie and I were screened with a metal detector. I could already see the prosecutors and detectives huddled near their end of the table as I slid into a row. A woman seated beside me said that earlier today, the jury had asked to hear Bob's April 7 call to his therapist, Jean Weidner, read back. In addition, they'd wanted to hear the complete John Doe transcript, but had been told they could only hear the sections read at trial.

The courtroom filled to capacity while we speculated about those requests. Bill Appel arrived with Bob, his brother, Ken, and Linda. A verdict this soon must have surprised the defense as well. Bob was dressed in blue jeans and a plaid shirt that peeked out from under his dark V-neck sweater. Linda, with a patchwork satchel thrown over her shoulder, looked like she'd just arrived from school. Again she stirred gossip. Near the defense section of the table, the small group gathered, listening to what appeared to be a pep talk from Appel. He patted Bob on the back. Ken squeezed his older brother's arm. A cautious smile grazed Linda's lips. Whatever Appel was saying was doing its job.

Eventually, Linda took a seat directly behind Bob, while Ken found one in the back row.

The minutes ticked by. At length, the door to the judge's chambers opened. Judge Greenwood entered and crossed to the bench, his black robe swishing. He stood behind his chair and nodded to the bailiff.

Bob had been first to his feet when the judge entered and remained standing beside Appel as the jury filed in. I could see Bob's hopeful eyes following them. Two jurors appeared to look him straight in the eyes. The others peered down at their feet.

The spectators around me were animated, trying to guess the outcome, until Judge Greenwood's stern glance elicited an immediate hush. Then, turning to the panel, he asked, "Members of the jury, have you reached your verdict?"

The athletic young man in the first row of the jury box stood. "Yes," he responded firmly.

"Would you give the verdict, please, to the bailiff?"

He complied.

The judge took the slip of paper from the bailiff, opened it, and silently read.

I watched Linda take several deep breaths as she glanced from the judge to the floor while Bob stood rigid, head bowed, awaiting his fate.

Poker-faced, Judge Greenwood's voice echoed through the courtroom, "We, the jury, find the defendant, Robert J. Bulik, guilty... of homicide by reckless conduct." For several heartbeats no one moved. A collective gasp of disbelief ricocheted around the room. Then chaos. Reporters rushed out to be the first to phone in the scoop. Spectators seated around me voiced vehement disapproval while a soft moan escaped Beezie's lips. I felt like I'd cannonballed off our Stormy Lake dock, plunging into the cold depths of the spring-fed lake, thrashing my arms to pull myself to the surface.

Shock had ripped across Bob's face, too. Tightlipped, Appel, also, looked stunned, his face drawn. Linda's body had sunk forward from her very apparent grief.

At the word "guilty," I'd watched the prosecutors' faces light up, but as homicide by reckless conduct had been read they'd grimaced. It was only a partial victory, a severe letdown.

Judge Greenwood admonished the unruly crowd. When we'd finally quieted, he asked whether Appel wanted to poll the jury.

He did. Suppressing his anger, the defense attorney said, "Ladies and gentlemen, my duty to my client is to ask you this: If you find him guilty of demonstrating a conscious disregard for the safety of another and a willingness to take a known chance of perpetrating an injury."

Calling each juror by name, Appel asked whether this was his or her verdict. Two male jurors seemed uncertain or confused by the "conscious disregard" portion of the question, and hesitated before finally giving their approval to the guilty verdict. One of them appeared to weep. The young foreman, who was last, replied with resolve, "Yeah!"

Bob shook his head in defeat. It was over.

Based on the State's request, Bob's bond was revoked. Until sentencing, he would once again reside at the Brown County Jail.

"Would you like to make any statement, Mr. Bulik?" Judge Greenwood asked.

Camera shutters clicked in the hushed courtroom as Bob purposefully rose from his chair. "Your Honor, I've lived under the Constitution of the United States here for thirty-seven years. For fourteen of those years, I swore to defend and uphold that Constitution. It's the first time, I can say, I don't know why the hell I did that! I'm not guilty, your Honor! I did not kill my wife, nor did I knowingly do anything to cause her death."

As an official started to place a cuff on Bob's right hand, his left wiped away the first tears I'd seen him display during the trial. Linda was then allowed to have a few words with him before he was escorted from the courtroom.

While the verdict sunk in, Beezie and I remained in our seats waiting for the crowd to disperse. We kept hypothesizing why the prosecution had lost their first-degree murder case. Appel must have done a good job putting some doubt in the jurors' minds. They'd also been sequestered for eleven days and so close to Christmas. Instead of fighting it out, perhaps they'd compromised on a quick decision so they could get out of Dodge!

I looked around at the departing spectators. None of them looked satisfied with the verdict. Comments flew: "Can you believe that son of a bitch was complaining? He should've been doing cartwheels across the courtroom with what he just got away with!" "There was no justice served here today!" "Hell! Even if he gets the maximum, he could be out in two and a half years! That bastard could even get probation!"

Last night's paper had printed the sentences to be doled out for each possible verdict. Ten years was the maximum for homicide by reckless conduct. With time off for good behavior, Bob would serve no more than six years and seven months. The best-case scenarios were parole after only two and a half years, or, Bob could even get probation and never set foot in prison.

Reporters had seized Appel as he packed up, asking about next steps. He said he was ready to file an appeal if that's what Bob wanted.

The media was also eager to interview the "winning team" and get their opinion on the verdict. Intense lights focused on the prosecuting attorneys and the detectives. Though outwardly calm, they were evidently upset. Lasee answered first. "I guess the jury had some difficulty finding Mr. Bulik intended to commit first-degree murder, but I'm not going to speculate."

"I thought the whole department did a solid investigation," said Sergeant Taylor. "That we'd crossed all our 'T's' and dotted all our 'I's,' but evidentially we didn't."

"Well," Captain Langan added, "I'm pleased with a finding of some sort of guilt, but personally, I think the verdict should've been more severe."

"We all know the verdict," Finne said harshly, "but sentencing is yet to come. I'm determined to obtain the maximum allowed by law."

Bob's brother looked as if he'd been holding in his anger. With his head bowed in the back row, Ken Bulik kicked the bench in front of him as he stood to leave. In the rotunda, a *Press-Gazette* reporter corralled him for an interview. We listened to Ken discuss the verdict, which he characterized as "not fair." He felt the trial had been a tale of two stories: "One was my brother's, which actually happened, and one they had time to dream up and make people believe ... He was so devoted to his children. He knew the consequences. Knowing that, there was no way he was guilty." Ken talked about the emotional effect the trial had had on his family. "It turned out to be a never-ending nightmare ... We never believed it would even go to trial because of lack of evidence."

Beezie was still bristling with righteous anger when we said our goodbyes. As I opened the outside door, a reporter nabbed me. "Mrs. Drews, you were one of Pamela Bulik's closest friends. How do you feel about the verdict?"

A gust of wind whipped at me. I shivered, trying to put words to my emotions. "I just feel so empty inside. I guess there's no verdict that could ever replace the loss of Pam's life." I turned my back on him and stepped outside into a whirl of snowflakes. I paused for a moment, attempting to calm myself, gulping in the freezing air, blinking hard. Holiday lights on lampposts sparkled against the backdrop of the dull gray afternoon. Christmas was now only twelve days away. I tipped my head to the heavens, letting the snow sooth my flushed face, and thought, I'll do my best, Pam, to celebrate your favorite time of year.

≈

The Jingle Bell Run was our last scheduled Fun Run for 1984. Friends arrived at the Lyties' home with bells strapped to their arms, waists, and necks for our annual two-mile jog over to Port Plaza Mall. Once there, we'd tromp from one end to another amid shouts of "Merry Christmas" to shoppers and store associates while depositing money in Salvation Army kettles.

Unlike other Fun Runs, everyone ran together, accommodating the pace of the slowest participants. The Kapalin kids would often lead the group, but tonight the whole family's absence was noticeable.

Our route to the mall passed the Brown County Jail. I looked up, wondering whether Bob was watching. Last year the entire Bulik family had taken part in this event.

Because Bill Appel had requested a pre-sentence investigation, Bob's fate would not be known until early February. His kids were still living with Linda. Wisconsin law didn't automatically take children away from a parent convicted of homicide. I knew Pam's brother had contacted Brown County officials about gaining custody. Bill Metzger fully believed that Bob had perpetrated first-degree murder. Of course he wasn't satisfied with the verdict, or any sentence Bob might receive. Nothing could ever replace the life of his only sibling.

I jogged along, my bells jingling in the frosty night air, thinking about 1984 and how it had changed so many lives. Pam was dead. Bob was behind bars. Their children were in limbo. And of course, Melissa Kapalin was not leading the way.

≈

The press characterized the Bulik trial as the most intensely watched in Brown County history. The final chapter was to begin on February 7, 1985—sentencing day. Bob's destiny now rested solely in Judge Greenwood's hands.

Beezie and I found seats in the stuffed courtroom. In my sixth month of pregnancy, I wriggled on the wooden bench trying unsuccessfully to find a comfortable position.

Bob, dressed neatly in a heather-gray sport coat over a white shirt and burgundy tie, was escorted over to the defense side of the shared table. Once his handcuffs were removed, he was seated next to Bill Appel. Bob's face looked sallow, but he appeared remarkably composed for a man whose future lay in the balance.

Royce Finne and Larry Lasee were stationed at the prosecution end of the table. Behind them sat Pam's father. Also in attendance was Virginia Williams, the probation/parole agent. She'd conducted one part of Bob's pre-sentence evaluation, comprised of two sections: her recommendation and a psychological evaluation ordered by Judge Greenwood. It had been performed by Robert Butler, Ph.D., the director of the psychology department for the Brown County Mental Health Center.

Missing from the courtroom was Bob's fiancée. That's how Bob had referred to Linda VandenLangenberg during his pre-sentencing meetings. In her interview, she, too, had admitted to having plans for marriage, but was unsure of a date.

The courtroom quieted when Judge Greenwood took the bench. To determine Bob's sentence for his conviction of homicide by reckless conduct, the judge said he would use the sentencing standards set forth by the Supreme Court:

1) The pre-sentence investigation recommendations;
2) The gravity of the offense;
3) The character and rehabilitative needs of the offender;
4) The need to protect the public.

Greenwood told the attorneys he'd read their briefs and had also received a deluge of letters, but before hearing their arguments, he first wanted to review the pre-sentence investigation report. It appeared the defense's request had backfired as the judge announced: The agent concluded that probation would not be appropriate because of inconsistencies and unanswered questions in Robert Bulik's life. Virginia Williams had noted that Bob had not been traumatized by his present offense, simply inconvenienced and exhibited no remorse at the loss of his spouse. "I'm quoting here," Greenwood said. "He remains a mystery, with some serious question marks." Because Bob was materialistic, Williams also believed a fine would be appropriate, but her recommendation had been diluted by the possible deprivation to the Bulik children.

Greenwood next referred to Bob's psychological evaluation. On January 8, 1985, Bob had appeared at the Brown County Mental Health Center in handcuffs and leg irons to complete a clinical interview and a number of psychological tests. Dr. Butler had noted that throughout, Bob appeared to try very hard to make an appearance of adequacy, control, and psychological effectiveness. His test results had portrayed a bright, socially skillful, and guarded individual, who would likely be seen as stubborn, oppositional, and self-centered. Neither Bob's history nor his psychological tests had shown evidence of any mental illness or severe emotional instability.

Dr. Butler had not recommended traditional inpatient or outpatient treatment since Bob did not see himself as needing such help at this time. From a psychological perspective, Butler could also not recommend probation, as (a) Mr. Bulik has little feeling of responsibility for his offense; and (b) has demonstrated marginal shame, guilt, or remorse in discussing his role in the death of his wife.

The judge next asked if there was any new evidence to present. Royce Finne politely declined while Bill Appel explained that he'd planned to have the Buliks' former neighbor testify. This morning, however, she'd instead dropped off a letter. Evidently frustrated, Appel said, "I'm sad, in the presence of the media, and treatment they've given this case, that it infringes upon the ability of people to come forward."

For the State's final argument, Royce Finne stood and addressed the judge. "I'd like to start my comments on the number of letters that the court has received on Mr. Bulik's behalf...Where were those people when they could come into court and give their opinions from the witness stand, so they could be cross-examined as the State's witnesses were forced to be? I am indeed sorry that Mr. Appel's troops in his letter-writing campaign are inconvenienced by the fact that trials in this country are open to the public. But that's the way it is."

The prosecutor said that after reading Bill Appel's brief, it had been evident that he'd felt the jury had believed the defense's version of the circumstances surrounding Pam's death. Finne adamantly shook his head. "That simply is not true! If the jury had, in fact, accepted Mr. Bulik's version at face value, he clearly would have been acquitted entirely."

Appel also claimed, Finne said, that Bob exhibited true remorse over Pam's death. The prosecutor's voice oozed sarcasm as he said that Bob had certainly shown remorse when, just weeks after Pam's death, he'd found the time and money to travel to the Bahamas and take summer trips with his new extended family, but hadn't found the time or money to place a marker on Pam's grave.

Finne next discussed the State's concern for the Bulik children. When Alex had been asked what effect the death of his mother had made on his life, he'd replied, "None." Even though Jean Weidner had recommended grief counseling for the Bulik children, the prosecutor said, Bob had not followed through. A social worker had been available at Danz School to talk with them, but the Bulik children had not been seen. For counseling to occur, Bob's permission had been required.

The pre-sentencing report stated that Pam's death had simply been an inconvenience to Bob. Finne said he agreed with its findings and added that even Bob's father had expressed surprise at how well his son had been coping with the death of his spouse.

"We owe something to Pamela Bulik," Finne beseeched the judge. "We have some responsibility to say to her, that while there is no reason for her death, there is some purpose or meaning attached to her life ... For this court to impose anything less than the maximum prison sentence upon Mr. Bulik would be an affront to the dignity of that woman's life!" Moreover, the prosecutor felt it would be the ultimate injustice if the system did not prevent Bob from deriving financial benefit from Pam's death. "We urge the court to sentence this defendant to a term of ten years in the state prison, and to fine him ten thousand dollars, the maximum allowed by law."

Pam's father next stood to address Judge Greenwood. William Metzger looked haggard. "I just hope that my emotion won't hinder what comes out of my mouth." He began to reiterate some of his comments that had been published in his January 18, 1985 letter to the *Green Bay News-Chronicle*:

"Nothing can ever be done to ease the pain of losing a child ... Pam had a feeling for Bob Bulik that is rare in most marriages, and I feel everything she did, from the time she met Bob, was to please him and to try to make him happy. Obviously, she failed, but that's no reason to punish her, and at the prime of her life.

"It's awfully hard to think that someone you love, as much as Pam did Bob, could do what he did to her in August of 1983, and again in April of 1984—and almost get away with it." Unfortunately, Mr. Metzger said, the August assault could not be introduced at Bob's trial. "If it could have, I think it almost certainly would have resulted in a first-degree murder conviction ... I have no feeling for Bulik, but I do feel so very sorry for my grandchildren, that, through no fault of their own, they will have to continue their young lives with a burden like this.

"I've never even received so much as a phone call from Bob Bulik since Pam's death. And to me, that is an admission of guilt." Mr. Metzger's eyes met the judge's. "Meager as the sentence may be, I sincerely hope that his prison term will be the maximum."

After Pam's father sat down, Bill Appel placed a hand on Bob's shoulder and stood. "The prosecution's recommendation today does not surprise me." Since the jury rejected the State's very public claims, Appel said he'd expected them to base their recommendation on disappointment and revenge. He then put on his glasses to read what the Supreme Court had to say about probation: It should be the sentence unless confinement was necessary to protect the public, the offender was in need of confined correctional treatment, or, if it would unduly depreciate the seriousness of the offense.

"The facts of this death, your Honor, clearly tell us that it is a very tragic event. Mrs. Bulik, I'm sure, was a very fine person. She has very fine friends." He gestured toward the spectator section. "I have some quarrel with their jumping to conclusions and prejudging. Basically they are fine people. I think we can measure her by that." Appel stated that he wanted Greenwood to compare the gravity of Bob's offense with other negligent homicide crimes, for example, the use of a weapon or vehicle, which carried a maximum penalty of two years; or homicide by intoxicated use of a vehicle or weapon, for which the maximum penalty was five years. Appel suggested that a death like Pam's should not be considered as serious an affront to society as one that involved guns, knives, or cars, which everyone recognized as dangerous to life and limb.

Appel next addressed Bob's rehabilitative needs. After reiterating his background, education, and job history, the attorney retrieved some letters. He criticized the pre-sentencing agent for having interviewed only peers of Bob's from "their side" like Mrs. Drews, Mrs. Gloudeman, Mrs. MacNeil, and Mrs. Madden. "That's why you got letters, your Honor." Appel began to read some, including one of Bob's students, a teaching associate, an individual who'd recently joined the Fun Run group, two reservists in Bob's former Green Bay unit, and a neighbor who had moved to Ohio. Appel said he'd brought those letters to the judge because the pre-sentence had not. "They don't tell you that Mr. Bulik is a man without remorse or repentance. They tell that he's a sensitive, kind, sincere, thoughtful individual, one who has earned their respect."

The last one Appel read was from the woman he'd hoped would've testified today.

> We, the Weglarz family, would like to plead for leniency in behalf of Robert Bulik. We were next-door neighbors for six and a half years, until August of 1983. Bob always impressed us as a shy young man … The big grin the kids would get from their dad when he would come to pick them up after school. The little manner in which he would correct a child's misbehavior. His involvement on many projects around the house and yard. The many sporting activities he shared with his family. All the nice things we know about Bob indicate to us that here is a man who … would never knowingly hurt anyone. We sincerely believe Bob and his children should be together again.

"We cannot bring Mrs. Bulik back today … We wish we could." But, Appel said, Bob's sentence would not only impact him, it would also affect his children. "Mr. Finne is wrong. I talked to the counselors … the teachers. Nobody has ever referred the children for any kind of help because they're doing fine in school. I'm not saying, Judge, that they aren't experiencing problems, and I frankly submit to you, the most imminent problem in their life right now is what's going to happen to their dad."

For the court to reject probation for Bob, Appel insisted that there must be a need for confinement and for correctional treatment. "We have to be honest and say that he's way beyond that … He is not a danger to society!" Incarceration would not be the appropriate punishment, the attorney said, when, due to the carbon monoxide, Bob had not known or could not appreciate what had been occurring the morning of April 7. "I don't see how punishment is going to help anybody." When the judge passed Bob's sentence, Appel asked him to think about the man and what the jury found truly happened.

With arguments complete, Judge Greenwood said he agreed with Mr. Appel. "I have to consider the facts in the light most favorable to the findings of the jury." He stated that they'd found Bob criminally responsible for Pam's death because of two courses of conduct: The first was when he placed Pam in bed, in a stuporous condition, without securing medical attention. The second was when he irresponsibly propped his stupefied wife next to the filled bathtub. "Mr. Bulik argues that the jury verdict is incorrect because they gave no consideration to the fact that he was under the influence of carbon monoxide poisoning." The judge leaned forward, folding his arms on the bench. "I disagree. The record is replete with a virtual symposium, if you will, of evidence on carbon monoxide poisoning, its insidious nature...and most particularly, how it has an individualistic effect on different people."

Moreover, Greenwood said, when Bob had given statements to the police at his home and at the station on April 7, he'd never complained of headaches or nausea, despite the fact that he'd testified to having been in a state of grief and shock. "But the jury didn't have to believe that...Credibility has always been one of the major problems in this case for both sides. That's why the case is really so unique." In addition, Greenwood said that Bob had never mentioned experiencing any carbon monoxide symptoms to Judge Duffy at the John Doe hearing. "The first time I ever heard anything about carbon monoxide poisoning and disorientation, on the part of Mr. Bulik, was in the trial...I also recall that Mr. Bulik's testimony exhibited a highly selective memory."

Greenwood believed that the decision to convict Bob of homicide by reckless conduct had been within the province of the jury, based on these facts:

- There was marital discord.
- There was a persistent paramour present.
- There were unsuccessful attempts to reconcile, through professional counseling.
- There was a motive for homicide.
- There was a crisis situation that existed.

- The jury found criminal conduct in Bob's complete failure to react to this crisis.

The judge stared sternly at Bob. "I can't understand how a magnificently conditioned thirty-seven-year old man, well educated, as Mr. Appel points out, could totally fail to do nothing... I'm prepared at this point to pass the sentence. But before I do, Mr. Bulik, you may address the court."

A subdued murmur fell over the room as Bob stood. Desperation had replaced composure on his face, now marked with shadows and heavy lines. "Thank you, your Honor... I really hope you haven't totally made up your mind yet... I have repeated, I am not guilty, and I would say that again today...

"You have all the information and letters, both good and bad. You have observed my behavior for seven months or so... You know about my family, probably better than the federal government does on their computers. You heard about my children and they are doing well... But it sounds like today, that it's not okay for me to be doing so well. My kids know me. They believe in me. They know there was no violence or abuse in our home...

"I also have to believe, they were probably the two smartest individuals to come and testify... They talked from experience about carbon monoxide... Abby had to slide on her butt down the stairs and crawl across the floor... So when we share these experiences the kids know what I'm talking about... We can accept and live with ourselves, and we can feel good about ourselves, because we know the truth.

"I have grieved for my wife, grieved deeply. But that was quickly surpassed by a need for survival from my first-degree murder charge. I've also grieved with my kids... I would never take their mother away from them! I would also like more than anything to reverse the contributions my actions made to Pam's accident. I can't. But they were not deliberate. I did not hold her head under the water." Bob's pained eyes met the judge's. "I think the jury found that. I didn't know I was jeopardizing a human life when I—"

"Let me say something," Greenwood interrupted. "The jury didn't believe you."

"I understand that, your Honor."

"I see. All right. Just so you are clear on that."

"I'm not sure they understood how individualistic carbon monoxide could be either ... Pam was not unconscious. She was groggy when I helped her sit down next to the tub—"

"The jury has considered that," Greenwood hastily cut in.

"Yes, your Honor." Bob looked grim.

"These are arguments that would have been presented to the jury, but I'll listen."

Bob nodded. "I'm concerned about the other adjectives—the propping up, and the dragging, and the setting down ... fabricated not from my story, but by the prosecution. And it's a matter of semantics that I feel I've been convicted ... I was not aware that she was in a life-threatening situation sitting next to the tub with eight inches of water in it. The kids and I have dealt with that, and we understand and honestly believe that it was an accident.

"1985 has Alex turning to a teenager and he goes to junior high. And Abby becomes eleven years old. I want to be there to help them through a difficult time in their life, any teenager's life. I have suggested to make my repayment for my actions in a positive way, based on my experience. Perhaps community service at a place like Rawhide Boys Ranch, working in varying new ways of life, new ways of living, being allowed to be a father to my children.

"If you have any questions, your Honor ... I'd be willing to answer them now. And I did say that to the police the day of my wife's death. I'm willing to answer any questions, be willing to take a lie detector test that they asked for."

An undercurrent of surprised whispers rippled through the room as Bob turned toward the prosecutors and said, "This might all have been unnecessary if they'd given me one."

Unbeknownst to the public, on April 7, 1984, Bob had signed a consent form to take a polygraph test about his involvement in

Pam's death, which the police had never administered. Prior to the trial, even though Appel had argued that Bob's consent bore "directly on his credibility," Greenwood had sided with the State. He'd ruled that no evidence could be presented about Bob's polygraph refusal in 1983, and no evidence could be offered about his desire to take one in 1984.

Now, turning back to the judge, hands outstretched in supplication, Bob implored, "I don't know what more the judicial process wants of me other than what I've already given. I have to trust once more in the fairness of your judgment."

He sat down, trying to keep his tears under wraps. Bob had made his last attempt to claim his innocence and beg for leniency.

A hush fell over the court as Judge Greenwood began, "Before I pass the sentence, I'm considering the alternatives available to me. At one time I seriously considered a medium fine in this case, but I think I'm going to change my mind... I'm not going to impose a fine."

A low hum again materialized.

The judge's stern look silenced it before he explained his reasoning. Greenwood said he'd taken into consideration that Mr. Bulik was a first-time offender who had a stable work record, had educated himself, and had a record of military service, though of course, that had been jeopardized by his felony conviction. And, after having been released on bail, Bob had returned to face trial. In considering all of these factors, the judge said that a fine might be unfair, not because it would take money away from Bob, but because it might work to the detriment of his children. "Also," Greenwood added, "it's highly improbable that he would be able to pay a fine."

The judge peered over his glasses at a hopeful Bob. "I reject probation..."

Bob's shoulders fell as noise erupted once more.

"I am convinced that Mr. Bulik does need correctional treatment. But most particularly, it depreciates the severity of this felony. Now, if you'll stand up, Mr. Bulik, I'll pass sentence..."

My breath rose as I plodded along the shoveled sidewalks on Monroe Street. In my seventh month of pregnancy, I was reluctant to give up running. It remained my best way to think. My gynecologist continued to give me his blessing, though had cautioned me to watch my footing. With my abdomen expanding, my center of gravity kept changing. So far, the biggest problem seemed to be bending over to tie my Nikes.

It had been almost a month since Bob's sentencing hearing. In this week's mail I'd received a letter from the Brown County District Attorney's office bringing back memories from that day. I could still picture Bob as Judge Greenwood said: It was the judgment of the court and the sentence of the law that Robert J. Bulik, be sentenced to the Wisconsin correctional system for a term of ten years, the maximum allowed by law.

Amid the explosion of cheers, jeers, and applause I'd watched my former friend, fellow runner, and the object of Pam's ardent love, shuffle away in cuffs toward his unimagined new life.

Today, before leaving the house for my run, I'd reread Royce Finne's personal note:

> Lynda—we are truly grateful for your help and encouragement. We could not have put the case together without the assistance of Pam's friends. My only regret is that I'll never get a chance to know Pam personally, as others will not. Perhaps that was the worst crime Bob committed.

Reflecting on his words, I jogged along, lightly resting a hand on my baby, who, like Royce had said, would never personally know Pam. Suddenly, I skidded, hitting a patch of ice below a dusting of snow. As my feet slipped out from under me, my hands thrashed wildly, trying to keep my balance. Still airborne, I struck the unforgiving pavement, hard.

19

Between Then and Now

Before 1984, I'd felt our close-knit running group was invincible. That year's tragic events had forever altered my belief. Beezie and I'd always said that we'd write a novel about that period in our life. When I retired, thirty years to the day from when I'd started at IBM, we'd begun. When the story changed into a true account, however, I continued on my own.

Back in the mid-eighties, Pam's death and Bob's trial had taken a toll on so many lives, especially their children's.

After sentencing, Bob was placed in maximum-security at Dodge Correctional Institution in Waupun and allowed three visits a week. Linda and his children could sit across from him and hold hands, but hugs and kisses were allowed only at the start and end of a visit. With access to a gym equipped with weight-lifting machines, a basketball court, and an outdoor recreation field, Bob had the opportunity to stay in shape.

About two weeks after Bob's sentencing, Pam's father was sent to a mental health center to undergo analysis for alcohol dependency. Earlier that week, after Pam's stepmother had told him she'd contacted a divorce attorney, William Metzger had grabbed and loaded a 20-gauge shotgun and announced, "There'll be no divorce." He'd aimed the gun at his wife who'd managed to secure it and call the police. Before Pam's father was evaluated, a judge had found probable cause to try him for endangering safety by conduct regardless of life. Like his son-in-law's charge, it could carry a maximum of ten years in prison.

While dealing with his sister's death and his father's problems, Bill Metzger was still trying to gain custody of Abby and Alex. "I desperately wanted to adopt the kids and take them away from that guy." Bill and Bonnie had contacted social services in Bellevue, Washington, to set up the home visit and study. But in late March, Linda VandenLangenberg applied for a marriage license at the Dodge County clerk's office. Prison authorities approved the wedding, which took place behind the correctional institution walls in the spring of 1985. Since the new Mrs. Bulik's status took priority over the Metzgers', she would retain custody of Bob's children.

In July of 1985, Bill Appel filed Bob's appeal. Afterward, Judge Greenwood received an anonymous letter that conveyed the feelings of many in the community:

> Dear Judge Greenwood:
> I see in the papers that Mr. Bulik is going to appeal his conviction. What does he expect? He got off cheap with the sentence that you gave him. I think he has no reason to get it reduced. I remember when his attorney tried to get you to put him on probation and you told Mr. Appel that this was not an accident. I agree with you. If you have any influence, on the up-coming decision, keep him in prison the full term or at least until 1990, on good behavior. Don't let him get away too cheap. He will at least learn that thy [sic] shall not kill.

Pam's father died in August of 1986 and never knew that his son-in-law's appeal was turned down. By this time Bob had been moved into Waupun's medium-security section. He'd also requested a transfer to a minimum-security facility close to Madison. As expected, Bob's parole agent told the press that his client's institutional adjustment had been excellent. He was currently working as an assessment and evaluation clerk.

Since Bob was a model prisoner, I felt certain that both he and

Linda had expected Bob to make parole at his first hearing in April of 1987, but that didn't happen. The prosecutors' office solicited letters to keep Bob behind bars. I wrote one, and so did nearly all of Pam's friends and family. Dr. Wellens's letter said:

> I'm very much opposed to his release at this time … It would have a detrimental effect on society. The community has certain standards … The jury and the judge made their decisions in this case. For the parole board to disregard that would be pretty capricious. The community needs time to heal and it hasn't healed yet.

After Bob's parole was denied, he'd received his transfer to Oak Hill near Madison where he participated in a marriage enrichment seminar, hinting at an undercurrent in the Buliks' marriage. That's also when Bob initiated his letter-writing campaign to Judge Greenwood requesting a sentence reduction. If there were new factors, the judge had the power to modify it.

In Bob's first letter, dated October 12, 1987, he enclosed an article from the May 1985 *Runner's World* magazine, which discussed the beneficial effects warm water had on human physiology. Bob also included an article on carbon monoxide from the January 1985 issue of *Woman's Day* magazine. He ended his letter with:

> I am fully aware that I should have acted differently on the morning of my wife's death. I have apologized to those most directly affected and have asked for their forgiveness — and for the forgiveness of God.

Based on the State's input, Greenwood told Bob that no new factors were up for consideration. The content of the magazine articles had already been argued to the jury.

Two weeks later, the *Press-Gazette* reported that the former Linda VandenLangenberg had initiated divorce proceedings, stating that her marriage to Bob Bulik was "irretrievably broken." Plainly, it hadn't turned out to be what she'd imagined. Bob wouldn't be paroled any time soon, Linda had been saddled with his children, and she'd assumed Bob's house payments and other debts. On November 2, 1987, Bob wrote his next letter to the judge. It included the new factor of his impending divorce. He said there was a family problem that "I had wanted to work on (and still do) closer to home and perhaps solve after my release. Unfortunately, my wife does not want to wait that long." Bob said the divorce would result in his two children—Alex, fifteen, and Abby, thirteen—having no legal status. "They would undoubtedly be candidates for separate foster placement. My father died in July 1987 and the only other relatives... live out-of-state."

Bob provided an enclosure showing that the average length of incarceration for homicide by reckless conduct was about thirty months. "As of November 1987, I have served thirty-six months of my sentence. I will have served a total of forty-two months before I next see the Parole Board." Bob suggested that continued incarceration no longer punished just him, but also punished his children.

Bob's divorce proceeding took place before Judge Greenwood responded. Linda testified that counseling couldn't save their marriage. When the divorce judge asked Bob if that was so, he answered, "I've taken her word in all other regards, so I must take it here also." When their divorce settlement was published, Bob again was strapped with mortgage payments. There was no doubt he'd been passionate about Linda, but he'd also loved that house and wasn't ready to lose it, too. Linda agreed to pay him $500 a month rent and would remain there, with his children, promising to act as their legal guardian until his release.

On March 16, 1988, Bob again wrote the judge.

> The children have been victims, or near victims, throughout this ordeal. If I had done nothing that April night of 1984—e.g. had not woken up in the middle of the night, Pamela would still have died from carbon monoxide poisoning. If I had done nothing that night, according to the pathologist, I would also have died—to a few people in Green Bay that doesn't sound too bad. But if I had

done nothing that night, Alex and Abby would also have died of carbon monoxide poisoning instead of just suffering its moderate affects. If I did nothing else right, in the dark of the night, in a carbon monoxide saturated environment, my initial actions saved my two children.

I have never before asked to be recognized for those initial actions that, in fact, saved my children. Yet I do fully understand that I should have been aware that Pamela was in danger and that I should have acted differently—I am...serving my punishment for bad judgment.

I would once again ask that you consider my request for modification of sentence...I have a job offer in Green Bay, a home to return to, and two children that need a parent in their lives.

By September 18, 1988, while still awaiting the judge's response, Bob was transferred closer to Green Bay. His new home was inside the Winnebago Correctional Center, a minimum-security facility located near Oshkosh. Bob again wrote:

At the time of our divorce Linda assured everyone that she would continue to care for my children until I was released. She has since changed her mind and told the children that they would not be welcome when she moves in with her new boyfriend at the end of September, and to ask the neighbors if they couldn't move in for "a while." I feel this emotional abuse is grounds for asking that Linda be removed as the children's guardian. But that also places yet another kind of stress on the children as a foster placement becomes necessary—and an additional stress on the social services agencies. Both burdens could be relieved by a sentence modification.

Bob added that he was currently attending UW-Oshkosh on a school-release program from Winnebago Correctional Center to pick up the continuing education credits he needed to retain his teaching license. He was also participating in a prison running program and attending road races throughout the state. He hoped to enter the upcoming Milwaukee Lakefront Marathon.

Friends of ours had bumped into Bob on the Oshkosh campus. At the Green Bay Kellogg's Classic Race, I'd been shocked to see him among other prisoners, all wearing their Winnebago Correctional running garb. I'd averted my eyes, and Bob had done the same.

During October of 1988, Bob's children were placed in separate foster homes in the Buliks' neighborhood. The Metzgers had decided not to step in. "I would not be a babysitter for the remaining time Bob was in jail," Bill said, "only to pass them back to him." The Madden family had become Abby's foster parents. Sylvia had hoped that Alex could have remained with his initial foster family, but it hadn't worked out. His next placement was outside the neighborhood. At Preble High School, Abby had a lot of support from the staff, including Rod Leadley who'd transferred from Edison Middle School.

In November of 1988, the judge received yet another update from Bob. He reminded the judge of his many unanswered letters and said, "In the past months I have taken on a number of responsibilities." In addition to attending college, Bob said he'd recently co-authored a professional journal article titled, "Recreational Needs Assessment of Youthful Offenders in the State of Wisconsin." He'd also completed the Milwaukee Lakefront Marathon and was performing chauffeuring duties for other inmates on school and work release programs. However, he said, "The responsibility I would most like to take on is that of full time parent for Abby and Alex."

In December of 1988, Bob received this response from Judge Greenwood:

> While I share Bulik's concern for his children, and appreciate his input...I am satisfied that this matter is more appropriately within the forum of the Parole Board. Motion for modification of sentence is denied.

December appeared to be a rough month for Bob. His letter-writing campaign to Judge Greenwood had been for naught, he'd had to sell his home, and Linda remarried on December 29. She headed off on a honeymoon with her third husband, a Brown County probate official, who was a personal friend to many of the local detectives and attorneys.

With no other recourse, Bob could only hope that the parole board would release him in April 1989. It didn't happen. They decided that he hadn't served enough time for his crime, though noted that he would be freed on his mandatory release date in April 1990. At that stage, he'd continue under state supervision until November 1994, the end of his ten-year term.

At age forty-two, after six years of confinement, Bob was released with an acceptance into at least one doctoral program. He moved into a duplex in Green Bay, reclaimed his children, and was also ready to reclaim his teaching job.

While Bob was in prison, the Wisconsin Teacher's Association had renewed his license. They now realized it had been done in error. This issue landed in court. Bob subpoenaed his parole agent, Steve Daniels, to testify on his behalf. That was not a smart move. During their meetings, Steve said he'd found Bob to be self-centered, arrogant, and condescending—a man who didn't like authority or want to be "lumped in with other criminals."

Additional witnesses testified to feeling that educators and the community would not be comfortable working with Bob. Richard Herlache, the special education supervisor for the Green Bay Public Schools said Bob's conviction had made it almost impossible for him to perform as a teacher in Green Bay. An article in the October 2, 1990 issue of the *Press-Gazette* quoted Herlache as saying, "The community convicted him of something greater than the court has done."

Bob's Wisconsin public teaching license was permanently revoked.

In the years that followed, Bob earned his Ph.D., secured a teaching position at a university outside of Wisconsin, and married for the third time.

"Since this tragedy occurred, we've seen the kids only four

times," Bill Metzger said. Shortly after Pam's death, Alex and Abby had come out and spent a week at the Metzgers' lake home near Seattle. No one had discussed the situation and the kids had a great time water skiing, boating, and relating with their cousins. Alex and Abby had acted like this had just been a regular visit to their aunt and uncle's.

The Metzgers didn't see either child again until Alex came to their eldest daughter's wedding in 2001. This helped break the years of separation. While waiting to enter the church, Bonnie had turned to Alex and whispered, "I sure wish your mother was here."

Bob Bulik after securing his Ph.D. and a university teaching position.

"I wish she were, too," he'd quietly responded.

In 2004, the Metzgers' second daughter was married. This time, both Alex and Abby attended. By then Alex was married, and the Metzgers met Abby's fiancée. Bill admitted, "Whenever I'm around them my anger gets stirred up all over again. I can't feel close to them because I never have been. All I have is sympathy. I pulled Abby's fiancée aside and asked him to tell me what Abby thought about the loss of her mother. He made it sound very objective, a matter-of-fact dark part of her life."

When Pam died, Collin had been two, while the MacNeil and Madden children had been around the same age as the Buliks'. I had never known Alex and Abby the way Beezie and Sylvia had. They'd both stayed in touch, especially with Abby. Before her wedding, we three women went through our recipes to find those handwritten by her mom. I found the ones for chocolate chip cookies, carrot cake, garlic bread, and cauliflower salad, all in Pam's distinctive script. Sylvia presented our combined recipe cards to Abby when the Maddens and MacNeils attended her wedding. Beezie decided to go for Abby's sake. Bob had excitedly approached the MacNeils, his hand held out to Bruce. Caught off guard, Bruce didn't know what to do and awkwardly shook it. Beezie turned away.

The Metzgers didn't attend the Bulik children's weddings. Bill said he couldn't be anywhere near Bob. "I have never discussed that situation about Pam with either one of the children. I am convinced that Abby, certainly, and to a degree, Alex, have been convinced that this was just a terrible accident. I think they have a pretty decent relationship with Bob. They certainly realize that their father went to prison, but believe it was probably just a miscarriage of justice. Bob's been able to convince them that the court got it all wrong."

≈

Back in the eighties, I'd believed Bob had been guilty of first-degree murder. After more than twenty years I met with other principals who'd shared this experience, to ascertain what they now believed.

Unable to locate Sergeant Jim Taylor at his familiar haunt, I was told he'd retired. The new chief of police was James Arts, my husband's former East High School cross country runner.

The years had been kind to Taylor. His hair was slightly thinner and he'd gained a few extra pounds, but not too many. I first asked him whether he still thought Pam's death was premeditated.

"I'm 100 percent positive her death was an intentional homicide!" Taylor said, pounding the table. "I have no doubt whatsoever! I never met Pam. She was being treated that night in August. The next time I saw her she was dead. But to this day I believe she was a heck of a nice person." He leaned back, catching my eyes. "I think six months before her death the train left the station heading toward her murder. August was important because that's when Bob made his trial run." Taylor believed that Bob had planned that the mysterious stranger would reappear in April and finish what he'd started in August. The intruder had already been there once—why not a second time?

The computer Alex had been using, Taylor said, had actually belonged to Freedom High School. Unbeknownst to Bob, Pam had brought it home on Friday, April 6, 1984, for their children's use. Taylor believed that's why Alex had still been awake, thus foiling Bob's original plan. "Daddy walked in the back door surprised, asking, 'What are you doing up?' Bob ran the house. When he told the kids to go to bed at nine o'clock he expected them to follow orders."

**April 7, 1984 photo showing the computer and
monitor that Pam brought home
from Freedom High School.**

I asked Taylor about Bob's statement at his sentencing hearing where he'd said that, on the day of Pam's death, he'd agreed to take a polygraph test. Over the years, this had bothered me. It didn't seem something a guilty person would do. Taylor couldn't remember why the department hadn't followed through. Most likely, they'd felt that Bob would've been familiar with the polygraph procedure since Pam had taken one in August when Bob had refused. During the months before Pam's death, there'd been plenty of time for Bob to figure out the secret behind it. A polygraph wasn't a scientific test and could be tricked with some practice. A liar could beat it by secretly enhancing their physiological reaction to the control questions by, for instance, doing mental arithmetic, fantasizing, or biting the side of their cheek. The actual questions about Pam's death would then have been compared inaccurately, resulting in false results. "The judge knew that as well," Taylor said. "That's why Bob's agreement to take a polygraph was suppressed before trial."

The former detective gave me something new to stew over. A friend of his had served some time with Bob. The prison had a deal that allowed inmates and their spouses to meet for marriage counseling. This inmate's wife had phoned Taylor after a session, all shaken up. She and her husband had been assigned to a group that had included Bob and Linda. When the counselor had talked about issues that could lead to divorce, Bob had jokingly said something like: There are other ways to dissolve a marriage besides divorce. Taylor told his friend's wife that there wasn't anything he could do with her information—Bob had already been tried and convicted.

In his office, near the courthouse, I spoke with Royce Finne, who had since moved into private practice. Still sporting a renegade attitude, he hardly seemed to have changed. He certainly remembered the Bulik case—the most difficult one he'd tried up to that point in his career. Back in 1984, first-degree murder carried a maximum of twenty-two years in prison. Today it carried a mandatory life sentence, so defendants often pled out. Even if Bob had been convicted now, Finne believed he still would not have done so. "Bob had a huge ego and felt he could get away with it."

Following his release, Bob had met with his parole officer monthly in a building right across the street. Finne appeared irked when he said, "I think Bob parked in front of my office window on purpose."

Finne had long believed that Pam's December 1983 memory loss had been drug induced. Like Taylor, he felt the August incident, as well as that December episode, had been trial runs for her eventual murder. The attorney had conjectured that on the night of Pam' death, Bob had put his sleeping pill in her beverage before Pam had gone to bed. Since she'd planned to run a half marathon in the morning, Finne felt she would never have taken that pill herself. He still believed that Pam hadn't entered the van of her own accord. When Bob eventually pulled her out, Finne thought that Bob had run the water and immediately put her into the bathtub while she was still unconscious. Perhaps that had been the reason why Pam's green sweat suit bottom and underwear had been wet, but contained no urine residue. "All I can say is Bob's new wife better keep a pair of swim fins and a snorkel handy!"

Finne sounded a bit like Bob's former swim team coach, Randy Albright, who said that Pam's death still bothered him. He knew what a good swimmer she'd been, and said it was hard to drown in a swimming pool, much less a bathtub. Pam would instinctively have tried to survive—unless she'd been held under.

I visited the Law Enforcement Center, the current home of the Brown County district attorney's office. Assistant DA Larry Lasee greeted me, a smile on his face. His firm handshake brought back memories of our earlier meeting before we'd known Bob's verdict.

Lasee told me that he still had no doubt that Bob was guilty of first-degree murder. Due to the extreme measures he'd gone through to plan Pam's death, this remained one of the prosecutor's most memorable cases. "In this community, we don't get crimes so sophisticated and calculated. Bob, however, did botch it up. Pam was supposed to die in the van."

During the Bulik case, Lasee said he'd had a fine working relationship with Royce Finne. "But it was Royce's case." If it had been Lasee's, however, there'd been one thing he would've done differently. In the closing argument, he'd wanted to challenge the jury to read Pam's journals cover-to-cover before reaching their verdict. If they had, Lasee believed the jury would never have considered that Pam might have taken her own life.

Before Robert Langan retired, he'd been promoted to deputy chief of detectives and eventually to assistant chief of police. In his Green Bay home he reflected on the Bulik trial. "I don't know what more we could've done. I think we went to court with a great case. We all felt confident that we could paint the whole picture, and first-degree murder was the only alternative…Royce Finne will remember it his whole life. He kind of blames himself for the timing, for bringing in the out of town jury. He believes Bob Bulik didn't get his just due."

While the jury deliberated, Langan said they could've sent the judge a note to get an interpretation about Pam's earlier head injury, but they hadn't. Langan felt it had been a high-pressure time around Christmas. "The other choices, second-degree and homicide by reckless conduct, were put out by the prosecution team at the last minute. Maybe they shouldn't have been, but if they hadn't, maybe Bob would've totally walked."

Had the Christmas season affected the jurors' decision, as others liked to believe? After tracking down three of them, we all met for dinner in West Bend, Wisconsin. Across from me sat Peter Smith*, the jury foreman. In 1984 he'd been twenty-five, the tool and die maker and triathlete. During jury selection, Bob had seemed familiar to Peter. In the midst of the trial, he'd finally placed Bob. The summer of 1984, Peter had completed a triathlon that had drawn about 600 participants. It had dawned on him that he'd either run or biked a portion with Bob. Peter assumed Linda had been there, too. When he'd been selected for the jury, he'd anticipated that the trial might run until Christmas or even beyond. While in Green Bay, Peter said he'd received no salary from his job. In turn, the state of Wisconsin had compensated each juror with only twenty dollars a day.

In 1984, Alice Musser* had been the twenty-three-year-old newlywed, who'd watched the *Fatal Vision* mini-series, while at twenty-two, Kyle Nebal* had been the only single juror and had worked in the vehicle body shop. As the last juror selected, he'd been unhappily surprised to discover that the trial was to take place in Green Bay. Believing he'd be home within the week, he'd packed accordingly.

All three were glad they'd been picked for the jury—it had been quite an experience. They agreed that all the lawyers had been very good. Without any prompting, they remembered many details about Bob and Linda, but nothing about Pam—not even her name. They didn't feel that they'd gotten to know her.

During deliberations they'd made it simple: Bob had planned it and killed Pam, had killed her without a plan, did nothing to help her, or not guilty. Peter said they'd first chosen a foreman. No one had volunteered, so he'd eventually raised his hand and gotten the job. They'd taken an immediate vote. Two had felt that Bob had been "guilty as hell." Peter had been one of them. He'd had occasion to take sleeping pills and had found it difficult to rouse himself—even by morning. He didn't think Pam could've awakened during the night. In his camp had been the female teacher's aide. Two jurors had thought Bob had been totally innocent. One had been the male volunteer for the West Bend Rescue Squad, who'd also been the runner. The other had been the female homemaker, who'd watched the *Fatal Vision* mini-series, too. The remaining jurors, including Alice and Kyle, had been undecided. "At that point," Peter said, "I was worried that Bob was going to get off."

The majority had gradually started to believe that Bob should not just walk. Because he'd been in the military and trained as a marine, he should have known how to handle an emergency situation. It should have been as ingrained as breathing.

They'd dismissed Bob's having parked his car at Preble High School, unable to decide whether he'd been hiding it from neighbors or innocently surprising Pam. They'd also considered the prosecution's claim that Pam's insurance money had been part of the motive, but had rejected it as not being enough to trigger first-degree murder.

They all said it had been difficult, at best, to make a decision without having answers to many of their questions, but they'd ended up by compromising on homicide by reckless conduct. They'd thought Bob was guilty for having taken no action to save Pam.

I asked how they'd reached their verdict so quickly. Did they think the trial's proximity to Christmas had been a factor?

None of them believed it had affected the deliberation time or their decision.

After the verdict, they'd been escorted out of the courtroom into a throng of Green Bay media. Because the jurors had been fearful of how "whacked out" Bob might be when he got out of prison, all had said, "No comment" to keep their names and photos out of print.

In addition to a Stein Supper Club placemat, signed by each juror, Peter handed me a large yellow envelope he'd saved from 1984. On the trip back to West Bend, they'd each been given an individual packet prepared by Mabel Tuttle, the clerk of courts. Inside was a letter of appreciation "for having been such diligent jurors and for having given of your time during this Holiday Season." She'd also enclosed copies of the trial articles from the Green Bay newspapers.

Within the envelope, I located the first *Press-Gazette* article, dated Monday, December 3, 1984. After skimming it, I read the following excerpt to the three:

> One thing jurors won't hear is the story of an alleged break-in at the Bulik home in August 1983. Bulik claimed that his wife was struck on the head and he was knocked unconscious by a stomach punch. Greenwood ruled Thursday that testimony on the break-in will be excluded.

They vaguely remembered having been confused after reading that article. When I explained the incident, they were all upset. "Why weren't we told this during the trial?" And, "If we had known, would it have made a difference in the verdict?"

Peter said, "One thing I learned from this whole ordeal is that the jury doesn't get to hear all the facts!"

Marsha Knoebel, the mother of my son's friend, clerked for a now semi-retired Judge Richard Greenwood. As I waited to meet with him I explained why I was there. She laughed and said it was such a small world. She and her husband, Keith, a Green Bay cop, owned the duplex that Bob had rented after he'd been released from prison. He'd slightly altered the spelling of his last name. Her husband had done a background check before leasing to Bob, and it had come back clean.

Judge Greenwood entered and ushered me into the jurors' room assigned to his court. It was the same one that had been used to determine Bob's fate. I asked the judge what he thought about the jury's decision in Bob's trial.

"It was their question of guilt, not mine," Greenwood firmly stated.

Over his lengthy career, he said he'd had a number of memorable cases. In one that stood out, the defendant had been found guilty of first-degree murder despite the absence of a body—almost unheard of. His second most memorable case had been Bob Bulik's. The judge still mused on it. "This was a puzzling case."

In response to my question about his ruling on the August incident, Greenwood said this "Whitty-type Evidence" was often introduced by the district attorney's office to show that the defendant had acted in a similar fashion on prior occasions. As a judge, it had been up to his discretion whether to allow it, and he'd made his decision.

Brown County Coroner Genie Williams was now retired. We met at her home to discuss her memories of the Bulik case. She felt Pam's death had been "beautifully planned out." Genie believed that until Bob had walked in and found Alex at the computer, he'd still had things aced. "Bob got impatient that night and carried it through. If he'd waited and tried another time, he might have succeeded."

In her years as a Brown County coroner, she'd seen many suicides in cars. It was a rare instance when the victim changed seats, unless the process was taking too long and the victim got bored or uncomfortable. No matter what the defense said, Genie didn't believe that Pam would've started the van from the passenger seat. When Bob had removed Pam from the van, she'd been in a coma. At that time, Genie felt he had put her in the "pool."

In response to questions about carbon monoxide, Genie said, even if Bob's blood had been analyzed on April 7, it would not have changed the outcome. No matter what his carbon monoxide level may have been earlier, by the time she and the police had arrived, that poison would've been diffused from his body and the house. "There were windows open. Bob was in and out of the house. The garage wasn't airtight. He had opened one side of it to use the van."

As a coroner, she was used to seeing people grieving after the death of a spouse. "Bob wasn't like the many others I have dealt with. On April seventh, as he left the house for the police station, the last thing he said to me was, 'Please make sure you close the windows.' It certainly wasn't the usual thought after your wife has just drowned in the bathtub!"

Of course the community had speculated whether Linda VandenLangenberg had been involved in Pam's death. The detectives had considered that option as well. From day one Sergeant Taylor had thought that Linda might have been involved, but could never prove it. When Bob had called 911, hung up, and then picked up the phone again, Taylor thought he'd been calling Linda to say, "It's over."

While Bob was in prison, Taylor had helped Linda with some issue and the two had talked. At one point, she'd told him, there hadn't been anyone in the world she'd hated more. Now Linda even sent him Christmas cards.

Robert Langan thought Linda was quite a character. "Every time she sees me she gives me a hug." Her current father-in-law had been deputy chief of detectives and Langan's first boss.

Both Robert Langan and Jim Taylor told me to give Linda a call. They felt she might talk with me. The last time we had talked was eons ago when she'd joined Pam and me on that July 1983 run. I called Linda and we chatted on the phone for about an hour. She said she'd been filled with regrets since Pam's death, but had managed to deal and get through them. If she hadn't taken a certain turn in her life, she knew things would have been different. She said she'd done a lot of soul searching, gone to counseling, and remained friends with many who had been involved in the trial. The most caring individual was Bill Appel, who'd always believed in Bob's innocence. She'd also remained friends with Bill's wife Kathy.

I asked Linda for her thoughts about Bob's part in Pam's death. She was, of course, biased, she said. She had to believe in Bob's good and in who he was, although she still thought it was crazy that he'd left the house to take the children to the mall. "But that was Bob."

Linda said he was a private man. There was a mystery about him. He wasn't a team kind of guy. No one would step up for him.

Afterward, Linda said she'd tried to have a life. The head of the Green Bay Schools special education instruction and the parents of her students had stood behind her. There had been no grounds for her dismissal. When she'd run for a city council position, Green Bay's mayor had supported her. At that time, Linda said, everything had resurfaced, but she'd managed to get through it and win the election.

Before hanging up, Linda told me she still held herself accountable for what had happened.

I told her I appreciated her candor and believed, had this tragedy not occurred, most likely, we would have been friends.

≈

I'd listened to other people's opinions and now came back to my own. Did I still believe Bob was guilty of first-degree murder? During my research, seven discoveries had surprisingly caused me to reassess my previous belief.

First was the August incident. Like others, I'd felt this had been Bob's trial run—but had it been? Sylvia told me there'd been a blond student that she and Bob had taught at Preble. He'd had emotional problems and lived near the Buliks. Although Sylvia never felt he could've been involved, the 1983 Green Bay Police incident reports never mentioned that he or anyone else had been questioned. It appeared the authorities had only focused on Bob. This seemed wrong. I'd asked Robert Langan what he thought. Even though he felt the odds had pointed Bob's way, Langan agreed that the police should've done some additional legwork to check for other potential suspects.

Second was Bob's premeditated plan to kill Pam. In the police interviews I'd noted that Abby's best friend, Allena Teixeira, had been invited to spend the night of Saturday, April 7 at the Buliks'. Because this had been a common occurrence, rather than Saturday night, the two could have been giggling up in Abby's room on Friday when Bob arrived home at 10:30. Alex had also returned from roller-skating at 9:45 on April 6. This had been a popular Friday night activity for kids his age. With all the sugary treats from the rink's concession stand, it would've been unusual for any eleven-year-old to immediately jump into bed. That same night, a number of Fun Run couples had gone out for fish. If I'd called Pam, I believe she would've hired a sitter and joined us, as she had done in the past. Like the rest of us, she would have returned home after 11:00. If Bob had intended to kill Pam, as an intelligent man, he would not have chanced being seen by his children, their friends, or a sitter. To ensure that his entire household would've been asleep, Bob would have arrived home at a much later time.

Third was when Pam's bruises had actually occurred. During Finne's rebuttal statement, I'd believed his conclusion that they'd been inflicted before Pam was taken out of the van. But the prosecutor had hedged his claim with "to the extent it's accurate." Dr. Skarphol had testified that the 50 percent diffusion figure was based on breathing fresh air over a four to five hour timeframe, but the Buliks' home had carbon monoxide in it. Also, the four to five-hour age for Pam's bruises had been based only on Dr. Young's testimony. Dr. Skarphol had said that the age range was from one and a half to six hours old, while Dr. Fodden had stated three to five. If the bruises had been, say, three hours old rather than four, Pam's ultimate carbon-monoxide level would have been closer to 70. At this figure, Pam could still have been alive. Based on these two factors, individually or in combination, Pam's bruises could have occurred during her rescue.

Fourth was Pam's state of mind. The police records noted that, at about 6:30 p.m. on Friday, April 6, Pam's neighbor, Mary Teixeira, had received a call from Pam. She'd mentioned being "depressed and down" about her marriage problems and canceled their plans to take their daughters out for pizza. Reservist Dan O'Connell had testified that when he'd landed in Denver, there'd been a page for Bob Bulik. Assuming that had been Pam and that she'd also called Linda's school earlier, what thoughts had been consuming her mind? On our last run, she'd mentioned that she and Bob had been discussing a possible move, so as to be closer to Denver. Even though I hadn't liked the idea, I'd realized that this could have provided her family a fresh start without Linda hovering nearby. When Bob arrived home at 10:30 on April 6, this would have confirmed Pam's disconcerting speculation. Had she slid into this intense state of anxiety knowing that her hopeful future had again been destroyed?

Fifth was Bob's assertion that carbon monoxide affected his reasoning and memory. At Bob's sentencing hearing, Judge Greenwood had stated that the first time Bob had mentioned being affected by carbon monoxide had been at his December trial. It appeared as if Bob had worked with Appel to develop this line of defense. But in Bob's John Doe transcript, before he'd hired an attorney, I discovered the following question asked by Finne and Bob's response:

Q: Evidently, Pam had not said anything to you that morning?

A: No ... That's what I recall. I also recall, I guess, being rather foggy-headed that morning. And as I think back over things, I'm assuming it's from what carbon monoxide might have seeped into the house. Probably the reason why the kids were sick, sick to their stomach with headaches, and probably why I cannot remember a lot of the specific details that you have asked about that evening.

I also located the article Bob had mailed to Judge Greenwood from the January 1985 issue of *Woman's Day* magazine, titled "One Family's Winter Nightmare" and written by Laurence Alpert, M.D. The story seemed to mirror many aspects of Bob's. When carbon monoxide from a faulty furnace had escaped into the home of a David Block, he recalled stumbling around in a dreamlike state, falling on stairs, losing all sense of time. Even though his wife had lain beside him in bed, unconscious, glassy-eyed, he had not been aware she'd been dying. Earlier his daughter had yelled that the heat had been off, but by then, he'd been totally disoriented and had lost his ability to reason. A neighbor had come over, however, she hadn't immediately dialed 911. After a few minutes, her reflexes had slowed, her thoughts had muddled. Doctors later said they usually saw corpses rather than survivors.

Sixth was Bob's rationale for soaking Pam's legs. The additional article Bob had sent Judge Greenwood had been from the May 1985 *Runner's World* magazine. In it, a group of physicians, sports chiropractors, and physical therapists discussed the value warm water provided prior to running. They said that heat increased the extensibility of the tissue in the joints so stretching was more effective in a whirlpool. Runners could also use the hot/cold approach to injury prevention where the hot tub could be used prior to the run and ice used afterward. At a recent UW-La Crosse alumni cross country weekend, I'd wanted to verify this. I'd asked a few of the guys who'd also achieved all-American status: "Have you ever soaked your legs in warm water before a competitive race?" Some said they had, and for the same reasons cited in the *Runner's World* article.

Finally, seventh was Bob's concern for his children. I'd believed Finne's rebuttal claim that Bob had taken his kids to the mall at 9:30 a.m. so that they would not have been in the home to discover their mom. But in the police records, three interviews could dispute Finne's timeline. First, Sue Burnham* said, she and her son, Scott, had driven down the Buliks' driveway at about 10:15 a.m. on Saturday April 7 to ask Alex to accompany Scott to the mall. Because Alex hadn't been ready, the boys had agreed to meet by Port Plaza's big clock at 11:30. Scott had confirmed that his friend had arrived at about that time. The police had also interviewed Nancy Marohl, a neighbor and the former wife of an IBM colleague of mine. On the day of Pam's death, Nancy said she'd seen Alex Bulik walking their dog at about 10:35 a.m. Finally, Allena Teixeira said she'd been all set to leave for the mall and had been walking over to the Buliks' when Bob had driven up at 10:55.

These seven factors have created some reasonable doubt in my mind—especially doubt that Bob planned to murder Pam. However, that still doesn't absolve him of his homicide by reckless conduct conviction. Bob never disputed that he'd placed Pam next to their filled bathtub while she'd been groggy. He alone had given her the opportunity to slip, strike her head, and drown.

Many years ago, Bob's peers had judged him and meted out punishment for that. He has also duly served his time. Our legal system has been satisfied, although, in all honesty, if Pam hadn't suffered eight months of mental abuse fueled by Bob's constant deceit, she would still be alive.

~

Near dusk on the anniversary of Pam's death, Beezie and I drove north on the high ridge of Bay Settlement Road. Last year, persuaded by Kathy Kapalin, I'd joined her to run the Dick Lytie

Spring Classic along this same route. Mark Ernst, an East High runner whom Jim had coached, was the new race director. He and his wife, Debbie, owned In Competition, a local running and biking store, and had renamed the half marathon in Dick's honor. Unexpectedly, at the age of fifty-nine, our gentle running guru, surrounded by his multitude of friends, had collapsed and died of a heart attack at our weekly Fun Run.

The Kapalin family had emerged from their devastating loss of Melissa with quiet enduring strength, a constant aid through their lifelong pain. At Melissa's funeral, Kathy had asked the congregation to promise that they'd never forget her. Our family, including Collin's brother, Christopher, who'd ignored my fall and arrived on May 19, 1985, had honored that pledge.

Shortly after Pam's death, Beezie had unsuccessfully tried to find Pam's grave. At the sentencing hearing we'd found out why. Neither of us had made a second attempt until now. Both of us preferred to remember Pam by the way she'd lived. Today, we simply wanted to see if Bob had ever marked her place of rest.

We entered the heavy doors of the Good Shepherd Mausoleum. In the eerie darkness, a young woman was working at her desk. We introduced ourselves, and Beezie and I explained our mission.

The woman recalled the tragedy and removed a folder from a cabinet. According to their records, Pam's marker had been placed a year and a half after her death. At that same time, Bob had canceled his adjoining plot.

The woman handed us a map after circling the location of Pam's grave.

The earth was spongy from days of rain. The sweet smell of soil rose from the ground and the trees were hazy with new growth. Beezie and I checked the grid and started our pilgrimage toward Pam's gravesite. After a few wrong turns we discovered it.

Kneeling, I swept away dried leaves to uncover the marker. "Hey, girl," I whispered, studying the simple engraving—Pam's name and the dates of her birth and death. Tears I'd been saving filled my eyes. I stood to find Beezie crying, too, and gave her a hug.

Then, turning toward the vista, we silently remembered.

Over the water, the light of the setting sun was the color of peaches. From this vantage point I could see a portion of the last course I'd run with Pam. Her final logged words were on Sunday, April 1, 1984:

Five with Lynda. Went good at 7:00 a.m. Sunny, beautiful day. Her optimism makes me feel good. I wish I had and hope I'm gaining self-assurance and satisfaction.

Welling up in my throat was that memory of Pam, jogging beside me, honoring me with her wonderful grin as we laughed, complained, reminisced, and marveled at our special bond.

Dr. Ronald Rook, an orthopedic surgeon, once said, "I do not run to add days to my life—I run to add life to my days."

And so did Pam.

Run at Destruction
Reading Group Guide

1. The theme of running gives the promise of a runner's high and creates this feeling of being invincible. After Pam's death, this feeling of invincibility changed for Lynda. Is there an event in your life that created this same realization?

2. How did Pam's early years growing up affect her? Knowing this, are there some lessons to be learned about raising your own children or assisting with your grandchildren? Are there issues that the Buliks' three therapists worked on with the couple that might provide you some help within your own marriage or someone you know? Self-esteem, communication issues, image issues, etc.

3. If you knew a friend's spouse was having an affair, how would you handle this? Did Lynda do the right thing by holding back from telling Pam?

4. Do you have a friend like Pam, whose problems seem to take over your life? The comment Lynda made that it seemed like Pam needed to die before Lynda could get her life back seems very cruel. Discuss if others have felt this way about a friend and how they have handled it.

5. Physical abuse is easier to define. Do you believe Pam was physically abused? Do you consider what Pam went through with Bob, mental abuse? Do you have friends in this same circumstance that might benefit from professional help? Discuss the situations.

6. Do you believe Bob was responsible for the August incident? Discuss the judge's decision concerning its admissibility at trial.

7. After Pam's death, would you have given Bob the benefit of the doubt until hearing the trial testimony, or jumped to conclusions like Lynda and the community? How much do you feel the media swayed the community? Was the judge's decision to bring in an out-of-town jury correct? Why or why not?

8. Do you agree with the verdict? What are the key influencers that helped you make up your mind?

9. Do you believe the injuries Pam sustained could have knocked her unconscious? Why or why not? If not, discuss why Pam ended up in the van.

10. Has anyone known someone that experienced carbon monoxide poisoning? Discuss if you believe Bob's story concerning its affect on him in relationship to your own experience.

11. Did the seven discoveries in the last pages alter your original thinking? If so, discuss which ones did.

12. Do you think the prison system should allow the freedom Bob Bulik seemed to have while he was incarcerated? Why or why not?

13. If an individual served their sentence for a crime against someone you loved, could you forgive them? Why or why not?

14. Many people have affairs or are affected by one and their marriage does not end with the same result as the Buliks. Why do you think their situation drove them to their ultimate destruction?

About the Author

Lynda Drews, a Wisconsin native and dedicated runner, recently gave the commencement speech at the University of Wisconsin La Crosse, her college Alma mater. One lesson she shared with the graduates was: "to journal your life." When Lynda, a marketing executive, made the decision to retire after her thirty-year career, she returned to an earlier passion. *Run at Destruction* is the outcome.

Lynda and her husband, Jim, a retired guidance counselor and an accomplished runner, have two sons, Collin and Chris, and a golden retriever named Bailey. The family has lived in Green Bay since the mid-seventies and helped launch the local running movement. The city now hosts the nation's fifth largest 10K, the Bellin Run.

www.lyndadrews.com